HAMMERSMITH

LIBRARIES

Fulham Library
598 Fulham Road
London SW6 5NX
748 3020 Ext 3877

Please return this book to the Library from which it was borrowed on or before the last date stamped. Fines will be charged on overdue books at the rate currently determined by the Borough Council.

28. NOV. 1988		
29. DEC. 1988		
10. FEB. 1992		

Renewal may be made by post, telephone or personal call, quoting details immediately above and the last date stamped.

The Social History of Religion in Scotland since 1730

CALLUM G. BROWN

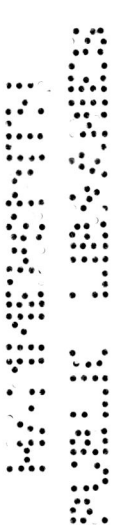

Methuen
LONDON AND NEW YORK

First published in 1987 by
Methuen & Co. Ltd
11 New Fetter Lane, London EC4P 4EE

Published in the USA by
Methuen & Co. in association with Methuen, Inc.
29 West 35th Street, New York, NY 10001

© 1987 Callum Brown

Typeset in Great Britain by
Scarborough Typesetting Services
and printed at the
University Press, Cambridge

All rights reserved. No part of this book may be reprinted or reproduced or utilized in any form or by any electronic, mechanical or other means, now known or hereafter invented, including photocopying and recording, or in any information storage or retrieval system, without permission in writing from the publishers.

British Library Cataloguing in Publication Data

Brown, Callum
The social history of religion in Scotland since 1730. – (Christianity and society in the modern world)
1. Scotland – Church history 2. Scotland – Religious life and customs
I. Title   II. Series
306'.6'09411   BR782
ISBN 0-416-36980-4

Library of Congress Cataloging in Publication Data

Brown, Callum G., 1953–
The social history of religion in Scotland since 1730.
(Christianity and society in the modern world)
Bibliography: p.
Includes index.
1. Scotland – Church history – 18th century. 2. Scotland – Church history – 19th century. 3. Scotland – Church history – 20th century. 4. Scotland – Social life and customs – 18th century. 5. Scotland – Social life and customs – 19th century. 6. Scotland – Social life and customs – 20th century.
I. Title   II. Series.
BR785.B76   1987   274.11'07   87-1714
ISBN 0-416-36980-4

For my parents

Contents

List of tables	viii
List of figures	ix
Preface	xi
List of abbreviations	xiii
1 Perspectives on Scottish religion	1
2 From religious monopoly to religious pluralism: the changing denominational structure, 1700–1980	22
3 Patterns of religious adherence	57
4 Religion in rural society, 1730–1890	89
5 The challenge of the cities, 1780–1890	130
6 The 'social question' and the crisis for religion, 1890–1929	169
7 Religion in the secular century	209
8 Conclusion	249
Bibliography	257
Index	265

Tables

1	Churchgoers by denomination, 1835/6 and 1851	61
2	The denominational structures in Scotland and England, 1851	63
3	Growth rates of the main presbyterian churches, 1860–1928	64
4	Non-presbyterian dissenters in Scotland, 1790–1959	73
5	Proportion of religious marriages by denomination, 1855–1970	76
6	Churchgoing rates of Scottish towns, 1851	82
7	Churchgoing rates, 1835–1891	83
8	Social composition of rural dissent in the Lowlands	110
9	Social composition of Dundee and Perth Glasite Congregations, 1771/2	149
10	Social composition of John Street Relief/United Presbyterian Church, Glasgow: based on fathers' occupations in baptismal roll	150
11	Proportion of brides and grooms unable to sign marriage books in religious ceremonies, 1871	151

Figures

1	Comparative regional strength of the main presbyterian churches in 1891	66
2	Comparative parish strength of the churches in Orkney, 1891	68
3	Membership of the minor presbyterian churches, 1900–70	71
4	Density of Catholics in population in 1755, 1851 and 1984	75
5	Churchgoing rates 1851, by county	78
6	Churchgoing rates 1984, by region or sub-region	79
7	Church and Sunday-school membership per capita, Scotland and Glasgow, 1800–1970	86
8	Proportion of marriages religiously solemnized, 1855–1984	87

Preface

Despite or perhaps because of the partisan nature of Scots' interest in their religious past, Scotland has not figured prominently in the wide debates prevalent in the rest of Britain, Europe and North America concerning the social history of religion: debates on the role and structure of churches in modern industrial society, about who and how many went to church, about the status of religion in popular culture, and about the nature, timing and causes of secularization. The thinness of research on these issues in Scotland means that this book is necessarily preliminary and flawed. It proposes a framework for debate and research beyond the confines of sectarian myopia, and if it arouses constructive disagreement, then a purpose has been served.

Many individuals have given freely of advice and information over the past ten years, including Dr David Bebbington, Dr Steve Bruce, Professor John Butt, Mrs Olive Checkland, Mrs Helen Dunbar, Dr W. Hamish Fraser, Dr Peter Hillis, Dr Margaret Mackay, Dr Allan MacLaren, the Rev. Andrew MacLean, Dr Bob Morris, the late Rev. Ian Muirhead, Dr Alan Robertson, Dr Bob Scribner, Ms Alison Todd, Dr Graham Walker and Professor John Ward. I am extremely grateful to the late Professor Sydney Checkland and Dr Bob Holton for introducing me to religious history as social science whilst supervising my doctoral research on Glasgow, and to the Economic and Social Research Council for awarding me a graduate studentship. The following people kindly allowed me to use unpublished research material: Dr M. Monies, Mr A. T. N.

Muirhead and Dr D. B. Murray. I am grateful to Century Hutchinson Publishing Group Ltd for their permission to reproduce 'Pisky, Pisky' from *A Breath of Border Air* by Lavinia Derwent. I am grateful also to Dr Tom Devine for commenting on an earlier draft of chapter 4. My greatest debt is to Dr Hugh McLeod who was an extremely patient and knowledgeable editor who gently pushed me to sharpen ideas and reconsider outrageous assertions. To all of these and others whom I have neglected to mention, I extend sincere thanks. All remaining errors and shortcomings are entirely my responsibility.

Lastly, I reserve special gratitude to two people who knew the agonies of this book: Mrs Irene Scouller, who with extreme forbearance typed and retyped the manuscript, and Jayne Stephenson who had to live with this project too long.

Abbreviations

CRA	Central Regional Archive (Stirling)
NSA	*New Statistical Account*
OSA	*Old Statistical Account*
PP	*Parliamentary Papers*
RSCHS	*Records of the Scottish Church History Society*
SHR	*Scottish Historical Review*
SRA	Strathclyde Regional Archive (Glasgow)
SRO	Scottish Records Office (Edinburgh)

1
Perspectives on Scottish religion

Introduction

The Mull of Kintyre is a long and narrow peninsula which extends southwards from the west Highlands of Scotland. It has traditionally been part of the Highlands in culture, economy and at one time language – Gaelic. Yet its principal centre, Campbeltown, lies on a latitude twenty miles south of Scotland's industrial metropolis of Glasgow and is only some thirty miles from the coast of Northern Ireland. Kintyre is an anomaly of geography, claimed once as an island by the Lord of the Isles and used by merchants, migrants and pop stars as a half-way stop between the rural north-west and the more urbanized Lowlands, and between Ireland and Scotland. As the movement of people, ideas and methods of economic production has quickened in pace over the past two and a half centuries, Campbeltown has collected a variety of churches and religious traditions which make it a useful microcosm of organized religion in Scotland.

In 1980 Campbeltown contained three congregations of the Church of Scotland and one each of the Roman Catholic Church, the Free Church, the United Free Church, the Scottish Episcopal Church, the Open Brethren, the Salvation Army and the Jehovah's Witnesses. At other times it has also had congregations of the Methodists, the Baptists, the Congregationalists, and the Good Templars. Some of these denominations bear witness to past migrations. Irish Catholics mingled with Highland Catholics from the Western Isles and western mainland to form a community whose numbers increased markedly in the 1820s. The Established Church of Scotland maintained two congregations – one for Highlanders whose services were held in Gaelic and one for English-speakers and incomers from the south. The 'English' congregation catered initially for Lowland presbyterians who were introduced as settlers in the 1650s, but their extreme presbyterian or 'covenanting' tradition led them to form dissenting congregations after 1760 known as the Relief Church, the Secession Church and the Reformed Presbyterian Church. Similarly, the Highland congregation of the Established Church split at the time of the spectacular national Disruption of 1843 when over a third of the clergy, elders and adherents seceded. Above the Highland line, the Free Church of Scotland which resulted became closely identified with the Gaelic-speaking lower orders, whilst in the central Lowlands it became led by the middle classes.

The Scottish Episcopal Church also represented a Highland tradition in Campbeltown, though a different one. Episcopacy and the rule of bishops had been the ecclesiastical system of the Established Church at various periods between 1560 and 1690, but the eventual victory of presbyterianism in the late seventeenth century reduced episcopalianism in southern Scotland. In the north however it was a strong remnant which supported the Jacobite cause of the ousted Stuart monarchs through successive rebellions down to 1745. The ignominy and government suppression suffered after these revolts further reduced episcopalian support particularly amongst the Highland peasants, but large numbers of aristocracy and the gentry remained loyal to a Church which grew closer in doctrine and temper to the 'high church' wing of the Church of England. The Scottish Episcopal Church came to represent, and in the Highlands and much of the rural Lowlands is still seen to represent the landed classes at prayer.

In this way Campbeltown rests at the meeting point of several major religious and ethnic traditions in Scotland. The town demonstrates how the country has been and still is characterized by significant regional differences in church life – of which the Highland–Lowland division is but one. Some denominations thrive in certain areas or in little pockets surrounded by hostile religious traditions. To a great extent Scotland's topography helps to account for this. The country varies from the fertile arable farmland of the Lothians in the east through to the vast expanses of mountains and moors in the inaccessible territory of the Highlands in the north. In addition Scotland includes around 700 islands off the western and northern coasts, lying in some of the most treacherous waters in Europe. In such conditions relative isolation was achieved by many communities, and even today some parts of the western mainland are best approached by sea. Consequently, strong though small communities were often able to maintain allegiance to various distinctive denominations and traditions and to resist encroachments from unwelcome incomers.

If topography created the barriers for religious diversity to be sustained, Scotland's diversity in economy and social structure provided the conditions in which the varied pattern could be nurtured and changed. By common acknowledgement the country was an economic backwater of Europe until the eighteenth century, singularly failing to match the prosperity of most other nations bordering on the North Sea. Though relatively active in mercantile trading on both eastern and western coasts, its domestic economy for the most part languished in subsistence farming with only a small manufacturing output. But from the late seventeenth century an accelerating momentum of agricultural improvement, growing trade and manufacturing transformed the economic life of many regions, creating highly productive farming in the south-east and commercial and industrial activity in the western Lowlands around Glasgow. Few parts were untouched by this wind of change, with even the remote Highlands and Hebrides going through various changes from cattle production in the eighteenth century to kelp at the beginning of the nineteenth, and then to a divided economy where large landowners used estates for 'sheep walks' and deer forests whilst the peasant population turned under some duress to crofting and fishing. Even in places where large cities and industrialism seemed far away, the cash nexus and the oscillations of the capitalist free market came to be factors increasingly influencing people's lives. But the sharpest change was in manufacturing towns and villages, of which Campbeltown was not unusual. Commercially organized fishing developed there as it did in villages all around Scotland, but at the same time the parish economy acquired commerce and manufacturing characteristic of the new industrial order of the Lowland cities: small trades, commerce, shipping, whisky distilling, textile manufacture and coal-mining.

The range of occupations created great variation in standard of living, popular culture and religion. Members of different social groups and even occupations developed a propensity to adhere to specific churches or to none. Whilst many landowners adhered to the Episcopal Church and others to the Established Church, crofters gave allegiance to a puritan presbyterianism which swept them into the Free Church in 1843. Irish migrants, whether working as seasonal harvesters or as permanent factory-workers and labourers, were predominantly Catholic. Herring fishers, noted in the 1790s for dissoluteness and drunkenness, developed a strong evangelicalism between the 1850s and 1920s which swept significant numbers into the Open and Close (or Exclusive) Brethren, the Congregationalist Church and the Methodist Church. Tradesmen such as masons, wrights and butchers, and some groups of textile workers adhered strongly to dissenting presbyterianism, and notably to the Relief and Secession churches. With time the tradesmen developed into an important section of the Victorian middle classes, and those two churches united in 1847 to form the strongly bourgeois United Presbyterian Church. Although such correlations of occupation and church were by no means uniform throughout Scotland, the creation of new denominations and sects often came to reflect the new social divisions created by economic and social change after 1780.

Another consequence of the multiplication of churches during the economic transformation of Campbeltown, as of Scotland, was a decline in the power of the Established Church. The release of population from the supervision of the state church created large numbers who found no home in any church. Clergymen became conscious of the 'unchurched' in a way they rarely had in pre-industrial society and it was the working classes whom they identified as the irreligious and immoral. The Rev. Dr John Smith, Church of Scotland minister of Campbeltown in the early 1790s, voiced a concern which was to become general amongst the British clergy in the nineteenth century:

> One circumstance in the general character of the lower class of people, both in town and country, according to the complaint and experience of their clergy, consists in the little attention paid to every thing beyond their worldly interests, and a woeful ignorance in matters of religion; . . . and . . . a more than usual neglect in attending public worship. . . .[1]

The alienation of the 'lower class of people' is a recurrent theme in the social history of religion in industrial society. The growth of factories, of divided social classes and of large and anonymous cities seemed to generate social problems and social divisions which adversely affected proletarian churchgoing. Like Dr Smith, ministers catalogued various 'causes' which attracted remedial attention – such as the temperance and total abstinence movements which emerged in the 1830s to combat the effects of alcohol, giving rise later in the Victorian period to indigenous working-class organizations like the Templars. This search for causes was still strong in the 1950s when television, bingo and the motor car were isolated as reasons for marked decline in church attendances. A commentator in Campbeltown recorded at the time:

> At the beginning of the twentieth century many people went to church in the forenoon, afternoon and evening and also for prayer meetings on certain weekdays. . . . Many can recall times when the churches were well filled, but empty pews are now a commonplace: perhaps not more than a third of all the professing members attend regularly. . . .[2]

What had once been associated with the working classes was now general. The causes of non-churchgoing were no longer poverty and intemperance but instead a socially widespread disinclination to waste valuable work and leisure time on the Sabbath.

Since the eighteenth century Scottish society has experienced rapid and profound changes. The population has risen more than five times, the economy has gone through various transformations, and social relationships and popular culture have been altered radically. Religion could not remain untouched by such transformations. In Campbeltown as elsewhere the denominational structure adapted to changing social structure and to constantly evolving aspirations of the people. There were great difficulties for the churches in keeping pace, and the very instability of modern society seemed to threaten the tradition of communal worship and the relative tranquillity of the agrarian life upon which piety and faith were founded. But the decline of religion did not follow automatically from the onset of these changes. Scots continued to attend church in large numbers, continued to read the Bible and memorize the Catechism, and religious ideas about morality and behaviour remained prevalent. Piety and faith were recast in a new mould which has not altogether been destroyed by the advance of modern secular society. Moreover, religion in Scotland has had an important bearing on national consciousness. For a people whose sense of nationhood was removed early in the eighteenth century, religion remained one of the few facets of Scottish civil life in which a collective identity could survive.

Religion and the Scottish Identity

Many historians and other commentators have found features of Scottish religion and the Scottish churches to be distinctive. So dissimilar are the religious heritages of Scotland and England, for instance, that they are frequently referred to as the origins of the social and cultural differences between the two countries. Yet there is little agreement on this issue. There is disagreement about the extent of religion's contribution to Scotland's character; there is disagreement about how far the country can be taken as uniform given the great regional variations in social and religious life within it; there is disagreement about exactly what features of theology or ecclesiastical government give Scottish religious life its distinctiveness; and there is even disagreement over which church tradition – presbyterianism, episcopacy or

Roman Catholicism – lies at the root of Scottish character. Despite this, the relationship between religion and the Scottish identity has been a prominent theme in the treatment of the country's history.

Campbeltown's list of churches in 1980 is not a complete inventory of Scotland's religious groups, but it does reveal immediately a distinctive church history. Some of the names are familiar in England and Wales, but many of them, such as the Catholic and Episcopal Churches, do not relate directly to southern counterparts but instead are products of independent traditions. Since 1780 immigrants have brought new churches and religious cultures to Scotland but a distinctive religious 'complexion' has remained. Incoming churches have often felt the need to establish separate Scottish organizations and to adapt their liturgies and, some have argued, even doctrines to suit native inclinations and customs. Whilst the majority of the people adhered to indigenous presbyterian churches, Scottish 'branches' of denominations as diverse as the Catholic, the Episcopal, Methodist, Baptist and Congregational Churches have all had separate Scottish governments or practices during at least part of the last two centuries. In this way the Scottish church structure and its religious traditions have sustained an outward appearance of distinctiveness and even peculiarity.

Such distinctiveness need not be considered unusual in a country of under six million inhabitants. What would be considered unusual is that it belonged not to a nation but to a comparatively small regional population within a larger nation-state of some sixty million people. It is a region which has lacked its own resident head of state since 1603 and which has been devoid of a legislative assembly since 1707. Scotland's political and economic independence was lost at the Treaty of Union at the latter date when the northern kingdom was fully absorbed in the British state, leaving only the legal system, the state church and the educational system as significant institutional vestiges of national consciousness.

In the absence of political independence, then, religion has become attributed as the principal agent of national consciousness. On one level it has frequently been used as the basis for the stereotyped Scot – even if the elements in the stereotype are contradictory. The Scots are regarded as in many ways the peculiar products of the Calvinist heritage of a poor and semi-barbarous country only partially enveloped by the civilizing tendencies of modern society; as Samuel Johnson remarked to Boswell on their Scottish tour of 1773, 'Sir, we are here as Christians in Turkey.'[3] The heritage demanded so much of the individual in terms of religious behaviour and moral 'respectability' that the people were divided into the good, the bad and the hypocrites. The Scots seem dour, determined that the purpose of the Reformation was, in the words of a recent Scottish poet, to 'eliminate Purgatory by getting it over while we're still alive'.[4] They have long been noted for thriftiness, a kirk minister having instigated the savings-bank movement in the 1810s and the Scots until recently having preferred interest-earning deposit accounts rather than cheque accounts at banks. At the same time, Scots on holiday are noted as spendthrifts on hedonistic entertainment on 'Fair' or trades fortnights to Blackpool and Benidorm. More generally Scottish industrial culture has long been portrayed as consisting of tenement slums, heavy drinking and a 'rough' popular culture. From the late 1830s onwards it was an axiom of social reform that the worst confluence of physical and moral degradation was to be found in Scottish cities. J. C. Symons, an assistant Royal Commissioner on handloom-weaving, stated in 1839: 'It is my firm belief that penury, dirt, misery, drunkenness, disease and crime culminate in Glasgow to a pitch unparalleled in Great Britain.'[5] For many in Scotland and in Britain as a whole, Glasgow, the Gorbals and more recently Easterhouse were bywords for everything in urban and industrial society which was antipathetic to Christian belief and morality.

Yet Scotland is also noted for the survival of puritanical attitudes. Teetotalism has arguably remained stronger in Scotland than in England, and the staunch Sabbatarianism of the Highlands and Hebrides is indicative of a more general strictness in religion and behaviour in that part of the country. Puritanism appeared to attain a political significance in Scotland unmatched in most of mainland Britain, as in 1922 when a candidate of the Scottish Prohibition Party defeated Winston Churchill in a parliamentary election in Dundee. There has been a noted predilection for hell-fire preaching and strict moral codes enforced by stern church courts. The Calvinist emphasis on the doctrine of predestination, whereby the individual cannot know nor influence his or her salvation, has been used to explain features of the Scots as diverse as their glumness, their aggression to succeed in worldly affairs, and their Rabelaisian qualities. The ironies were acutely observed in the early nineteenth century by the poet James Hogg, the Ettrick Shepherd, when he wrote of the Scots: 'Nothing in the world delights a truly religious people so much as consigning them to eternal damnation.'[6]

Stereotypes of the Scots are consequently somewhat confused and the power of the religious contribution is even more uncertain. But commentators have long ascribed to religion an unusual strength in the development of modern Scotland. It has been suggested that in the absence of an indigenous political and constitutional system religion acted in a number of key ways to fill the void in the national consciousness, thereby developing or sustaining distinctively Scottish patterns of behaviour, thought and popular culture. In this way Scotland has been seen as one of a number of regions within European countries where the secularization of religion has been held in check by the association of religion with a thwarted political nationalism.

At an institutional level it has been suggested that the ostensibly democratic nature of presbyterian church government permitted the supreme court of the Established Church of Scotland, the general assembly, to become a surrogate Scots parliament after 1707; as one ecclesiastical historian put it early this century, 'the kirk has been the embodiment of Scots character'.[7] A committee of the general assembly itself stated proudly in 1968 that 'The Church of Scotland has consistently upheld Scotland's historic nationhood and identity', and many recent historians have concurred in this view. Democracy seemed to be enhanced by the Disruption of 1843, when a third of the Established Church walked out. One historian has seen this event as 'partly fuelled by something very close to nationalism',[8] and by others as surrogate political protests by the bourgeoisie and the proletariat. Despite differing interpretations, there is general agreement that it was a major political event resulting in the creation of a second large general assembly – that of the Free Church of Scotland. The two assemblies met simultaneously in Edinburgh every May, and speakers referred to the meeting 'over the way' in a manner consciously redolent of the Houses of Lords and Commons in London; Robert Louis Stevenson observed that 'the Parliaments of the Established and Free Churches . . . can hear each other singing psalms across the street'.[9] These assemblies attracted wide public attention as the printed reports and debates were not confined to ecclesiastical matters but extended in some depth into issues such as housing, education and social welfare. By drawing from the ranks of the eldership individuals with professional expertise as social reformers, businessmen and politicians, the presbyterian churches appeared to become central both to the investigation of social issues and to the formation of public policy. A notable example was the agitation of the housing committee of the Free Church general assembly between 1857 and 1866 which nurtured electoral support for the Lord Provosts of Edinburgh and Glasgow in undertaking slum-clearance work in their cities, and which contributed to the decline of the bothy system which housed farm servants in allegedly immoral circumstances.

Set against this view of powerful church assemblies is the very cause of their apparent strength – the geographical distance from the civil legislature in London, and the submergence of presbyterian representation at Westminster beneath the alien religious traditions of the Church of England and the various elements of English and Welsh nonconformism. Certainly in some spheres such as education and the drinking laws Scottish affairs have continued to be subject to special legislation ever since 1707, and the Scottish churches could have significant influence over the terms and timing of Acts of Parliament. One case in point was the introduction of prohibitive drinking laws in 1853 which closed Scottish public houses on Sundays more than twenty years before England obtained a similar measure. But even when Scottish legislation remained separate, Parliament did not bow automatically to Scottish wishes. There was clear electoral support for a state system of education in Scotland in the 1850s, due largely to the strength of presbyterian dissenters who wished to end the preferential status of the Established Church's parish schools. However, the votes of Scottish MPs were repeatedly overwhelmed by English MPs amongst whom the nonconformists were opposed to state education. In the event the Act establishing state education in Scotland came only in 1872 once England and Wales had already implemented their own system. In this way, the church assemblies may have been able to act as forums for quasi-legislative debate, but their real political power was severely circumscribed.

On a more local level there is greater evidence of the religious influence in public administration. From the Scottish Reformation of 1560 onwards the ruling committee of the parish church, the kirk session, grew in power *de facto* if not *de jure* as the magistrates' court in criminal law. Despite some decline in its power, the kirk session remained a compelling force in many communities well into the nineteenth century. More generally, the churches continued to exert enormous power in local government in spheres such as the drinking laws, poor relief and education. Clergymen and church representatives continued to be prominent in these fields even after the apparent 'secularization' of public administration: by their election to school boards and *ad hoc* education authorities between 1873 and 1929, by election to parochial boards and parish councils from 1845 to 1929, and by sitting as elected councillors on licensing boards.

In these and other ways, the civil establishment in Scotland was and remains strongly presbyterian in composition. This results in a widely held perception of a lingering theocracy. A newspaper columnist wrote exasperatedly in 1978:

> It is difficult for tolerant, liberal-minded chaps like myself to grasp the reason why the majority of Scots, the non-church-goers, should have, with the connivance of the state, a close-mouthed, eighteenth-century Presbyterianism so heavily imposed upon them.[10]

The role of such a puritanical presbyterianism has been a recurrent theme amongst historians and commentators on modern

Scottish society. Some have seen it as a capitalist yoke imposed on the working classes by a ruling élite who wished to enjoy the fruits of a sober and compliant labour force. More broadly there has been a tendency to regard the Scottish churches, with the exception of the Episcopal Church, as more egalitarian than English churches. The kirk is seen as one of the venues in which class divisions have been overcome, where democracy is seen to reign, and where class antagonisms have been eased. The apparent absence in Scotland of a church–chapel division which split many communities in England and Wales along class lines, and popular acquiescence to kirk morality and discipline, are taken as evidence of a socially cohesive quality to Scottish presbyterianism.

The assignment of such far-reaching attributes to presbyterianism must be treated with considerable caution. For one thing Catholic and episcopalian writers would deny that presbyterianism was the only religious source of Scottish identity and native character; they can point out, for instance, that the majority of Scots were non-presbyterians until at least 1700. At another level there must be caution in accepting that Scottish society was homogeneous – even before the industrial revolution. Many writers infer from the relative passivity of the peasantry during the agricultural revolution that Scottish society was more united than that of England or Ireland, and proceed to identify Calvinistic presbyterianism as the cause. But passivity does not necessarily imply homogeneity, and in the case of religion there has been a tendency to exaggerate the cohesive powers of presbyterianism and to understate the extent and intensity of social division created by the rise of both presbyterian and non-presbyterian dissent. Far from exemplifying social unity and passivity, the Scottish churches were the vehicles for expressing many of the antagonisms within the society at large. Presbyterianism was racked by interminable secession between 1750 and 1850, giving rise to a multiplicity of denominations which in local communities often acted as focuses for class identity. Moreover, social conflict of a serious and seemingly ineradicable nature arose out of the Protestant–Catholic confrontations in Lowland society. The bigotry of 'Orange' and 'Green' had origins in Scotland's history of the sixteenth and seventeenth centuries, but the arrival in the nineteenth century of large numbers of Irish immigrants of both religions reinvigorated ecclesiastical and popular tensions. Since the middle of the eighteenth century the English-speaking world, including Ireland, has turned to Scotland as the crucible of the schisms between presbyterians, episcopalians and Catholics. Communities in the United States, Canada, Australia and New Zealand have been primed principally by Scots on the fine doctrinal points which split the presbyterian community, and the anti-Catholic 'crusade' has always turned to the land of John Knox as the source of its mission.

There is a final and equally contentious role attributed to presbyterianism in Scotland: that of encouraging the country's dramatic economic growth of the eighteenth and nineteenth centuries. Max Weber referred only briefly to Scotland in his book, *The Protestant Ethic and the Spirit of Capitalism* published early this century. Subsequent contributions to the debate Weber fostered have paid meagre attention to what appears a classic case of a Calvinist country which underwent rapid economic growth. A major study by Gordon Marshall has attempted to illustrate the importance of presbyterian doctrine to entrepreneurs' activities between 1560 and 1707, and whilst the validity of his findings could well apply to the eighteenth and nineteenth centuries there is a paucity of similar systematic investigation beyond the period of Scotland's relative economic backwardness. The role of 'this worldly asceticism', ascribed to Protestants by Weber, is highly debated and probably unsuited to conclusive verification or falsification, but there are serious doubts anyway about whether Scottish presbyterians of the period of the Industrial Revolution were distinctively Calvinist. As we shall see in chapter 5, there are some grounds for believing that the entrepreneurial and business classes, not to mention sections of the lower-middle and working classes, overthrew Calvinist theology in favour of Arminianism and an open evangelicalism of a Methodist variety.

The tale of uniqueness in Scottish religious life has developed in several directions. The cultural ambience of Scotland seems to many to be alien to England, though Scottish writers overlook strong similarities with Wales. The emphasis has been on the

Scottish divergence from a 'British norm' and the 'religious peculiarities of Scotland' were reinvestigated from a new angle in the 1960s and 1970s with the rise of Scottish nationalism. Since then presbyterianism has been seized upon as the one remaining distinctive feature of Scottish society which seems capable at least of explaining the survival of national consciousness within what has been for over two centuries a mere region. The Welsh have their language; the Scots, with few Gaelic speakers, have their 'National' Church. Two hundred years of promoting British industrialization and forging the British Empire did not extinguish the Scottish identity, for, as many see it, 'God was securely in his heaven, perceived in a distinctively Scottish way'.[11] Along with the kilt, Robert Burns and the bagpipes, presbyterianism has been taken as an export of a Scottish rather than a British culture. But as the next section contends there are weighty reasons for giving equal if not greater credence to the impact upon religion of Scotland's absorption after 1707 into the greater Britain.

The British dimension

After the Union of Parliaments in 1707 the economic development of Scotland fell rapidly in step with that of England, taking advantage of the same trading opportunities within the nascent British Empire and employing the same technological breakthroughs, transport innovations and production methods. The agricultural and industrial revolutions unfolded in Scotland in tandem with the rest of mainland Britain. Scotland's leading agricultural counties, especially in the south-east, more than kept pace with advances in farming, and the Lanarkshire cotton industry based in Glasgow emerged in the 1780s only ten years behind that of Lancashire. As the age of cotton gave way in the 1840s to the age of steam, the Glasgow area remained a leading British industrial centre with large-scale production in iron, steel, shipbuilding, locomotive manufacture and all forms of engineering. The Scottish economy became diverse and dynamic with manufacturing spreading out through the Lowlands to places like Dundee where jute dominated and to Fife where coal-mining grew dramatically in the late nineteenth century. Scotland had its regional and local specialisms but it vibrated like every other part of Britain to the general rhythm of the world's first industrial nation. At the same time Scotland encountered the same social consequences of rapid economic change: dramatic population growth, urbanization, factory production and the social divisions it created, and the problems of poverty, health, housing and sanitation. The formation of political parties and social movements occurred within a larger British dimension: the popular unrest of the Revolutionary and Napoleonic periods; the Chartists, trades unions and the rise of the late-nineteenth-century labour movement; and the British parties of the Whigs/Liberals, Tories and the Labour Party. The evolution of Scottish responses to social problems was part of a British development which involved philanthropy and municipal intervention in the nineteenth century and the piecemeal growth of state welfare policies in the twentieth. Whilst legislative enactments and administrative enforcement were often specially adapted to Scottish requirements, the fortunes of Scottish political, social and economic life were inextricably linked to those of England and Wales. In such circumstances it is vital to place the social history of modern Scottish religion within this unfolding British experience.

The 1707 Union preserved presbyterianism in the Established Church of Scotland. This was undoubtedly a major difference from England, Wales and Ireland where the Established churches were all episcopal. However, the significance of this peculiarity was progressively diminished. Within five years the Anglican-dominated Parliament withdrew the legal powers of kirk sessions over persons of other faiths and specifically granted freedom of worship to Scottish episcopalians. This eradicated the principle of a state monopoly of religion in Scotland, bringing her into line with the English policy of religious toleration, and granting legality to any who should wish to leave the Church of Scotland. More broadly, religious toleration and the fashion in high circles for what opponents called 'lukewarmness' in religion spread northwards from England during the eighteenth century as the Scottish landed classes and a small but influential section of the presbyterian clergy became aligned with English taste and politics. This led to the dominance of the Moderate Party in the general assembly of the Established Church from the 1750s until 1833. English aristocratic influence and Enlightenment thinking and manners encouraged Moderates to weaken presbyterian doctrine, rhetoric and style. They discarded much of what they perceived as harsh Calvinism in preaching and church discipline in favour of refinement and elegance, moderation in religious enthusiasm, and philosophizing rather than remonstration in pulpit discourse. Although not necessarily in the majority amongst Scottish presbyterians, the Moderates became a firm if critical arm of government, enjoying the patronage of the rural landed classes.

The opponents of the Moderates were the Evangelicals who formed a 'Popular Party' in the Church of Scotland and increasingly defected to form dissenting churches in the late eighteenth century. This evangelical reaction was simultaneous in timing to the rise of evangelicalism and Methodism in England and bore strong similarities in social appeal and in religious temper. Both were reactions against perceived laxity in religion amongst the social élites and attracted support from many who were being affected by economic change: from the lower orders whose lives were being disrupted by the advances in agriculture, commerce and manufacturing, and from the new entrepreneurial classes who were in the vanguard of the spirit of innovation. By the 1790s the essential unity of interests had led to strong links between Scottish and English evangelicals. Preachers were exchanged, joint campaigns mounted (such as William Wilberforce's anti-slavery movement), and co-operation established in promoting the work of evangelization through home and foreign missions. The decades around 1800 were difficult times for evangelical innovation in the wake of the French Revolution and radicalism at home, and English evangelicals gave noteworthy support to Scottish colleagues who were the objects of intense suspicion for Moderates in the civil and ecclesiastical establishments.

The evangelical interchange between England and Scotland developed from those beginnings to be a major feature of British

Perspectives on Scottish religion 17

ecclesiastical life in the nineteenth and early twentieth centuries. By the Victorian period, Moderatism and 'lukewarmness' were discredited and the self-stylization 'evangelical' came to be an avowal of Protestant orthodoxy, uniting the vast majority of nonconformists and Methodists in the south and presbyterians in Scotland. Evangelical campaigns to reform urban and industrial society by extinguishing immorality and promoting godliness and churchgoing were widely accepted by local and national government as the basis of public social policy. The leading Scottish minister Thomas Chalmers became famous for his opposition to state-supported charity which he saw as diminishing Christian responsibility and self-determination, and Scottish evangelicals exported ideas and innovations for tackling the decay of religious life evident in the crowded and insanitary slums of industrial districts. Amongst such innovations were city missions (the concept first fully developed in Glasgow in 1826), the temperance and total abstinence movements (first introduced to Britain from America at Greenock in 1829), ragged schools for destitute children (notably in Glasgow in the late 1830s and in Edinburgh ten years later), religious revivalism (with Moody and Sankey's first major success coming in Scotland in 1873–4), and youth movements like the Boys' Brigade (which was founded in Glasgow in 1883). By the 1860s leading evangelical laity in Scotland were at one with their brethren in England in pursuing municipal office and later membership of school boards to implement the 'civic gospel' of improvement in housing, education and public utilities.

The trend towards the incorporation of Scottish churches in British ecclesiastical life continued in the twentieth century. Religious responses to the rise of the labour movement, to the decay of evangelicalism, world war and economic depression became increasingly matters of British inter-denominational concern. Joint committees, conferences and reports proliferated, doctrinal and political issues generated much inter-church debate, and ecumenical initiatives were instituted from the 1950s to explore possibilities of denominational union amongst Scottish and English churches in various permutations. At the end of the day it must be said that cross-border amalgamation of major churches has not materialized and is unlikely to do so; but then such unions have tended to be confined within traditions of the Reformed Church: within Methodism, English congregationalism and presbyterianism, and Scottish presbyterianism. Whilst most Scottish denominations have maintained separate governmental structures, the ecclesiastical atmosphere became charged with issues thrown up overwhelmingly in a British context: abortion, homosexuality, nuclear weapons and unemployment. Moreover, the Church of Scotland, representing 90 per cent of Protestant church members, has since the 1960s become rapidly infused with English episcopal characteristics in liturgy and style. In the last ten years there has been a significant spread of lavish church decoration, the use of responses in prayer, and a celebration of the Christian Year in a manner hitherto proscribed by presbyterian tradition. The vast bulk of Scottish presbyterians have during the twentieth century been shifting at an accelerating rate towards 'high churchism', and despite the survival of distinctive presbyterian government, Scottish Protestantism is rapidly converging with an English-style episcopalianism.

Consequently the discreteness of the Scottish church structure should not mask the profound significance of British ecclesiastical life over the past two centuries. But of even greater importance has been the converging social experience of religion. The movement of people to cities in the late eighteenth and nineteenth centuries created identical problems throughout Britain in providing new churches and clergy in the districts where the need was greatest, and it was the Established Churches of England and Scotland which were the most hampered by their rural roots, their links with the rural landed classes and by legal impediments associated with their established status. With a shortage of urban churches and aristocratic dominance, many of the new middle classes found the state churches unsuited to their social aspirations and ideology and turned instead to dissenting congregations. In Scotland as in England the urban bourgeoisie sought religious identity in evangelicalism in the same way that they sought political identity in the Liberal Party. Proletarian congregations of an evangelical disposition were also formed in many industrial communities of England, Wales and Scotland, whilst large numbers of the working classes lost association with organized religion through want of money, clothes and a welcoming atmosphere in 'respectable' middle-class churches. This framework of social dichotomies became general in British cities, and the prescribed solutions by way of evangelization, mission churches to the working classes and religious voluntary organizations were equally applicable in Glasgow and Edinburgh as in Manchester and London. An essential conformity of interest, practice and precedent evolved both north and south of the Tweed, and the evangelical movement straddled the Protestant life of the nation to dominate as the aggressive face of industrial Christianity.

In other ways the social history of religion in Scotland came to be part of a larger British picture. The Catholic Church in 1780 was in both England and Scotland numerically weak, but with large-scale Irish immigration through west-coast ports it developed into a major denomination. The Irish immigrants were often poor, driven out by high rents and potato blight, and they sought refuge and work mainly in industrial and mining districts. Cities such as Liverpool and Glasgow, already sharing similar economic bases and social problems, became even more alike in their religious composition and sectarian divide. Indeed, significant parallels can be drawn between Lancashire and Lanarkshire in industrial development, class structure and religious life, and in both counties Irish immigration posed identical problems for the Catholic Church in the provision of churches and priests to minister to the spiritual needs of a denomination marked by its overwhelmingly proletarian composition.

It has already been noted how many commentators regard the Scots as 'more religious' than the English. Statistics of religious adherence and practice are an unreliable measure at the best of times, but they do lend some support to this argument. The sole government census of religion on 30 March 1851 showed Sunday attendances at church to represent 60.7 per cent of Scottish population and 58.1 per cent of English and Welsh population. In a non-governmental and less complete series of censuses in 1979–84, adult church attenders as a proportion of population was estimated at 11 per cent for England, 13 per cent for Wales and 17 per cent for Scotland. At face value these suggest a considerably higher level of churchgoing in Scotland than elsewhere. However, a major cause of the high Scottish figure for 1979–84 is the large concentration of Catholics in west-central Scotland, and comparison of areas with less divergent denominational composition reveals reduced differences; in the high Catholic areas of Lancashire and Strathclyde, for instance, the rates of churchgoing were 16 per cent and 21 per cent respectively.[12] When similar and other factors are applied to the results of the 1851 census, the 2 or 3 per cent difference between Scotland and the rest of Britain becomes insignificant and, by the standards of enumeration and local variation, meaningless. But what is clear and much more significant is that there has been an overall decline in churchgoing between the two censuses. This is important because many parts of the western world have indicated a much less marked decline or, in the case of the United States, a growth in churchgoing between the nineteenth and twentieth centuries. It indicates that Scotland has shared with England and Wales a very similar and major decay in active church connection amongst Protestant churches during the twentieth century. In other words, the over-arching implications of social, economic and cultural change upon popular participation in religion have been uniform amongst all three constituents of mainland Britain.

It would be folly to argue that in all respects the religious life of Scotland has lost its individuality and character. But it would be equal folly to neglect the importance of Scotland's place in British development over the past 250 years. Scottish churches have shared with others on this island the consequences of industrialization, rural depopulation and more recently industrial decline. The nomenclature may be different in Scottish church life, and theology and doctrines may have differed (though decreasingly as time has passed), but the problems the churches faced, the strategies they adopted, and popular involvement in organized religion were as much characteristic of British experience as they were distinguishing of Scottish society.

Notes

1 *OSA*, x, p. 560.
2 C. M. MacDonald (ed.) (1961) *The Third Statistical Account of Scotland: The County of Argyll*, Glasgow, Collins, 291.
3 R. W. Chapman (ed.) (1970) *Johnson's Journey to the Western Isles of Scotland* . . ., London, Oxford University Press, 205.
4 Alasdair Maclean (1984) *Night Falls on Ardnamurchan: The Twilight of a Crofting Family*, London, Victor Gollancz, 198.
5 Quoted in A. K. Chalmers (1905) *Public Health Administration in Glasgow*, Glasgow, 8.
6 J. Hogg (1824) *The Private Memoirs and Confessions of a Justified Sinner*, London, Oxford University Press, 1970 edn, 201.
7 J. Watson (1907) *The Scot of the Eighteenth Century: His Religion and His Life*, London, 23.
8 H. R. Sefton (1982) 'The Church of Scotland and Scottish nationhood', in S. Mews (ed.) *Religion and National Identity*, Oxford, Basil Blackwell, 549.
9 R. L. Stevenson (1879) *Edinburgh: Picturesque Notes*, London, 16.
10 Jack Maclean, *The Scotsman*, 9 September 1978.
11 S. and O. Checkland (1984) *Industry and Ethos: Scotland 1832–1914*, London, Edward Arnold, 10.
12 P. Brierley and F. Macdonald (eds) (1985) *Prospects for Scotland: Report of the 1984 Census of the Churches*, Edinburgh, MARC/NBSS, 5, 84–97; P. Brierley (ed.) (1980) *Prospects for the Eighties: From a Census of the Churches in 1979*, London, Bible Society, 74.

2
From religious monopoly to religious pluralism: the changing denominational structure, 1700–1980

It is characteristic of the development of industrial society for the denominational structure to alter dramatically. In part modern economic growth has been accompanied by the movement of people between country and town, region and region, and country and country, creating new mixing of ethnicity, culture and religion. This was as apparent in Scotland as in Western Europe and North America in the eighteenth and nineteenth centuries, and accounts in the main for the growth of non-presbyterian churches in the Scottish Lowlands and particularly industrial districts. But urbanization and industrialization had a more profound impact upon indigenous religions by destabilizing the relative tranquillity of rural society in which one state church had traditionally dominated. Even if Established churches rarely achieved their ideal of monopoly during the pre-industrial period, religious nonconformity was regarded as deviant not only in a religious but more importantly a political sense. The loosening of the social fabric which accompanied the agricultural and industrial revolutions effectively destroyed the realization of such an ideal. Shifting population, new patterns of work and leisure, and the creation of new social divisions based on the factory and the impersonal employer–employee relationship fomented heterogeneity, social segregation and a pluralism of occupations and activities. In the same way, religion diversified into a multiplicity of denominations and sects, and in this pluralism of churches were to be found significant reflections of the new social divisions.

From religious monopoly to religious pluralism 23

This chapter approaches the complex and unique church structure of Scotland in this context of social change. Section (b) deals with the presbyterian churches which all developed out of the Established Church of Scotland. These were what Robert Louis Stevenson described in the 1870s as Scotland's 'large family of sisters where the chalk lines are thickly drawn' between 'people who think almost exactly the same thoughts about religion'.[1] The doctrinal and theological issues which divided the presbyterian churches were of small matter in relation to the schisms in Protestantism or Christianity as a whole, but they split the indigenous Scots in serious ways. Section (c) turns to the non-presbyterian churches which grew after 1780 as a result of recruiting predominantly amongst immigrants from Ireland, England and Europe. For many communities of incomers and their offspring religion became a point of cultural and ethnic identity which gave shape to other antagonisms in modern Scottish society. But though the pluralization of the denominational structure was very much a product of social and economic changes after 1730, the foundations of doctrinal division and of geographical variations in religious adherence lay in the sixteenth and seventeenth centuries, and it is important to look first at the legacy of this period.

(a) The legacy of the early-modern period

The Scottish Reformation of 1560 was a relatively peaceful entrée to the more violent excesses of the seventeenth century which only abated with the accession of William and Mary in 1689. Whilst Roman Catholicism was securely overthrown everywhere bar a few isolated communities in the north and north-west, the century and a quarter following the Reformation witnessed a protracted struggle between presbyterians and episcopalians for control of the Established Church. Presbyterians like John Knox were the main instigators of the reformed kirk, and they were resolute that episcopacy was merely 'popery' in another guise and that it should not be countenanced. Episcopacy was seen as the religion of royalty and aristocracy and but a short step from Catholicism; Queen Mary, James VII and the Old and Young Pretenders were Catholics, and James VI, Charles I and Charles II had strong episcopal leanings. The entire Stuart line, with the exception of Queen Anne, seemed intent to impose the rule of bishops over the Scottish church, and presbyterian doctrine hardened against anything seen as tinged with popery: the episcopal prayer book, liturgy, and celebration of saints' days (including Christmas which presbyterians prohibited). The episcopal intrusions of Charles I in the 1630s led to 'covenant theology' which placed the presbyterian church and its individual members in a contract with God to uphold undeviatingly the moral law of Scripture. Puritanism was claimed as the preserve of presbyterians whose resolve to resist the episcopacy of the 'upper ranks' was stiffened by the bond or covenant, which gave succour to those who took up arms to preserve the faith.

The covenant became a claim to righteousness which legitimated the flouting of monarchical decree and by extension all rule by the 'unjust'. In this way presbyterians and covenanting became a focus and a means of social protest. This is not to suggest that the presbyterian–episcopal confrontation was generally or even principally class struggle. Early-modern Scottish society was too underdeveloped economically to display the divisive characteristics redolent of industrial society. Equally, episcopacy was not the monopoly of the gentry and aristocracy, but enjoyed the support of a sizeable proportion of the peasantry. Episcopalians predominated in the northern half of the country and in rural areas rather than burghs. Similarly, presbyterians were not confined to one section of society but included many landowners and a large proportion of the professional and commercial classes. More generally, it can be misleading to divide the population into episcopalian and presbyterian before the eighteenth century as the vast bulk of the laity 'blew with the wind' in the seventeenth century, accepting the rule of either faction when it was in power locally. Between 1560 and 1690 the government of the Church of Scotland changed five times: roughly it was episcopal from 1560–1592, 1610–1640 and 1661–1690, and presbyterian at the intervening dates and after 1690.

Despite this popular adaptability, there emerged from the early-modern period some distinct differences in the composition and ideology of episcopacy and presbyterianism. These differences were not ubiquitous geographically, nor permanent throughout the period. None the less, they were significant for what was to follow in the middle of the eighteenth century. Presbyterianism became associated with an extreme puritanism which laid stress on observance of moral law. The Church became in periods and places of presbyterian rule the unrelenting inquisitor and persecutor of a wide range of civil and religious offences. This puritanism was accepted slowly in Lowland Scotland, finding its earliest support from the burgess class in the larger towns like Edinburgh, who found in presbyterianism an ideology which promoted their social standing, their business principles and the virtue of hard work. It was only after 1600 that the 'Godly society' fanned out into the countryside where the peasantry adopted a more rustic and plebeian concept of presbyterianism. During the seventeenth century, and especially the 'Second Reformation of 1638-50' which later zealots looked upon as the zenith of godliness in Scotland, kirk discipline and the unrelenting preaching of the Word established wider acquiescence, unity and enthusiasm in Lowland counties. The lower orders became the 'muscle' of presbyterianism, forming mobile mobs to remove episcopal clergy from their parishes in the years after 1690. Whilst the Highlands, Hebrides and north-east remained fairly solidly episcopal, in the south-western and central counties the bulk of the peasantry became presbyterians and covenanters. They resisted episcopal gentry and monarch alike in the 1670s and 1680s by armed guerilla warfare, keeping their faith alive by meeting in hillside conventicles and praying societies. It was amongst this group that the basis of modern presbyterian dissent was laid.

The 'hillmen' or 'society men' regarded the presbyterian church that was restored in 1690 as corrupt and unworthy. With a handful of sympathetic clergy, they stood back from the state church without actually leaving it entirely. They described themselves in a manifesto of 1692 as 'the poor, wasted, misrepresented remnant of the suffering, anti-popish, anti-prelatic, anti-erastian, anti-sectarian, true Presbyterian Church of Scotland'.[2] Their struggles with episcopal landowners, particularly in the south-west, made their outlook one which combined religious and social protest. On one occasion their movement emerged as active resistance to economic change. In 1724 peasants in Kirkudbrightshire opposed the enclosure of open fields by landowners. For four months, the 'Galloway Levellers' overturned dykes marking out new fields where once common fields had existed. In a manifesto affixed to the door of Borgue Church they proclaimed that it was 'directly opposite to the law of God and man that the poor should be destitute of bread upon God's earth' and that God 'hath denounced fearful judgements against all oppressors'.[3] The Levellers were led by an unidentified hill preacher and the covenanting tradition was central to their ideology and self-justification. It was but a momentary violent resistance, for the weight of the state, the landowners and the Church of Scotland was against them. Troops moved in to quell the disturbances, ending one of the few instances of revolt against agricultural improvement in eighteenth- and nineteenth-century Scotland.

It is perhaps doubtful to claim, as one labour historian did, that the covenanters were involved in class struggle with their episcopalian landowners as early as the 1670s and 1680s.[4] None the less, there does seem to be cause for identifying a shift in the covenanting ideology of the peasantry from one centred on resistance to religious persecution in the seventeenth century to one more broadly focused by the second quarter of the eighteenth century on unease with change in rural society. Throughout the early-modern period there can be detected in the struggles of the kirk a significant popular participation. Although Scottish society was perhaps more homogeneous than English society, presbyterianism came in part to represent a plebeian culture where the right to 'sit under' a minister of popular choice was defended as Scriptural and legal right. In the 'society men', in occasional instances of religious revival, and in hostility to the intrusion of episcopal and 'popish' practices, there was an episodic and inchoate resistance to the loss of what was regarded as popular culture. In 1736 the first dissenting presbyterian church, the Secession Church, absorbed the vast bulk of the covenanters of the south-western and central counties, and in so doing acknowledged that it was taking possession of 'the Lord's oppressed heritage' and subsequently made covenanting a qualification of membership. In this way the covenanters were the precursors of presbyterian dissent of the modern period, canalizing latent social divisions and antagonisms into the religious sphere.

The emergence of Scottish religious dissent was very much a product of the eighteenth century. Nonconformism of the sort known in sixteenth and seventeenth century England was alien to Scotland where the Established Church remained contestable territory for all groups but the Catholics. The result was an important tradition of internal and informal dissent in Scotland in which groups could drift in and out of close harmony with the prevailing party in the church. Not only did this tradition survive into the nineteenth century, it permitted the continuation of the concept of a 'recoverable' Established Church which could be reclaimed from perceived corruption at an opportune moment by the maintenance of 'true' presbyterianism in dissenting churches and sects. The focus of intellectual disagreement was the qualified nature of establishment in the Church of Scotland. Unlike the state churches of England, Ireland and Wales, the monarch was not the head of the presbyterian church but was accorded observer status at the meetings of the supreme court, the general assembly. Consequently the Lutheran notion of 'twa kingdoms' – that of the monarch and that of Christ (i.e. the church) – was adopted. Presbyterian churchmen were sensible of the need for a civil magistrate to govern society and defend the church, but independence from his intrusions was jealously guarded. The nature and extent of the church–state relationship, thus imperfectly defined, remained an issue for disputation. In the context of the economic changes of the eighteenth and nineteenth centuries, social aspirations became identified with presbyterian freedoms and fomented denominational schism. In this way the seventeenth-century presbyterian struggle with Catholic and episcopal monarchy could be translated into a vocabulary of general resistance to social authority.

On the threshold of the agricultural and industrial revolutions, Scotland was not a homogeneous society in religion. In the central and southern Lowlands there were significant differences in the cultural interpretation of presbyterianism – between the urban professional and business groups and the rural peasantry. In the Lowlands north of the River Tay episcopacy was strong and resisted presbyterian invasion. In the isolated Highlands and Hebrides, presbyterianism was exceedingly weak and even episcopacy and Catholicism were submerged in a widespread semi-pagan religious culture. Such differences had not given rise to true dissent, perhaps in part because of the inefficiency of persecution. It was the economic and social changes of the eighteenth and nineteenth centuries which were to introduce a belated but very rapid and extensive process of pluralization in religion.

(b) The presbyterian churches

The Established Church of Scotland was the origin of all the dissenting presbyterian churches. Its form of government and doctrine were laid down in its principal subordinate standard, the Westminster Confession of Faith of 1643, to which practically all of the dissenters adhered. Thus there was little which separated the presbyterian churches in doctrinal terms. Dissent arose because of perceived laxity in Established Church adherence to the expected standards and because of differences over the extent of the church–state relationship. Initially the dissenters were not opposed to the principle of a state church, only to the prevailing party which governed it. But from the end of the eighteenth century there was a gradual and inexorable shift to a 'voluntaryist' position – or belief in the separation of church and state. Thus, the Established Church came under constant pressure from defection and the political influence of dissent to break the various ties which defined its establishment status.

The Church of Scotland, as the example to which most of the presbyterian churches adhered, is organized as a democratic or ostensibly democratic hierarchy. The congregation of each parish elect (in theory) lay elders and a minister to act as the kirk session; in practice elders often became self-perpetuating whilst ministers could be chosen by lay patrons until 1874. The kirk session is the congregational court in matters relating to discipline and religious provision, supplemented in some congregations by a deacons' court which may have oversight of financial matters. Kirk sessions of a district send some elders and all ministers to sit on the presbytery which supervises the clergy and is first court of appeal. In turn, presbyteries send representatives to provincial synods, which in the Established Church have been the least important court, and presbyteries (and until 1925 royal burghs) send representatives to the national general assembly which meets annually (usually in Edinburgh in May) in full session and in smaller 'commission' form at other times. All the courts above the kirk session are composed as nearly as possible of equal numbers of ministers and elders, known more prosaically as 'teaching elders' and 'ruling elders' respectively, and no distinction is drawn between them in terms of rights to speak or vote. Similarly, those appointed as chairmen, usually called 'moderators' or sometimes 'preses', hold no special powers or authority. So opposed is the presbyterian tradition to the concept of bishops that except for the parish minister, who is automatically the moderator of the kirk session, moderators are customarily elected for short periods such as one year. In such ways, the system was on the surface expected to be receptive to protest and responsive to the popular will.

Amongst the many constraints upon this democracy, the most controversial and profound was the system of patronage whereby an hereditary owner of the right of presentation selected and installed his choice of minister in the parish church. Patronage was associated in the seventeenth century with episcopacy and was abolished in 1690 since it conflicted with the presbyterian concept of 'the call' in which parishioners signed an invitation to a favoured candidate for a vacant pulpit. But the British parliament reintroduced patronage in 1712 as part of the larger package of inducements to the Scottish landed classes to forsake the Jacobite cause. The general assembly opposed its return but was mollified by the power of presbyteries to overrule a presentation. Until 1730 the Church sided with popular feeling and there were few disputed presentations. But a few did end in violence, presaging the more widespread controversies of the later eighteenth and early nineteenth century. At Bathgate in West Lothian in 1717 there was 'the unseemly spectacle' of a minister selected by the patron 'being guarded to church upon a Sabbath by files of dragoons, amid the noise of drums, and the flashing of swords'.[5] Such occasions became more numerous after 1729 when the courts of the church started to back patrons and resulted in the defection of four ministers in 1733 to form the Secession Church.

An important division was emerging in Scottish presbyterianism. On a theological level, there was a trend amongst some ministers, mostly in rural parishes, to adopt a more relaxed attitude to the standards of presbyterian discipline, preaching and morality. By the 1750s this group emerged as the Moderate Party in the Church of Scotland which sought a rational basis for religious belief in view of Enlightenment thinking, and which despised 'enthusiasm' and excess in religion. On a political level the Moderates became associated with government, being seen as an agency of the state and of the Whig government in particular. On a social level, the Moderates were the party of the landowners who came to favour the refinement in taste, 'lukewarmness' in religion and anglicization required to become members of the larger British ruling class. In this context, patronage became a device to ensure the political correctness of the clergy and of the general assembly. Though probably in the minority amongst the clergy, the Moderates had powerful support and were well organized, and controlled the Established Church until 1833. Consequently, the ideals, outlook and manner of an increasingly English-orientated Scottish landed class dominated in the Church's supreme court.

The opposing Popular or Evangelical Party was larger but less influential and more divided because of its varied social composition and confused ideological alignment. The agricultural revolution of the eighteenth century was creating a large section of rural and small-town society which was becoming alienated from the landed classes. By the 1790s the rise of factory labour and the emergence of urban middle classes created two further groups who shared little in common with each other or with the peasantry, but all three were alienated from aristocratic Moderatism and turned to evangelicalism for their religious identity. Patronage was anathema to all of them, but beyond that the movement was not denominationally united. Large numbers of the rural lower orders left the Established Church in the 1760s

From religious monopoly to religious pluralism 31

and 1770s as a result of often violent patronage disputes which rent parishes asunder. They formed congregations of the Secession Church or, less often, the Relief Church which came into being in 1761. By 1766 there were claims in the general assembly of 120 dissenting churches with 100,000 adherents, and though religious tensions eased in the last two decades of the century, presbyterian dissent remained strong in agricultural counties of the Scottish Lowlands. In growing commercial and industrial towns and cities the Church of Scotland faced loss of adherents too, firstly in 1740–80 to small sects of a congregationalist bent and after 1780 to the Relief and Secession churches.

The loss to the Established Church is difficult to calculate and varied enormously on a local basis. By the 1790s more than 70 per cent of the adult population of Jedburgh in the Borders had joined dissent whilst a more representative figure for industrializing districts might be drawn from the suburbs of Glasgow (the Barony) where the proportion was one-third. In Lowland parishes the dissenters were comparatively thin on the ground in the southwest but were by 1800 accounting for about a quarter of the population elsewhere. With considerable growth of cities and industrial parishes, the national proportion of dissent had risen appreciably by the 1830s. In the middle of the decade the Established Church could attract only 41 per cent of the churchgoers in Edinburgh, the least industrial of the larger cities. Contemporary calculations by those sympathetic to the Established Church tended to weight statistics against dissent. One 1826 compilation arbitrarily doubled the number of Established Church adherents – 'for anomalies' – but still showed that a fifth of the population were dissenters; a reworking of the data would suggest a more realistic figure of 38 per cent, of whom three-quarters belonged to dissenting presbyterian churches. Consequently, around 29 per cent of the total Scottish population, and about 32 per cent of the population of the Lowlands, were presbyterian dissenters by the 1820s.[6] Quite clearly the scale of the loss was enormous, surpassing the level of nonconformity in early nineteenth-century England.

The position of evangelicalism was not confined to the churches already mentioned. Arguably the greatest proportion of evangelicals remained in the Established Church in the late eighteenth and early nineteenth centuries, maintaining a stress on faith as an element in salvation and urging the Moderate-dominated general assembly to pursue conversion through foreign missions and church extension and missionary activity at home. Established Church evangelicals were predominantly urban, attracting middle-class support, but their influence was severely checked by identification with the dissenters during the difficult times of the French Wars of 1793–1814. Both Moderate clergy and the government spied upon Established and dissenting evangelicals as 'democrats' and 'revolutionaries'. One Moderate informant of the government wrote in the late 1790s that 'the whole of this missionary business grows from a democratical root', and commented that even evangelicals' Sunday schools were 'calculated to produce discontent, to foster an aversion to the present order of things'.[7] Though few evangelicals were French sympathizers, their cause was severely retarded until after the end of the Napoleonic Wars. But their numbers in the Established Church were growing as a result of urban expansion, and they toppled the Moderate Party from control of the general assembly in 1834 – in part because of increased evangelical representation from the newly formed burgh councils which were entitled to send assembly commissioners. Between 1834 and 1843 there was, between Moderates and Evangelicals in the Established Church, an intense and bitter contest known as the Ten Years' Conflict, in which the dominant Evangelicals vainly sought government legislation and support for their position on patronage and evangelization. An evangelical Veto Act of the 1834 assembly permitted congregations to veto a patron's choice of 'intruded' pastor, but the civil courts rejected the alternative 'call' as having no legal foundation. Parliament's repeated refusal to pass modifying enactments, and the government's rejection in 1842 of an evangelical 'Claim of Right' to spiritual independence from the state, made schism inevitable. On 18 May 1843 the Evangelical Party dramatically walked out of the general assembly in what was known as the Disruption, taking with them 38 per cent of the clergy and possibly 40 per cent of adherents, and constituted the Free Church of Scotland.

From religious monopoly to religious pluralism

The Established Church, already weak from the growth of older dissenting churches, was severely reduced in strength and status. The Established Church was deprived by the Disruption of its most active lay and clerical members, retarding evangelization schemes such as Sunday schools and the temperance movement until at least the 1870s. The 1851 Religious Census showed that the state church could attract only 32.2 per cent of attendances compared to 31.7 per cent for the Free Church and 59 per cent for presbyterian dissent as a whole. In the space of just over a hundred years the Church of Scotland had shifted from a position of near monopoly in religion to that of one denomination amongst several.

By the last quarter of the nineteenth century the Established Church could lay claim to the adherence of less than 15 per cent of the total population. Moderatism was effectively discredited within the Church where remaining evangelicals slowly grew in power, and the enormous political strength of the dissenters who, like English nonconformists, aligned with the Liberal Party, pushed the Church ever closer to disestablishment. Patronage still caused over sixty cases of disputed settlement between 1843 and 1869 and contributed to its abolition in 1874. Mounting desire for the reunion of Scottish presbyterianism compelled the severing of the state connection, and this was achieved slowly by parliamentary enactments between 1904 and 1926 dealing with doctrinal attachment to the Westminster Confession (which defined the church–state relationship) and the divesting of private ownership of church property. In October 1929 the vast bulk of presbyterian dissenters rejoined what was to be dubbed henceforth the 'National Church of Scotland'.

Since then the Church of Scotland has accounted for more than 90 per cent of Scottish Protestants. In that sense it is a church with a broad social composition and a wide geographical distribution. But for the whole period since 1780 it has represented a less cohesive and more heterogeneous denomination than other churches. It is in the dissenting churches that we can perceive more clearly some of the important social characteristics of Scottish religion.

The United Presbyterian Church (1847–1900) and its antecedents. The Secession and Relief Churches which originated in 1733 and 1761 respectively and which united in 1847 to form the United Presbyterian Church are the most potentially interesting churches for sociological enquiry. Unfortunately these are also the least studied of Scottish churches, largely because ecclesiastical historians have viewed them unsympathetically from a twentieth-century ecumenical standpoint as schismatics, fanatics and inward-looking sectarians who 'thought little of the unity of the Church' and whose prime concern was 'a determination to have their own way'. There has been equal condemnation from more liberal commentators – from Thomas Carlyle who described their clergy in 1866 as 'hoary old men', to twentieth-century historians who have described them as 'the cave-dwellers of Puritanism' and hair-splitters.[8] In short these churches and especially the Seceders have had a bad press which distracts attention from the scale and social significance of presbyterian dissent before the 1843 Disruption.

The four clergymen who founded the Secession Church in December 1733 were stunned by their popularity evident in a stream of petitions from praying or 'correspondence' societies craving 'sermon and superintendence'. The initial Seceders were mostly located in the counties of Fife, Stirling and Perth, but there was a powerful influx of old covenanting societies in central and south-western counties. The first Secession congregation south of the river Forth met in 1739 on a hillside in West Lothian when a minister joined a praying society which drew its attenders from a twenty-mile radius. The minister preached from Ezekiel 37 v. 26: 'Moreover I will make a covenant of peace with them; it shall be an everlasting covenant with them; and I will place them, and multiply them, and will set my sanctuary in the midst of them for evermore.' For the upholders of seventeenth-century covenanting, the coming of the Secession Church was a return from internal exile as rudimentary meeting houses were appointed and ministers selected from the small number who seceded in the 1730s. In its first two decades, the bulk of the Secession Church's growth was due to the accession of old covenanting societies who brought to the Church the taking of the covenant (which was made a condition of membership in 1743 though not strictly enforced), the reading of covenanting history, and the Secession's first divinity student. But between 1750 and 1780 new congregations emerged from patronage disputes in the Church of Scotland. Around six cases a year were handled by the general assembly of the Established Church between 1750 and 1770 with violence occurring on many occasions. Legal cases could drag on for up to six years, but most patrons stuck to their choice and completed the presentation leaving the thwarted parishioners to secede.

In this way, the apparently dormant tradition of covenanting resistance was revitalized after 1750 in the puritanism, fiery oratory, fierce discipline and internal rancour of the Seceders. They were tinged with millenarianism, calling frequent days of 'fast and humiliation' in reflection of 'the manifest and abounding Sins [of] the Day and Generation' ranging from 'Uncleanness of all Sorts' to 'evilspeaking, backbiting, envyings, grudgings' and 'Scandalous Sins and Miscarriages, that are breaking out among us of this congregation'. They prayed for the return of Christ to convert all from King George III to 'the meanest subjects', thus hastening 'the final overthrow of the man of Sin, the bringing in of the Jews, . . . and so bring about the iminent [sic] glory of the latter days'.[9] The Secession was the most divisive of the endemically schismatic dissenting churches of the late eighteenth century. The Seceders split in 1747 on the issue of the Burgess Oath introduced to Glasgow, Edinburgh and Perth in 1745 at the time of the Jacobite Rebellion to prevent Catholics from obtaining public office. The largest section known as the Antiburghers refused to submit to the oath since it implied recognition of the Established Church, and those who were willing to take it became known as the Burghers. Since refusal to take the Oath entailed a hefty fine, it is not surprising that Burghers were the more numerous of the two sections in towns and cities.

Although the Church of Scotland noted as early as 1766 the prevalence of dissent 'in the greatest and most populous towns', the Secession Church's main growth in the 1760s and 1770s was chiefly in Lowland rural parishes, thus explaining the strength of the Antiburghers. But the surge of rural support seems to have stagnated dramatically in the 1780s when parish clergy all over the Lowlands reported a decay in Seceders' 'blind furious zeal', 'forbidding asperity' and 'moroseness and acrimony'. An Established clergyman in Renfrewshire commented in 1790 that the 'Secession has not been very fashionable of late', and the Antiburghers noted it themselves. Their Stirling Presbytery appointed days of humiliation in 1789 to lament the passing of many leaders 'while few seem to be raised in their stead endowed with equal zeal'. A year later the same court mourned 'that in our several congregations the work of Christ is so low': 'instead of walking with God as a people married to the Lord, we have broken his bonds'.[10] As a result the number of disputed settlements in rural parishes fell considerably after 1780, and the Secession Church entered upon a new phase of its development.

In the last decade of the eighteenth century, the Seceders' strength started to shift towards urban districts in which artisan and lower-middle-class groups came to identify with evangelical dissent. Within the Secession Church this shift was marked by the emergence of 'New Licht' theology which split the Burghers and Antiburghers into four separate denominations between 1799 and 1806. The 'New Licht' (Light) eased Calvinist doctrine, stressing the offer of salvation, and at the same time moved considerably along the road towards advocating disestablishment of the state church. Whilst the minority 'Auld Lichts' were 'looking backward while the world was advancing',[11] the majority adopted a religious culture focused on individualism, 'respectability' and economic opportunity which was commensurate with their position in the expanding economy of Lowland Scotland. With the removal of the Burgess Oath in 1819, the two branches of the New Licht united the following year to form the United Secession Church and ten years later they abandoned support for state religion and became voluntaryists. Having started in the 1730s as a 'suffering remnant' in rural society, the Seceders had become within a hundred years a large religious group led by the aspiring and socially mobile in urban and industrial districts.

Like the Secession, the Relief Church had its origins in Fife but spread throughout the Lowlands and even into corners of the Highlands. Offering 'relief of oppressed Christian congregations' under the patronage system, the Relief was more liberal than the Seceders with a fairly free communion and a relaxed attitude to discipline and central church control. Its congregationalist leanings made it popular with a wide social spectrum in urban society, attracting rising entrepreneurs as well as textile workers and tradesmen. From the outset it lacked the rustic social stigma attached to the Secession, and its lax internal discipline and better relations with the Established Church allowed it to develop as a form of informal dissent. Many congregations joined the Relief as a temporary protest over a disputed presentation. A classic case started in 1761 when virtually the entire eldership and congregation of the Wynd Established Church in Glasgow left – some to form a Relief Church, others vainly trying to build a chapel-of-ease within the Establishment. Both groups united in 1766, and the bulk of them returned to the state church in 1774. At the end of the day, this incident produced new congregations of the Relief and Established churches and a small sect of independents under the control of David Dale, the founder of the New Lanark cotton mills, whilst the original Wynd congregation revived. The Relief Church was respectable where, in the late eighteenth century, the Secession was not; in Jedburgh, the formation in 1757 of what was to become a Relief congregation was a civic occasion attended by the magistrates in their regalia, and 40 per cent of the inhabitants including reputedly the entire town council joined it. In many towns such as Glasgow, Campbeltown, Hamilton and Clackmannan, the Relief Church achieved high status and popularity, and its appeal stretched to the American revolutionaries who found in its voluntaryism a religious counterpoint to political liberty. For some commentators, the 'Relievers' were the 'Scots Methodists'.[12]

The changing social composition and ideology of the Secession Church in the early nineteenth century drew it closer to the Relief, and the two united in 1847 to form the United Presbyterian Church: a powerful, strongly middle-class and by then predominantly urban denomination with some 518 congregations nationally. It achieved considerable political influence in Edinburgh and Glasgow, with many town councillors and several MPs.

In the 1851 Religious Census the United Presbyterian Church was the largest single denomination in Glasgow, claiming 23 per cent of attendances, and in the country as a whole they claimed slightly under one-fifth of churchgoers. From that position of strength in the mid-Victorian period they suffered relative decline down to 1900. Their doctrines were liberalized rapidly with a formal breach from Calvinism in 1879, but in a wider sense the distinctive testimony and ideology of the old dissenters was being eroded by the appearance of the rival Free Church with which they came to share an acute crisis in the late Victorian period, culminating in ecumenical union in 1900.

The Free Church (1843–1900) and the United Free Church (1900–29). The Disruption of 18 May 1843 was the most spectacular ecclesiastical event in modern Scotland. It created a large and influential denomination almost literally overnight amidst scenes of great excitement and public attention. All over Scotland, ministers left their manses and elders and congregations left their parish churches to meet the following Sunday in farmyards, graveyards, public halls, barns, gravel pits, on hillsides and on board anchored ships. The event was to become symbolic of a great sacrifice of money and security, and as the ultimate statement of social and religious self-determination. But the formation of the Free Church did not reflect a single split in society. In different regions and different types of community it was the product of varied social tensions and segregation.

The Free Church was dominated by its urban and middle-class adherents, many of whom were of a new and upwardly mobile generation of businessmen, agents and bank staff. In large cities like Glasgow the basis of the Disruption had been laid during the 1830s by the erection of Church of Scotland extension churches which had attracted large numbers of lower-middle-class attenders from city congregations of the older parish churches. But this pre-Disruption realignment was apparent in another way in the Borders and south-west where in the early 1830s the sons and daughters of Seceder parents were reportedly returning to the evangelical-controlled Established Church. Elsewhere, the Free Church attracted widespread support from areas where dissent had been weak hitherto. In Aberdeenshire the formation of the Free Church coincided with a wave of agricultural improvements and the Free Church became identified with the 'sufferers [who] are principally her members'.[13] And in the Highlands and Hebrides the progress of improvement and the Clearances had already generated an alienated and highly evangelical crofting community, and the peasants there entered the Free Church *en masse*.

The varied elements in the Free Church can be seen in the geographical pattern of secession amongst the clergy; this is customarily taken as a measure of lay secession for which no accurate statistics exist. A total of 454 (or 37.9 per cent) out of 1195 ministers left the Established Church, the largest proportions coming from urban districts and parts of the Highlands and Hebrides. In the city of Aberdeen all fifteen ministers 'went out', whilst in Glasgow and its suburbs the proportion was 25 out of 40, or 63 per cent. The further into the countryside, the lower was the secession. In the whole Presbytery of Glasgow which included rural parishes the figure dropped to 53 per cent, and in adjacent Dumbarton Presbytery it was a mere 22 per cent. In Edinburgh Presbytery 62 per cent seceded, but the overall figure for the Edinburgh province (Lothian and Tweeddale Synod) was 43 per cent. In the Borders where the Secession Church was strong and in the south-west where it was not, the Free Church walkouts were equally low – 25 and 20 per cent respectively. In the heartland of the Seceders in Fife, Perthshire and Stirlingshire the Free Church claimed a vigorous 47 per cent of ministers. In the north-eastern counties the 33 per cent secession was strongest outside of Aberdeen in the Inverness area, Moray and Nairn and in coastal fishing communities. The ministerial secession in the Highlands and Islands varied from 76 per cent in Easter Ross to 35 per cent in the Hebrides and West Highlands, but this is an unreliable guide to what was a fairly uniform defection to the Free Church by the peasant laity. Nationally, few parts were untouched by the Disruption with even the northern island groups of Orkney and Shetland experiencing a walkout of 32 per cent of the clergy. Only in places like the islands of Barra and South Uist where Catholicism predominated was the Free Church presence insignificant.

The strength and geographical breadth of the Free Church gave it cause to claim the status of 'the true old Church of Scotland'. But despite its social diversity, it was from the start a church dominated by the ethos and style of the bourgeoisie. This was reflected in the great concern that the Disruption would incur loss of status and income – 'ministers in one day signing away more than £100,000 a-year'.[14] Solidarity was maintained and fears allayed by careful planning from at least October 1842 when money was pledged and conclaves of supporters organized. The Sustenation Fund, the central source of Free Church ministers' stipends, was planned in advance of the Disruption, and after it the Church was managed on very strict business lines. The dependence on 'Christian liberality' sustained concern for its financial state, and success was judged year by year on the volume of donations to central funds. The amount of money raised in the first four years was staggering, and churches and manses appeared rapidly all over the country. Those members with money or the ability to secure loans came to dominate in kirk sessions of the new church, giving rise to a comment in an Established Church propaganda pamphlet in 1844: 'Money! money! with the "F.C." is everything'.[15]

The Disruption was a powerful and popular event of the grassroots amongst the evangelical movement in the Church of Scotland. The Rev. Dr Thomas Chalmers has long been regarded by ecclesiastical historians as the key inspirer and organizer, but it is clear that he was forced reluctantly to back the policies on which the evangelicals 'went out' and that he was too much a high Tory to understand or applaud the popular democracy unleashed. It is also clear that his much-quoted statement to the first general assembly of the Free Church that 'we quit a vitiated Establishment, but would rejoice in returning to a pure one' and that 'we are not Voluntaries', did not reflect overall opinion in the Church.[16] A small and vociferous band of supporters kept his view alive after his death in 1848 and prevented union with the voluntaryist United Presbyterian Church in the 1860s and 1870s, but from the outset the Free Church was drawn into close harmony with the dissenters. They were given the use of Secession and Relief churches in the months after the Disruption, became

From religious monopoly to religious pluralism 41

closely involved with the United Presbyterian Church in home and foreign mission work, and like other dissenters tended to support Liberalism. The 'Frees' were *de facto* dissenters and voluntaryists, and with the United Presbyterian Church reflected the social virility of the urban middle classes and their ideology of self-help and individualism.

However, the fact that the union of the Free and United Presbyterian Churches did not take place until 1900 is significant. From the 1880s a crisis developed in British evangelicalism – a crisis which will be examined in chapter 6 – and it pushed the two denominations towards amalgamation in the face of mounting difficulties; over 90 per cent of United Presbyterian kirk sessions and 95 per cent of Free Church presbyteries agreed to union. Although the new United Free Church became the largest church in Scotland in 1900, its rate of growth during the first quarter of the twentieth century lagged far behind that of most other churches. Throughout its entire but brief history, the United Free Church was negotiating a reunion with the Established Church that was accomplished in 1929. It was hailed at the time as a glorious event for the Scottish Church, but the spirit of ecumenicalism that has come to play such a prominent part in the twentieth-century reformed kirk had roots in fundamental difficulties afflicting late Victorian evangelicalism.

The minor presbyterian churches were products of the endemic divisiveness in Scottish presbyterianism. They form a confusion of splits and amalgamations rarely recorded in full in ecclesiastical histories and mostly ignored hitherto by social historians. Our understanding is thus fairly limited but some significant patterns are apparent. They fall into three major groups: those which emanated from the seventeenth-century covenanting tradition, most of which passed through the Secession Church and avoided its final embourgeoisement in the United Presbyterian Church; various indigenous Independent churches, which though not presbyterian in *government*, were closely harmonized with presbyterian evangelicalism; and churches, mostly of the Highlands and Hebrides, which emerged from the nineteenth-century Free Church as a result of its inherent social and ideological tensions. Characterizing most of these, and especially the first and the last, is intense puritanism and introversion which makes them bastions of old-style Scottish presbyterianism. The oldest of them, and the extreme Calvinist conscience of all Scottish presbyterianism, is the Reformed Presbyterian Church which comprised the descendants of the covenanters from the south-western and central counties. In 1714–43 the 'society men' had only one minister, and according to their own strict presbyterianism could not constitute a presbytery and appoint clergy as it would have signified 'bishop-like' qualities in their one pastor. Not surprisingly the bulk of them joined the Secession Church in the late 1730s to avoid extinction, and the remainder were saved from that fate in 1743 when a Secession minister joined them and permitted the formation of the Reformed Presbytery. Of all the dissenters the 10,000 or so Reformed Presbyterians went to the greatest lengths to distance themselves from secular affairs and the state. Though not 'voluntaries', they opposed erastianism and viewed successive British governments as unworthy. After several of their members were enfranchised by the Reform Act of 1832, the Church forbade voting in civil elections. They were also forbidden from starting legal actions, enlisting in the armed forces, and joining outside organizations – even missionary societies of which the Church actually approved. This was the cause of frequent schisms as sections of the membership became urbanized, upwardly mobile and affectionate of modern attitudes. Nearly half the congregations left in 1753 when they adopted the doctrine of universal atonement; aspiring middle-class adherents were estranged for becoming tax collectors, burgesses and excise officers (positions involving recognition of the state); and four congregations were lost in the 1830s over civil voting and swearing oaths of allegiance to Queen Victoria. After 1850 adherents found it difficult to swallow the social isolation and impotence implied by such tenets, and the bulk of the Church united with the Free Church in 1876. A minority stayed out, still surviving in 1980 with an ageing membership of 300 in Scotland but with stronger branches in Northern Ireland and overseas.

The minor branches of the Secession Church shared the covenanting tradition of the Reformed Presbyterians and suffered virtually identical problems. A succession of tiny remnants, mostly adhering to 'Auld Licht' theology but others stuck fast to various stages of Secession development, emerged from 1790-1829 and struggled constantly against the desire of members to adapt to modern life. From the 1810s they split apart in different directions with the bulk joining the Established, the Free, the United Presbyterian or Reformed Presbyterian Churches from 1839-52. A remnant called the Original Secession Church (former Antiburghers) survived with 3000 communicants in 1871 and just under 2000 in 1953. Their tradition of a suffering remnant was difficult to sustain. In East Campbell Street Burgher Church in Glasgow, for instance, the remarkable growth in wealth of its adherents in the early nineteenth century had to be compensated by refusing to install heating.

The Independent tradition emerged from Scottish presbyterianism between 1730 and 1770 amongst groups in society who were generally receptive to the economic opportunities of commercial and industrial life. Groups called the Glasites, the Old Scots Independents, the Scotch Baptists and the Bereans were strong in both town and country parishes of Fife, Angus and Kincardine on the east coast, and in towns stretching westward to Glasgow and Paisley. Their members were overwhelmingly rising manufacturers, such as the Sandemans of Perth and David Dale of New Lanark, and weavers, and attained great strength in some local communities. In Dundee the Glasites were the largest single denomination in 1790 claiming nearly a third of the total population. The same spirit of economic opportunity and independence also promoted the emergence of Scottish Independency led by James and Robert Haldane. Excited by Painite ideas and by popular evangelism, they initiated a wave of evangelical enterprises from 1796-1800 which established Sunday schools, day schools and tabernacles in many parts of both the Lowlands and the Highlands, Hebrides and Northern Isles. They were denounced by the government and by the Established Church as subversive, their supporters referred to by the general assembly in 1799 as 'persons notoriously disaffected to the Civil Constitution of the country'.[17] But with strong support from visiting English evangelicals like Charles Simeon, their denomination thrived though it split in 1808 into Congregationalist and Baptist Churches. Both bodies had mixed social compositions of urban middle classes, especially in Glasgow and Dundee, and peasant and fishing communities in the north-east, Orkney and some west-coast ports and islands. They maintained links with presbyterian dissent, and the Congregationalists actually united in 1896 with an offshoot of the Secession Church called the Evangelical Union. But in the main neither of them achieved high growth rates and have remained socially diverse and geographically scattered.

The Lowland Free Church was highly aware of the peculiarities of the Gaelic-speaking crofters in the nineteenth century. But the liberalization of the Church's doctrine in the 1890s, which led it to abandon Calvinist tenets, caused a secession of some north-western congregations who constituted the Free Presbyterian Church. This was followed in 1900 by the refusal of many Gaelic congregations to join the United Free Church. The Free and Free Presbyterian churches have continued throughout the twentieth century to enjoy the adherence of from half to two-thirds of the Protestant crofting population located mostly in the Hebrides, upholding seventeenth-century presbyterian standards which ironically never affected that area at the time. The Free Church is less strict than the Free Presbyterians and the two have an uneasy and sometimes hostile relationship, but together they have sustained the cultural distinctiveness of a part of Scotland that has never felt the full economic benefits of modern industrial society in Britain.

(c) The non-presbyterian churches

The Roman Catholic Church was by 1980 the largest denomination in Scotland in terms of churchgoers. This is a fact which has failed to sink into the presbyterian consciousness, and the Church is still widely regarded as an alien intrusion. But the faith that was nearly obliterated in Scotland at the Reformation and that experienced a very gradual removal of restrictive laws in 1793, 1829 and 1926 now accounts for some 43 per cent of all churchgoers and around 15 per cent of the adult population.

From religious monopoly to religious pluralism 45

In 1755 Catholics in Scotland were enumerated by Alexander Webster at 16,490, or just over one per cent of the population. The vast majority of these lived in a narrow band across the north of Scotland stretching from the islands of Barra and South Uist in the west through inner Hebridean islands such as Rhum, Eigg and Canna, the peninsulas of Knoydart, Morar, Moidart and Kintail, up the Great Glen to 'the Enzie' in Banffshire and parts of Aberdeenshire. A number of Catholic nobles enabled Catholicism to survive on their estates in the north-east, but the Catholics of the Western Highlands and Hebrides were almost uniformly peasants who after 1770 came to share with their Protestant peers elsewhere in that region a popular culture shaped by oppressive landlords, clearances and evictions. From 1770 Catholic migrations built up with priests organizing the establishment of a colony at St John's in Newfoundland (at a discreet distance from a colony of presbyterian Scots), but with larger short-distance migrations to growing Highland towns and settlements such as Fort William. Large-scale emigration schemes via Clyde ports to America were under way by the 1780s, and in 1792 the first major movement to the industrial Lowlands occurred with some 600 dispossessed Catholics from Glengarry in the Great Glen north of Fort William moving to Glasgow at the invitation of cotton manufacturers. Though out-migration has continued ever since, the Catholics of the Highlands have survived in communities distinctive in religion and culture both from their Protestant near-neighbours and from Lowland Catholics.

Irish immigrants of whom roughly two-thirds were Catholic first became a major feature in the south-west of Scotland where substantial numbers became, quite unusually, agricultural workers and even tenant farmers. Between 1810 and 1850 as many as 25,000 harvesters came annually to Scotland through west-coast ports, but for the most part Irish immigrants entered industrial-related employment ranging from 'navvying' on canal, railway and, in the twentieth century, hydro-electric construction, to cotton-spinning and -weaving, and coal- and iron-mining. The vast majority settled initially in Lanarkshire, Renfrewshire and Ayrshire, transforming the religious composition of the area. In 1778 there were reputedly only twenty

Catholics in Glasgow meeting semi-secretly for worship in a private house. The numbers rose to around sixty in 1791 and to 2300 in 1808, and the first resident priests since the Reformation arrived in the city from the north. With the introduction of cheap steam-boat travel from Ireland, numbers of Catholics in the city rose to 10,000 in 1820 and 27,000 in 1831, representing some 13 per cent of the population. The percentage of Irish-born people in Scotland reached 4.8 per cent in 1841, peaked at 7.2 per cent in 1851 after the potato blight, and then fell slowly to 3.3 per cent in 1921. However, the Catholic population grew by natural increase. It rose from around 1 per cent of total population in 1755 to 8.5 per cent in 1891 and 15.7 per cent in 1970. Despite a slight reduction in the 1980s, the consistently higher levels of church attendance amongst Catholics compared to Protestants during the twentieth century has brought their church close to being the largest in Scotland.

The Irish Catholic immigrants of the nineteenth century were more uniformly poor than most other groups, and many entered the lower end of the working classes. During the twentieth century social mobility amongst Catholics in Scotland has increased markedly over that of the Victorian period, but it is still true to say that the Catholic Church's adherents are more proletarian in composition than those of the Church of Scotland. In the context of a hostile presbyterian reception, the incoming Irish turned to the chapel and its activities for cultural and ethnic identity, and even in the 1950s it could be reported that the Catholic layman was 'still feeling himself after 100 years a stranger in the land'.[18] But the Catholic Church encountered great difficulties in rising to this role. Despite the removal of restrictive laws against priests, the holding of mass and the ownership of property by Catholics, Protestant sentiment prevented the restoration of an official church hierarchy until 1878. The Church in Scotland was short of resources with which to build chapels and its priests were probably the lowest paid in the country; in the 1830s, Glasgow priests' salaries were £40 compared to at least £100 for Secession ministers and as much as £425 for parish ministers of the Established Church. Partly because of its poverty and partly because its doctrines stressed the availability of pastors rather than buildings, the Church concentrated its efforts on providing clergy until the middle of the nineteenth century leaving the main part of its church-building schemes until after 1850.

The 'labour-intensive' nature of the Catholic Church's operations created its own problems. The indigenous Scottish Church had its traditional headquarters in the Aberdeen area and drew its priests from surrounding parts, but this 'Scottish' section was overwhelmed by the Irish influx of the nineteenth century. The Scottish Church was reluctant to recruit Irish priests and few attained promoted posts before the late nineteenth century. This caused periodic and sometimes severe ruction between Scottish priests and Irish laity, and between Scottish and Irish priests. Tensions were reduced after 1869 by the judicious appointment of a pointedly 'neutral' English Archbishop to the Glasgow archdiocese. However, the intrusion of Irish republican politics to Scottish Catholic affairs was, and to some extent remains a headache for the Church authorities; in the 1880s priests were disciplined for standing at municipal and school board elections as candidates supporting Irish Home Rule. This has put the Church under pressure from the presbyterian-dominated civil establishment to keep its house in order, but the Church's efforts in this direction did not prevent waves of approved anti-Catholic agitation from the Church of Scotland and other churches. One such outbreak in the 1920s and 1930s led the Catholic novelist Compton Mackenzie to comment: 'This fury of sectarian hate still rages more fiercely in Scotland than anywhere else on earth.' Official Catholic policy in Scotland in the 1980s is still to meet Protestant bigotry 'by the Church keeping a low profile'.[19]

As in most European countries, the decline in churchgoing in Scotland during the present century has been less steep amongst Catholics than amongst Protestants. General reasons can be adduced for this, such as the relative lack of compromise in Catholic doctrine in the face of growing secularism in popular philosophy and morality. This is very marked in Scotland where the Catholic Church and its adherents tend to be more conservative on moral issues like abortion and birth control than either Scottish Protestants or English and Welsh Catholics. But we might also identify a dynamic and efficient management in the last one hundred years which has, for example, permitted the Catholic Church to respond to population movements more quickly than the Protestant churches. Whilst the presbyterian churches have been burdened with 'over-churching' from the 1890s onwards, directing effort into the difficult tasks of amalgamating congregations and disposing of excess buildings, the Catholic Church has been increasing its number of churches by erecting modern ones in new housing estates and new towns. Although this far from explains the relative strength of Catholics' participation in organized religion, it is symbolic of the generally greater vigour of their faith in twentieth-century Scotland.

The Scottish Episcopal Church has in some respects had a similar modern history to that of the Catholic Church. Both started the period as churches of the Highlands, Hebrides and the northeast, and the Episcopal Church was regarded in the presbyterian Lowlands as a surrogate for 'popery'. Indeed it continued to drift more towards Catholicism and away from presbyterianism, deleting the word 'Protestant' from its Code of Canons in 1838, and courting Eastern Orthodoxy in its liturgy and doctrines. In the twentieth century large numbers of English episcopalian immigrants find even the presbyterian Church of Scotland more to their taste. In the eighteenth century the Episcopal Church was also politically identified with Catholicism. Episcopalians formed the mainstay of the Jacobite armies of the Catholic Stuart pretenders and, like the Catholic Church, were the object of penal laws which were repealed in the early 1790s. Thereafter, episcopalians were accepted back into the fold of respectable British politics – symbolically in 1827 when six bishops were received by George IV at Holyroodhouse in Edinburgh. Like Catholicism episcopacy was reabsorbed into Lowland and urban Scotland during the industrial revolution, but in the process it became a denomination more split by social and ethnic divisions than any other in Scotland.

These splits became evident early in the eighteenth century when the penal laws instituted against the Church and its adherents for supporting the Jacobite cause divided it into those clergy

From religious monopoly to religious pluralism

and congregations willing to swear loyalty to the Hanoverian monarchs and those unwilling; respectively the juring or 'English' chapels and the non-juring or 'Scottish' chapels. The latter were technically illegal but as Samuel Johnson pointed out, they were meeting freely by the 1770s in the strongly episcopalian areas of the north-east 'by tacit connivance'.[20] In the south, by contrast, the Church emerged in the eighteenth and nineteenth centuries with a varied social composition but dominated by an anglicizing upper middle class who eventually brought the whole Church into full communion with the Church of England. The first juring congregation in Glasgow was formed in 1750-1 with a membership of prominent manufacturers and merchants, two of whom attained high office on the town council. In the fashionable Clyde coast town of Helensburgh, residence for many of the wealthier Glasgow business families, the Episcopal Church included the titled gentry. The Church's cultured liturgy and decorous furnishings exuded a refinement and wealth which appealed to sections of the Scottish middle and upper classes. A very large proportion of the high nobility (86 per cent according to an estimate of 1843) and perhaps as much as two-thirds of the landowning classes generally were episcopal. In many parishes all the heritors of the Established Church were actually members or supporters of the Scottish Episcopal Church or of its equivalent the Church of England. Moreover, large numbers of the children of the *nouveaux riches*, educated at English public schools, seceded from the Church of Scotland in the mid-nineteenth century to swell episcopal ranks.

The Church's identification with the landed and middle classes made its relations with other social groups more difficult. There was a sweeping loss of peasant adherents in the Highlands, the north-east, Perthshire, Angus and Kincardineshire as presbyterianism grew in strength in the north of the country after 1750. In the Lowland industrializing districts recruitment of immigrant working-class episcopalians was very low. In Greenock in the 1840s the Anglican hatters from Lancaster, earthenware workers from the Potteries, glass-blowers from Newcastle, chain-makers from Liverpool and Lutheran sugar-boilers from Germany were all reportedly excluded from membership of the upper-middle-class

Episcopal chapel. More seriously in numerical terms, the episcopalians from Ireland seem to have been almost uniformly neglected by the Church. The City Chamberlain of Glasgow calculated in 1831 that there were 8551 of them in the city and its suburbs, and twelve years later an Episcopal clergyman estimated that there were some 10,000 in the same area devoid of religious provision. In some places the Church was more active in recruiting from the industrial working classes: for instance, amongst iron and steel workers in Coatbridge in the 1840s. But in the larger cities of Glasgow, Edinburgh and Dundee there seems to have been a general resistance to admitting Irish clergy, culture and people to the Church until late in the nineteenth century.

One major reason for this situation must be introduced. In Scotland, episcopalianism has always been seen as resting on the Catholic side of the Protestant–Catholic divide. In England, Anglicanism has had a more ambiguous position, whilst in Ireland the episcopal Church of Ireland has traditionally placed itself on the Protestant side. Indeed, Irish episcopalians were strongly Orangeist and undoubtedly contributed to the introduction of Orange lodges to nineteenth-century Scotland. Although documentary evidence for this might be scarce, it seems clear that Irish episcopalians with a strongly Protestant tradition could not possibly have come to terms with the pro-Catholic tendencies of the Scottish Episcopal Church.

The Church's relatively poor membership patterns in the twentieth century emphasized the debilitating effects of social division. Whilst it has been alert to opening churches in post-1945 new towns, it has suffered dramatically in the larger cities. In Dundee its membership stayed constant between the two world wars but then fell nearly 40 per cent by 1949 and by half ten years later. The scale of loss suggested not only working-class but also middle-class 'leakage'. Whilst 'high church' episcopalians often attend Catholic services as well, the growing use since 1950 of candles, incense burners and other Roman or Orthodox practices such as the weekly communion may well have alienated many.

But the Church has maintained greater strength in parts of the Highlands like Argyll, and in the north-east and rural districts generally. Congregations like that at Kirriemuir in Angus came to rely on landowners resident in out-of-town mansions, and in rural Perthshire the Church has been almost exclusively composed of the gentry who still award it 'considerable social prestige'. But since the eighteenth century the Church has lost significantly through episcopal landowners living in England and sitting in the 'laird's loft' in the parish church when in Scotland 'for the season'; as an episcopal clergyman noted in the nineteenth century, landowners supported the Established churches on both sides of the Border 'simply for the sake of example and propriety'.[21] This practice highlighted the socio-religious divide. A children's rhyme in an early-twentieth-century Borders parish noted the alien practices brought to the presbyterian kirk by episcopal occupants in the loft:

> *Pisky! pisky, A —men!*
> *Doon on your knees an' up again!*
> *Presby, Presby, dinna bend!*
> *Always sit on your hinnerend.*[22]

The Scottish Episcopal Church has never lost this identification with rural landowners and with a culture connected closely with that of the English upper classes. Its failure – arguably a deliberate failure – to broaden its social and ethnic appeal prevented it from sharing with most other churches in industrial Scotland the high growth rates of the eighteenth and nineteenth centuries.

The Methodist Church in Scotland suffered, like the episcopalians, from major ethnic divisions resulting from Irish and English immigrants of the nineteenth century 'bringing national habits, feelings and usages into conflict at the Quarterly and Leaders' Meetings'.[23] Some Methodist congregations relied on immigrants, such as malleable iron-workers from Staffordshire who moved to Airdrie, Coatbridge and Hamilton. But Methodism in Scotland depended more on native Scots, although its success was at best highly localized. The prospects seemed promising in the 1740s and 1750s with George Whitefield and John Wesley attracting large audiences of presbyterians during

Scottish tours. Methodist societies were set up all over Lowland Scotland, but mostly in the larger cities and textile and fishing villages. Handloom weavers and fishers were two prominent occupational groups, scattered on a diagonal strip from Shetland, where Methodism was particularly strong, south-westwards through coastal and inland villages of the north-east to the industrial districts of the west. The bulk of the Scottish membership was located in Glasgow, Airdrie, Coatbridge and Paisley. Glasgow and Airdrie districts accounted for 43 per cent of all Scottish members in 1819, and from the 1840s to the 1950s Glasgow continued to account for 20 to 30 per cent.

But from the 1760s Scottish Methodism failed to grow at the pace of other churches or of population as a whole. From 1767-84 annual growth of members averaged less than 0.2 per cent per annum compared to 5 per cent in England, nearly 6 per cent in Wales and nearly 8 per cent in Ireland. A surge in the decades around 1800 gave way to widespread contraction between 1810 and 1840 when congregations collapsed in weaving and fishing communities all over Lowland Scotland. The immediate cause of the collapse of the Methodist circuit in Dumfriesshire in 1836 was the scandal of the preacher selling a cure for VD, but a more general reason was defection to the dissenting presbyterian churches: to the Seceders and the Free Church. An Aberdeen preacher noted an 'extraordinary decrease of male members, especially amongst the intelligent and useful class' from 1835-1850.[24] Wealthier members tended to defect first leaving working-class adherents who could not pay preachers or meet the chapel debt. Despite increased mission work in the late Victorian and Edwardian periods, Scottish Methodist membership never rose above 15,000. In Glasgow by 1954 there were seventeen chapels but only 1468 attenders, representing only 1 per cent of all churchgoers.

Accounting for this general and seemingly unique failure of Methodism amongst an English-speaking Protestant manufacturing population has been a matter of some debate since the eighteenth century. On one level Methodist preachers coming north from England noted the Scots' desire for fully-ordained clergy rather than mere lay preachers; Wesley granted this concession in 1785 resulting in a doubling of membership in four years, but it was reversed after his death in 1791 with an immediate contraction of members. Scots, and especially the middle classes, felt that lay positions in the Church did not match the status given by the eldership in the presbyterian churches, and they certainly seemed to favour the dissenting presbyterian churches after 1830. More contentiously, Allan MacLaren has argued that the Arminianism of Methodism did not appeal to Scots' Calvinism, and that in reflection of this Methodists in Scotland vainly preached Calvinism and the doctrine of the elect.[25] But David Wilson, a Methodist preacher in Aberdeen, argued convincingly in 1850 that Methodists did not preach a limited atonement but merely failed 'to proclaim to perishing sinners a *full, free, present and assured salvation*' that was already becoming available in the presbyterian churches. The central issue, as he pointed out, was that the Free and United Presbyterian churches no longer taught a limited atonement but were preaching exactly the same as the Methodist Church and were stealing its distinctive preaching and its adherents.[26] Thus, accounting for the failure of Methodism in Scotland focuses on the character and doctrinal alignment of presbyterianism, and this will be examined in chapter 5.

The minor non-presbyterian churches. Scotland like any industrial society has acquired a variety of small churches. The Quakers date back to the seventeenth century, but their numbers have remained small and largely confined to the large cities and the north-east. Individual presbyterian ministers often led congregations into small denominations such as the Unitarians. The later nineteenth century brought an influx of East European Jews, many skilled in the tailoring, furniture and fur trades, who congregated in working-class districts like the Gorbals in Glasgow. Estimates of their numbers vary, but the largest community in Glasgow may have been 1000-strong in 1879, around 5000 in 1900 and perhaps 20,000 in the 1950s.

A variety of other churches appeared after 1850, mostly imported religions from England and, increasingly, the United States: the Mormons, Jehovah's Witnesses, the Church of the

Nazarene and the Salvation Army amongst many others. Perhaps most notable for their geographical spread and their strength are the Open and Exclusive (or Close) Brethren. In 1960 the Open Brethren numbered around 25,000 meeting in some 350 assemblies, and the Exclusives perhaps a further 3000. They became very strong in the inter-war period amongst fishing families in Orkney and the north-east, in mining communities in the central Scottish coalfield, and in other industrial districts in the Lowlands. They are also socially spread, the Open tending to be strongest amongst professional and business people in the cities and the Exclusives amongst the poorer fishing families of the Moray Firth Coast. The Brethren recruited from dissenting presbyterians and Methodists, and were in the same mould as the Congregationalists and Baptists who were also strong in the fishing communities. The Brethren assumed a strong anti-Catholic stance, some sharing the view with the Free and Free Presbyterian churches that the Treaty of Rome and the Common Market were 'popish' devices.

In many ways, several of the minor presbyterian and non-presbyterian churches since the 1880s have been 'religions of the disinherited'.[27] They adopted rhetoric and puritanism redolent of the covenanters and rural Seceders of the mid-eighteenth century, feeling themselves estranged from the benefits brought by economic change and social advancement. Amongst crofters, small-boat fishermen and miners, it was common to find congregations of the Brethren, the Free and Free Presbyterian Churches, the Salvation Army, the Church of Christ, the Evangelical Union, the Congregationalists and the Baptists adopting semi-millennialism and aggressive insularity. In large cities and towns, however, congregations of these churches have often been more wealthy, and especially since the 1940s. Middle-class congregations have come to dominate many of the mostly lowland sects which, though remaining small, have often experienced vigorous growth.

Notes

1 R. L. Stevenson (1879) *Edinburgh: Picturesque Notes*, London, 16–17.
2 The Sanquhar Declaration quoted in M. Hutchinson (1893) *The Reformed Presbyterian Church in Scotland: Its Origins and History, 1680–1876*, Paisley, 116.

From religious monopoly to religious pluralism

3 Quoted in J. Leopold (1980) 'The Levellers' Revolt in Galloway in 1724', *Journal of the Scottish Labour History Society*, 14 (May), 18–19.
4 T. Johnston (1946) *The History of the Working Classes in Scotland*, Glasgow, Unity, 92–6.
5 J. McKerrow (1841) *History of the Secession Church*, Glasgow, 34.
6 *Edinburgh Christian Instructor* quoted in J. Sinclair (1826) *Analysis of the Statistical Account of Scotland*, vol. II, London, Appendix p. 14. See also vol. I (1825, Edinburgh), 81.
7 Rev. William Porteous of Glasgow to Lord Advocate, 24 January 1797 and 21 February 1798, Edinburgh University Library, Laing MSS, LaII500.
8 A. L. Drummond and J. Bulloch (1973) *The Scottish Church 1688–1843*, Edinburgh, The Saint Andrew Press, 51; Carlyle quoted in J. Barr (1934) *The United Free Church of Scotland*, London, Allenson, 81; W. L. Mathieson (1910) *The Awakening of Scotland: A History from 1747 to 1797*, Glasgow, 233; W. Ferguson (1968) *Scotland 1689 to the Present*, Edinburgh and London, Oliver & Boyd, 126.
9 Leslie (Fife) Associate (Burgher) Congregation, kirk session, MS minutes 2 December 1744, SRO CH3/319/1; Stirling General Associate (Antiburgher) Presbytery, MS minutes 9 January 1781, CRA CH3/286/1.
10 ibid., 29 December 1789, 2 December 1790, CRA CH3/286/2.
11 A. Thomson (1848) *Historical Sketch of the Origin of the Secession Church*, Edinburgh and London, 151.
12 Quoted in G. Struthers (1843) *The History of the Rise, Progress and Principles of the Relief Church*, Glasgow, 254.
13 *Free Church Magazine*, 1848, quoted in I. Carter (1979) *Farmlife in Northeast Scotland 1840–1914*, Edinburgh, John Donald, 163–4.
14 T. Brown (1884) *Annals of the Disruption 1843*, Edinburgh, 91, 97.
15 Quoted in A. A. MacLaren (1974) *Religion and Social Class*, London and Boston, Routledge & Kegan Paul, 104.
16 T. Chalmers (1843) *The Addresses delivered at the Commencement and Conclusion of the First General Assembly of the Free Church of Scotland*, Edinburgh, p. 7.
17 *Principal Acts of the General Assembly of the Church of Scotland, 1794–1812*, 38–45.
18 R. C. Rennie and T. C. Gordon (eds) (1966) *The Third Statistical Account of Scotland; The Counties of Stirling and Clackmannan*, Glasgow, Collins, 270.
19 C. Mackenzie (1936) *Catholicism and Scotland*, London, George Routledge, 151; A. Ross (1980) 'The Church in Scotland', in J. Cumming and P. Burns (eds) *The Church Now: An Inquiry into the Present State of the Catholic Church in Britain and Ireland*, Dublin, Gill and Macmillan, 34.
20 R. Chapman (ed.) (1970) *Johnson's Journey to the Western Islands of Scotland . . .*, London, Oxford University Press, 15.
21 J. P. Lawson (1843) *History of the Scottish Episcopal Church*, Edinburgh, 433.

22 L. Derwent (1977) *A Breath of Border Air*, London, Arrow, 125, and idem (1985) *Lady of the Manse*, London, Arrow, 116.
23 D. Wilson (1850) *Methodism in Scotland*, Aberdeen, 19.
24 ibid., 14.
25 A. A. MacLaren, op. cit., 41; idem (ed.) (1976) *Social Class in Scotland*, Edinburgh, John Donald, 43.
26 D. Wilson, op. cit., 5-6, 22-6.
27 P. Thompson *et al.* (1983) *Living the Fishing*, London, Routledge & Kegan Paul, 258.

3
Patterns of religious adherence

The measurement of religion

Statistics of church adherence are an important tool for the historian in assessing the social significance of religion. They can assist in a variety of ways to illuminate the relative popularity of different denominations and the changing patterns of religious activity and inactivity. However, they cannot be used without considerable caution for there are major problems and dangers manifest in their application.

In the first place there was very little collection of national statistics of church adherence in Scotland before the mid-nineteenth century; only the Methodists for instance produced membership data annually between the 1760s and the 1860s. The concept of a church membership which could be counted and distinguished from non-members was essentially the product of modern industrial society. In the largely agrarian society of the early-modern period, where the Established Church was expected to be the monopolistic provider of ecclesiastical facilities, there was little interest in the numbers attending church or taking communion since it was assumed that all but the small numbers of heretics and schismatics were under the superintendence of the one and universal kirk. As a result statistical estimates before the 1790s in Scotland were invariably of 'papists' whom the suspicious presbyterians and the government were intent on monitoring. As far as the historian is concerned, pre-1800 statistics of Scottish religion are principally guides to political conformity rather than religious 'choice' in a modern sense.

From the late eighteenth century there was a developing interest in enumerating the people's religious preferences. The statistics collected were at first estimates, haphazard in their geographical coverage, and only gradually systematized between the 1830s and 1860s. An important motive for the churches' interest was denominational competition, especially on the part of the presbyterian dissenters during their heyday in the 1850s and 1860s. But increasingly in the mid- and late-Victorian periods there was an alarm at the extent of non-churchgoing and the size of 'the lapsed masses'. By the 1890s the religious condition of the people was an integral part of 'the condition of England' debate which enveloped Scotland also, and in the context of examining the nation's moral and physical well-being statistics of religion were taken to be 'unimpeachable witnesses to vigour, progress and interest'.[1] The historian must be cautious about sharing this alarm and reading into the figures the disappearance of a golden and usually rustic age for religious observance.

The problems do not stop there. Even when information was collected on numbers of church members and churchgoers there were frequent lapses in the reliability of enumeration, in completeness, and in continuity in defining categories. In counting church members for instance churches differed according to whether they used numbers of active members or eligible communicants. The Catholic Church, with no category of 'membership', has produced estimates of Catholic population (sometimes using a statistical base such as numbers of baptisms but sometimes relying on informed guesswork), whilst the Episcopal Church has produced data on communicants and baptized persons. The category of eligible communicants used by many of the presbyterian churches varied considerably between denominations and over time according to the strictness of the criteria for keeping names on communicants' rolls. In counting churchgoers there has always been the insurmountable problem of distinguishing attenders from attendances because of the practice of going to church more than once on a Sunday. Some counts of attenders included children whether they went to church or separate Sunday schools. Furthermore, some churches like the

Patterns of religious adherence

Glasites and the Brethren have been hostile to or uninterested in collecting statistics of any kind. Indeed, our knowledge of the numbers adhering to smaller dissenting churches is weak for all periods since the eighteenth century and has undoubtedly led to an underestimation of their strength.

Additionally there is a fundamental problem over the accurate and impartial measurement of religious adherence in Scotland. Government inquiries into religion were not conducted with the rigour and exactitude that were applied in other parts of Britain or in other countries. The two main investigations, the Royal Commission on Religious Instruction in 1837-9 and the Census of Religious Worship taken on 30 March 1851, left the collection of statistics to churchmen – with the result that the first was haphazard in its coverage and the second was incomplete. The 1851 religious census of Great Britain is a key source of information about churchgoing, the extent of church accommodation, and the relative size of denominations. But the Scottish section of the census is markedly more inaccurate than its English and Welsh counterparts. In relation to attendances there were no returns from 32 per cent of Established churches, 12 per cent of Free churches and 10 per cent of United Presbyterian churches. This creates an underestimation of churchgoing in the population as well as an imbalanced impression of denominational adherence. The absence of a proper state census of religion in Scotland forces us to use church-collected membership figures wherever possible since ironically they are more complete and reliable in what they show. However, the data from 1837-9 and 1851 remain at the forefront of churchgoing analysis as there is little alternative information.

These are just some of the problems in preparing statistics of religion for tabulation. But once they are assembled and all the qualifications made about reliability and comparability, it is important to be clear about what such data can demonstrate. Figures for membership and churchgoing reveal very little about belief – about its intensity or its content. Attendance at church does not mean someone is a devout Christian and non-attendance does not necessarily imply atheism or agnosticism. Non-churchgoing may well indicate exclusion or alienation from organized religion, or a combination of both, but it does not reveal unbelief. But in so far as our concern is for the *social* significance of religion, we must accept church membership and attendance as important measures in themselves. One implication of this is to distinguish between the two for they have separate and distinctive histories. It is possible to brandish figures of church membership which appear to demonstrate a rise in religious adherence; presbyterian church membership, for instance, rose from 21 per cent of total population in 1850 to 26 per cent in 1950. Yet figures of churchgoing provide evidence of a contrary trend; presbyterian church attendances on a Sunday, expressed as a proportion of total population, fell from 55 per cent in 1851 to around 9 per cent in 1959.[2] Statistics of religion can mislead and fool to an alarming extent, and we must not allow them to obscure or simplify the complex changes in the social experience of popular religion over the past two centuries.

Denominational adherence

One of the things that statistics of religion can show is the growth and decline of different denominations: their individual patterns of support and how they changed over time, and the geographical areas where each church found its greatest popularity. In most cases, however, it is not possible to extend such workings before about 1850 because of the lack of data. In the eighteenth century, for example, the high degree of informality to dissent led to some groups who were alienated from the Established Church still being classified as within its pale. In the northern half of Scotland episcopalians did not entirely abandon the state church for their own denomination, and in the Lowlands it was common practice for members of the Relief, Secession and independent churches to worship in parish churches. Although these denominations imposed heavy penalties upon members who 'heard sermon promiscuously', it is clear that large numbers of ordinary churchgoers were slow to accept the principle of membership of one denomination. Disciplinary cases continued well into the nineteenth century, testifying to the continuation of the practice. The parish minister at Stonehouse in Ayrshire commented in 1790: 'It is not easy to ascertain the precise number of dissenters from the Established Church, principally, because many scarcely know to what particular sect they belong.'[3] Whilst the practice of 'sermon tasting' never disappeared, the better provision of churches in rural and industrializing parishes by the middle of the nineteenth century had permitted the inculcation of a stricter notion of exclusive membership. Data from the Royal Commission on Religious Instruction in the 1830s and from the 1851 Religious Census, given in Table 1, give an idea of the relative strength of the Scottish churches. What is immediately apparent from the figures for Scotland's two largest cities is the weakness of the Established Church even before the Disruption of 1843. In both Glasgow and Edinburgh presbyterian dissenters were equal in number to attenders at the state church in the mid-1830s, whilst the influence of Irish immigrants was already dramatically changing the religious complexion of Glasgow where Catholics accounted for 13 per cent of churchgoers.

Table 1   Churchgoers by denomination, 1835/6 and 1851 (% all churchgoers)

	Edinburgh		Glasgow		Scotland
	1835/6	1851	1835/6	1851	1851
Established Church of Scotland	44	16	41	20	32
Presbyterian dissent:					
Free Church		33		22	32
Secession Church ⎫ United	21 ⎫		14 ⎫		
⎬ Presbyterian	⎬	27	⎬	23	19
Relief Church ⎭ Church	9 ⎭		13 ⎭		
Congregationalists	3	5	5	5	4
Baptists	4	3	2	2	1
Reformed Presbyterian Church	1	1	2	2	1
Others	4	1	4	3	1
Non-presbyterian:					
Roman Catholic Church	5	5	13	16	5
Scottish Episcopal Church	5	5	2	3	3
Methodist Church (all branches)	3	2	3	2	1
Others	1	2	1	2	1
	100	100	100	100	100

Sources: Figures based on data in Royal Commission on Religious Instruction, PP (1837) xxx, 12–13, and (1837–8) xxxii, 13; Census of Great Britain (1851): Religious Worship and Education, Scotland, PP (1854) lix.

But the figures for these two cities undoubtedly exaggerate the extent of dissent – and especially presbyterian dissent – in the country as a whole. Formal dissent was yet to materialize in the Highlands and Hebrides, whilst in the Lowlands dissent accounted for little over a third of the population. One national trend the Glasgow and Edinburgh figures do illustrate, however, is the downturn in the growth of the Secession and Relief Churches from the 1830s onwards. In both cities these churches failed to keep pace with population growth between 1835 and 1851, indicated by a decline in their proportion of churchgoers: a decline from 30 to 27 per cent in Edinburgh and from 27 to 23 per cent in Glasgow. This deceleration in growth was probably greater in country areas – a circumstance reflected in the fact that about a fifth of Scottish churchgoers in 1851 belonged to the United Presbyterian Church. But a concomitant of this, and perhaps a causal factor, was the striking number of dissenters produced by the formation of the Free Church. The Disruption sapped energy and self-confidence from the Established Church, and perhaps induced the high number of non-returns to the 1851 census. Thus, the census underestimates the number of those attending the state church, but whether the non-returning congregations had lower than average attendances is unclear. Making a statistical compensation for such non-returns is difficult in these circumstances. But even if every denomination is attributed with its own average number of attenders for each non-returning congregation, the Established Church would still have claimed less than 36 per cent of worshippers in 1851. Collectively, the presbyterian dissenters clearly outnumbered Established Church supporters and undermined the validity of the state church.

Table 1 demonstrates the sweeping transformation which the denominational structure had undergone in the late eighteenth and early nineteenth centuries. In 1700 the Established Church accounted for probably 95 per cent of churchgoers – including those served by episcopal clergy who were holding on to parish churches. Little had changed six decades later. Even if we accept the exaggerated estimate of 100,000 presbyterian dissenters in 1766, and allow for around 20,000 Catholics and an equal number of episcopalians, the Established Church could still claim that 89 per cent of the population was in at least *de facto* nominal adherence. The position in the second quarter of the nineteenth century is thus all the more striking, and is highlighted by a comparison with sizes of the major religious groupings in England (Table 2). The established church in each country was stabilizing its numerical strength after losses to dissent, but the Church of Scotland had clearly suffered more acutely than its southern counterpart.

Table 2 The denominational structures in Scotland and England, 1851 (% all churchgoers)

	Scotland	England	
Church of Scotland	32	47	Church of England
Presbyterian dissent	59	47	Nonconformists
Non-presbyterian dissent	9	6	Catholics and minor churches
	100	100	

Sources: The table is based on data in the Religious Census, Scotland, and on a tabulation by W. S. F. Pickering (1967) in 'The 1851 religious census – a useless experiment?', *British Journal of Sociology*, 18, 392.

But the tide was already turning back in favour of the Church of Scotland by the 1850s. The vigorous growth of 'old' presbyterian dissent – that is, all but the Free Church – seems to have been spent by the 1840s. In Glasgow this collection of denominations reached its peak of popularity in the 1820s and 1830s. In 1824 these churches provided 40 per cent of all pews in the city, but by 1851 this had declined to 35 per cent. The Secession and Relief Churches opened twelve churches in the city between 1781 and 1823, representing one new church for every 8700 new inhabitants between those years. By contrast, they opened only five churches between 1824 and 1847, or one new church for every 59,000 new citizens. Clearly, these denominations were failing to keep pace with the growth of either other churches or population. An important factor was the advent of the Evangelical regime in the Church of Scotland after 1833 which seems to have created a surge of popularity, attracting dissenters with a new vigorous evangelicalism and the offer of church accommodation in 200 extension churches built during the following nine years.

Evangelical policies may have attracted adherents to the Established Church in the 1830s, but the Free Church did not benefit for long after 1843. Table 3 shows that the Established Church rump had the highest growth of the three main presbyterian churches by the time membership data was collected in the 1860s. The rates of growth of the Free and United Presbyterian Churches were consistently lower than that of the Established Church for the entire period from 1860 to 1928 with the exception of the First World War. The slow growth of the United Presbyterian Church, composed of the Secession and Relief Churches of the pre-1847 period, is particularly noticeable. This and the sluggish growth of the Free Church present something of a paradox. The mid-Victorian decades from 1850 to 1880 were the high point of presbyterian dissent's influence in public affairs: in local and national politics, in the move towards state education, in charitable and social-policy activities, and in evangelization at home and abroad. By dint of energy, enthusiasm and 'Christian liberality', the Free and United Presbyterian Churches appeared to put the Established Church in the shade. Yet it is quite evident

Table 3 Growth rates of the main presbyterian churches, 1860–1928 (%)

	Church of Scotland	Free Church	United Presbyterian Church
1860–1870	1.80	1.11	0.72
1870–1880	2.15	1.16	0.72
1880–1890	1.32	1.02	0.66
1890–1900	1.15	1.08[a]	0.86[a]
		United Free Church	
1900–1910	0.79	0.28	
1910–1920	0.35	0.45	
1920–1928	0.63	0.16	

Source: Figures refer to the average annual growth rates in the communicants' rolls based on figures given in or produced by linear extrapolation from R. Currie *et al.* (1977) *Churches and Churchgoers: Patterns of Church Growth in the British Isles since 1700*, Oxford, Clarendon Press, 132–5.

Note: [a] Figures relate to 1890–99.

that within the presbyterian community the trend towards religious pluralism that had characterized the period from 1760 to 1843 was well in reverse by the 1860s. The Church of Scotland was slowly regaining ground in attracting members and adherents. In 1860 the Church of Scotland accounted for 48 per cent of presbyterian church members, the Free Church 32 per cent and the United Presbyterian Church 20 per cent; by 1891 the proportions were 53 per cent, 30 per cent and 17 per cent.[4] Although these figures exclude the smaller presbyterian denominations, it is unlikely that the general trend is distorted since most of these minor churches were experiencing stagnation or decline in membership and many of them were being absorbed by the larger churches.

The reversal of pluralization was a major phenomenon within British Protestantism in the later nineteenth century. In England the Anglican Church was certainly increasing its share of Protestant church membership after the 1880s at the expense of the Methodists and most nonconformist denominations, and possibly from the 1830s. But the process was slow on both sides of the border. In Scotland the numerical decline of presbyterian dissent after 1850 proceeded at a much slower pace than that at which dissent had grown during 1760–1840. The presbyterian dissenters remained into the 1920s a large and powerful force in Scottish church life. Moreover, they could be very strong in certain communities. Figure 1 shows the relative strength of the three main churches in the regions of Scotland in 1891. As can be seen, the Church of Scotland was dramatically weak in the north and north-west of the country, claiming the allegiance of only 3.9 per cent of presbyterians in the West Highlands and Hebrides (Glenelg), 6.4 per cent in Sutherland and Caithness, and 7.9 per cent in Easter Ross (Ross). In each of these three areas and to a lesser extent in Argyll and Moray, the position of the Established Church was overtaken by that of the Free Church. The Free Church's grip on the Highlands was remarkable, but elsewhere its support was fairly even – ranging from 19 per cent in the Borders (Merse and Teviotdale) to 30 per cent in Orkney. But in non-Highland areas support for the Established Church varied more than that of the Free Church. In the synod of Aberdeen the

SYNODS:
1 Lothian & Tweeddale
2 Merse & Teviotdale
3 Dumfries
4 Galloway
5 Glasgow & Ayr
6 Argyll
7 Perth & Stirling
8 Fife
9 Angus & Mearns
10 Aberdeen
11 Moray
12 Ross
13 Sutherland & Caithness
14 Glenelg
15 Orkney
16 Shetland

Church's members as % of total presbyterian church members:

- over 90%
- 70 - 90%
- 60 - 69%
- 40 - 59%
- 30 - 39%
- 20 - 29%
- 10 - 19%
- 5 - 10%
- under 5%

★ Indicates largest church in the region

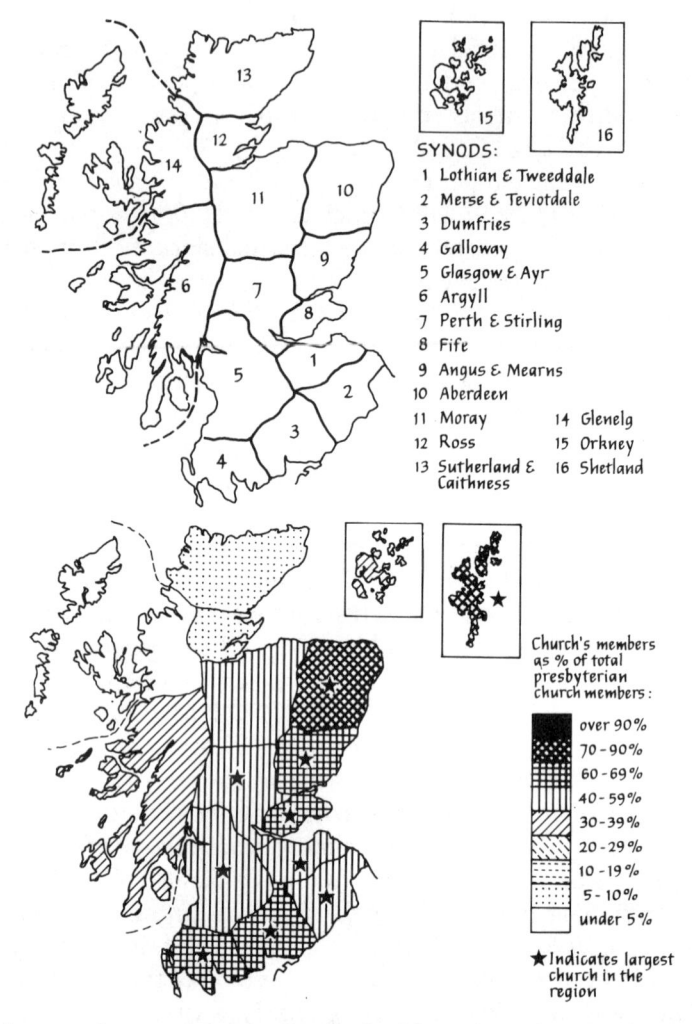

Figure 1 Comparative regional strength of the main presbyterian churches in 1891[1]

(a) Church of Scotland

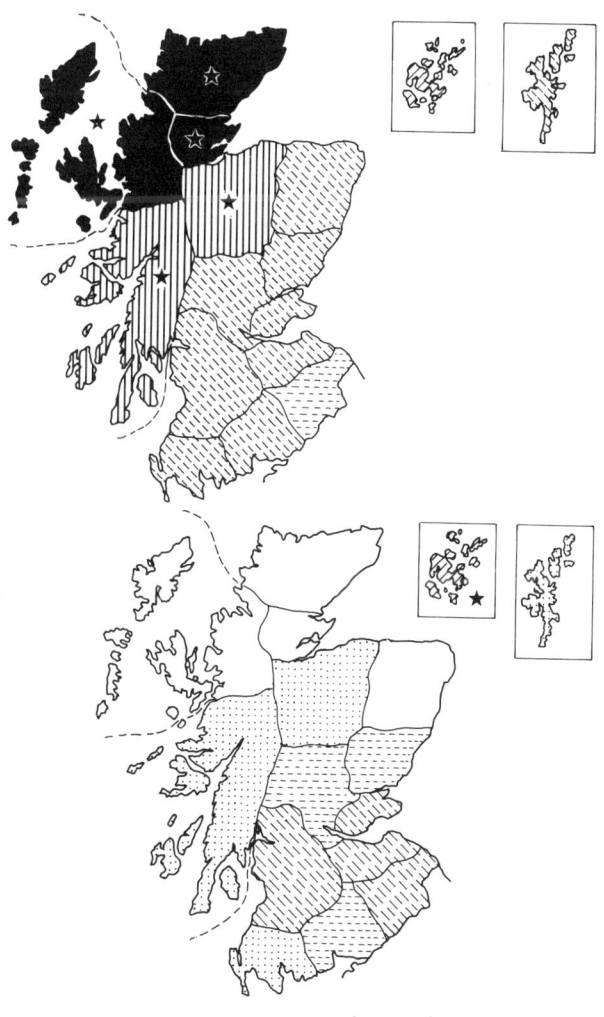

(b) Free Church of Scotland

(c) United Presbyterian Church

Source: Data calculated from Robert Howie (1893) *The Churches and the Churchless in Scotland*, Glasgow, p. 38.

[1] Calculated according to provincial synods of the Church of Scotland

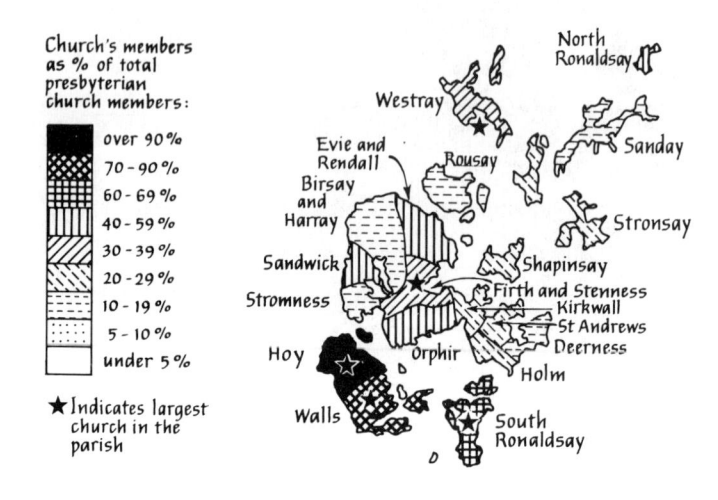

Figure 2   Comparative parish strength of the churches in Orkney, 1891

(a) Church of Scotland

(b) Free Church of Scotland

(c) United Presbyterian Church

(d) Baptists, Congregationalists and Original Seceders

Source: Based on data from Robert Howie (1893) *The Churches and the Churchless in Scotland*, Glasgow, pp. 35–6.

Note: There were 56 Episcopalians in Kirkwall (representing 2.5% of church members) and 7 in Stromness (representing 0.7%). There were also unrecorded numbers of Catholics and members of the Evangelical Union, with churches in Kirkwall and Shapinsay respectively.

state church could claim 70.9 per cent of presbyterian members, but in Orkney only 34.7 per cent. With the Free Church taking such an even proportion of members from the Established Church at the Disruption, the vital factor in regional variation in the Lowlands was the United Presbyterian Church. The United Presbyterians were virtually unknown in Highland areas by the late nineteenth century, and were weak in the south-west and the north-east. They were more numerous in the synod of Glasgow and Ayr which held 42 per cent of Scotland's population in 1891, making their church more urban in character than the other two. But in terms of density, United Presbyterians were most concentrated in a local population in the Orkney Isles. With 35 per cent of presbyterian members the United Presbyterian Church claimed Orkney as the only part of the country where it was the largest single denomination.

This regional 'snapshot' in 1891 is not entirely satisfactory for it conceals some important features of the historical geography of religion in Scotland. For instance there are reasons for believing that there had been changes in the regional strength of the three churches over the preceding half century. The high number of Secession congregations formed in the north-east between 1800–40 suggests that there must have been a marked decline of United Presbyterian membership in ensuing decades to leave figures of 4.5 per cent for Aberdeenshire and 11.5 per cent for Angus and Mearns in 1891.

In addition the regional pattern does not demonstrate the high degree of local variation in the balance between the three denominations. In the Highlands and Hebrides the regional statistics are probably fairly accurate representations of district situations, but elsewhere there were enormous differences. Figure 2 illustrates the complexity of adherence in a relatively small area. In 1891 the United Presbyterian Church was the largest denomination amongst the 30,000 inhabitants of the Orkney Isles; out of 12,887 members of all churches, 4301 (or 33.4 per cent) belonged to the United Presbyterian Church. But of these, 1215 worshipped in one church in the islands' capital of Kirkwall, and a further 1379 were located in another three parishes. In other words, 60 per cent of United Presbyterian members were concentrated in only four

Patterns of religious adherence

of Orkney's nineteen civil parishes, contributing to highly diverse structures of church affiliation in separate and sometimes adjacent communities. Such diversity was perhaps accentuated in an island group where isolation could sustain variations in denominational alignment. But in Lowland districts of the mainland of Scotland diversity could result from different degrees of industrialization and urbanization. Protestant dissenters were strongest in districts with considerable built-up areas and industrial manufacturing, with the Free Church's support being more evenly spread than that of the United Presbyterian Church, whose membership tended to concentrate in cities and larger towns, whilst adherents of smaller denominations often attained high density in smaller industrial villages.

The decline of the smaller dissenting churches has been a marked feature of the twentieth century, as Figure 3 shows. Whilst such churches have survived in small pockets in mining and fishing villages, on a larger scale in the Highlands and Hebrides, and have generally sustained a presence in the larger

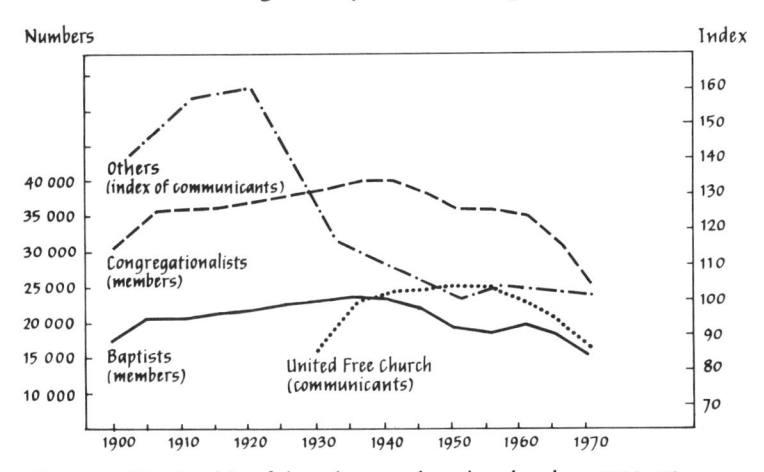

Figure 3 Membership of the minor presbyterian churches, 1900–70

Source: Figures are from or derived from R. Currie *et al.* (1977) *Churches and Churchgoers: Patterns of Church Growth in the British Isles since 1700*, Oxford, Clarendon Press.

Note: The index for 1900–1950/3 includes the Free Church, the Free Presbyterian Church, the Reformed Presbyterian Church and the Original Secession Church; the index for 1950/3–1970/1 excludes the Original Secession Church 1950/3 = 100.

cities, national adherence has in the main fallen. The Congregationalists, the Baptists and the United Free Church (Continuing) have declined more slowly – and only after 1940 – but taken collectively the hard-line presbyterians of the Free Church, the Free Presbyterian Church and the Original Secession Church have progressively declined in popularity since 1920. Such small churches can, however, experience periods of sharp growth through the work of a few energetic ministers and lay helpers, but their general isolation from other churches tends to limit their growth potential in Lowland areas and confines their appeal to geographically or occupationally isolated communities.

Throughout the growth and decline of presbyterian dissent since 1740, there has been a steady rise in the numbers adhering to non-presbyterian churches. As Table 4 shows, these churches were particularly weak in the eighteenth century, their members being located mostly in the Highlands, Hebrides and north-east where Scottish Catholicism and Episcopacy were largely concentrated. Diversity in church adherence is customarily associated with towns and cities, but in religious terms at least Scottish urban areas were extremely homogeneous before 1800 whilst many country districts in both Highlands and Lowlands had significant sprinklings of non-presbyterians. In Glasgow in 1778 there were reportedly less than twenty Catholics and probably fewer than 500 episcopalians, together representing less than 2 per cent of the city's population. In the Highland county of Inverness, on the other hand, Catholics alone accounted for more than 5 per cent of the people in 1755. During the nineteenth and twentieth centuries this situation has been reversed. By 1851 most of the minority churches had their base in cities such as Glasgow, Edinburgh and Dundee, whilst in country areas their strength tended to be much less. There are qualifications to this, however. The 1851 religious census showed that the Mormons were more numerous outwith the larger cities, usually in small industrial villages. Indeed, many of the small sects – both presbyterian and non-presbyterian – had a greater appeal in small communities which had experienced recent growth of population. The larger churches were often slow off the mark in forming congregations and erecting places for worship, and in this way

Table 4 Non-presbyterian dissenters in Scotland, 1790–1959

	1790		1851		1914		1959	
	Adherents	% of total population	Churchgoers	% of total churchgoers	Adherents	% of total population	Adherents	% of total population
Roman Catholics	25,000?	1.6	79,723	4.6	546,000	11.4	787,170	15.5
Episcopalians	12,000?	0.8	43,904	2.5	146,073	3.0	106,478	2.1
Methodists	1,356	0.1	21,675	1.2	9,651	0.2	14,146	0.3
Jews	10?	(0.0006)	35	(0.002)	10,000?	0.2	20,000?	0.4
Mormons			3,407	0.2	700?	(0.01)	784	(0.02)
Brethren					5,000?	0.1	28,000?	0.6
Seventh Day Adventists					280?	(0.006)	500?	(0.01)
Jehovah's Witnesses							2,876	(0.06)
Others	500?	(0.03)	3,243	0.2	3,000?	(0.06)	5,000?	(0.09)
Totals	38,866	2.5	151,987	8.7	720,704	15.0	964,954	18.9

Sources: A wide range of sources has been used, notably for the estimates. Most of the firm figures come from R. Currie *et al.* (1977) *Churches and Churchgoers: Patterns of Church Growth in the British Isles since 1700*, Oxford, Clarendon Press, and J. Highet (1960) *The Scottish Churches: A Review of their State 400 Years after the Reformation*, London, Skeffington.

Note: Figures accompanied by a ? are estimates.

proselytizing minor churches could form congregations quite quickly in rural parishes changing rapidly as a result of the arrival of manufacturing industry and migrating workers.

Immigration to Scotland was the single greatest cause for the growth of non-presbyterian dissent. In 1841, 4.8 per cent of Scotland's population was Irish-born; of these, perhaps two-thirds were Catholic and the remainder episcopalian, Methodist and presbyterian. Continued high levels of immigration from Ireland in the 1840s and 1850s were followed between 1880 and 1910 by a considerable influx of Jews from Eastern Europe and Russia. Since the 1880s there have been groups of immigrants from Lithuania, Poland and Italy, and over the last two centuries steadier flows from England and the United States. This has introduced new churches to Scotland: some of them characteristically 'modern', such as the new religions of America, but others ethnic variations on the Catholic Church. In the early stages of immigration, there was a strong tendency for incomers and their churches to congregate in certain communities. Perhaps more than half of Scotland's Jewish population in 1900 lived in the Gorbals district of Glasgow. Lithuanians collected at Bellshill. The Irish Catholics and their descendants displayed the same pattern of concentration. Over a third of all the Irish-born in 1841 lived in Glasgow and its suburbs, and the bulk of the remainder lived in the neighbouring counties of Lanarkshire, Dumbartonshire and Renfrewshire. But since then, as Figure 4 shows, Catholics have fanned out from west central Scotland – moving eastwards into the Lothians, West Fife and the Stirling area, northwards to Dundee, and southwards into Ayrshire and the Border counties. In some areas such as the Highlands, the proportion of Catholics has diminished, whilst in the north-east their density has stayed almost the same over the whole period since 1755. But in the rest of Scotland, the Catholic section of the population has grown – almost entirely by natural increase since the late nineteenth century when Irish immigration diminished considerably. From Glasgow the Catholic population has over-spilled, and increasingly it has moved not into other large cities but to smaller cities and towns: initially between the 1870s and the 1920s to rapidly expanding satellite towns of Glasgow and to

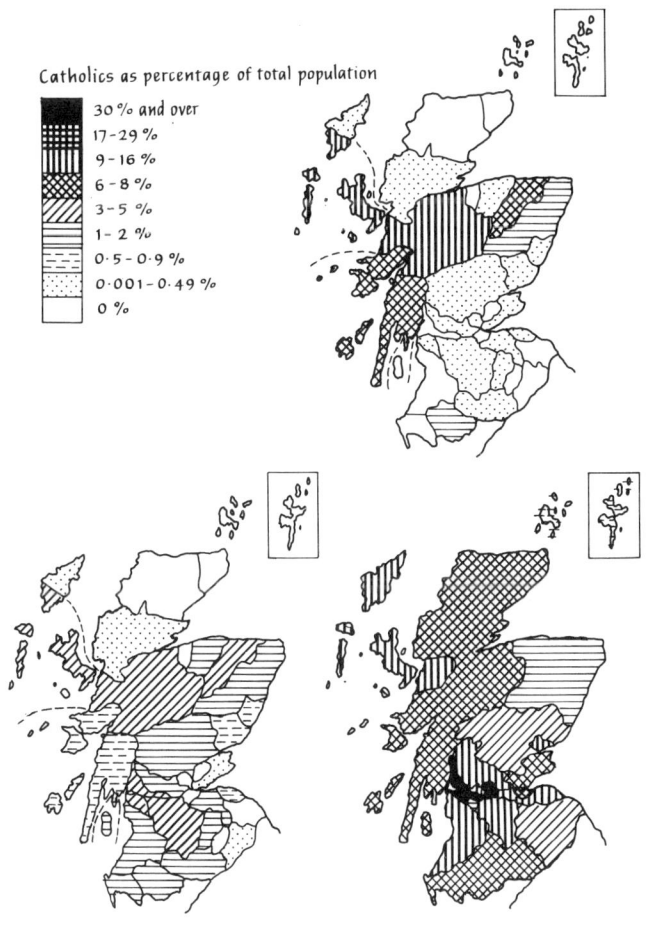

Figure 4 Density of Catholics in population in 1755, 1851 and 1984 (as % of total population)

(a) 1755, from Alexander Webster's census (adherents)

(b) 1851 (attendances on 30 March at all diets of worship, making a nominal allowance of 300 attendances for a county with Catholic chapels but no returns)

(c) 1984 (estimated Catholic population)

Sources: Based on data from R. H. Campbell (1965) *Scotland Since 1707*, Oxford, Blackwell, p. 10; Census of Religious Worship, 1851, *PP* (1854), lix; and P. Brierley and F. Macdonald (eds) (1985) *Prospects for Scotland: Report of the 1984 Census of the Churches*, Edinburgh, MARC/NBSS.

The Social History of Religion in Scotland

Table 5 Proportion of religious marriages by denomination, 1855–1970 (%)

Year	Church of Scotland Free Church, 1855–95 United Presbyterian Church, 1855–95 United Free Church, 1915	Catholic Church	Episcopal Church	Others
1855	84.2	9.3	1.8	4.7
1875	81.2	8.8	2.6	7.4
1895	78.7	10.5	3.2	7.6
1915	73.9	13.6	4.0	8.5
1935	71.6	15.1	3.0	10.3
1955	69.4	19.3	2.9	8.4
1970	67.0	22.9	2.8	7.3

Source: Figures based on data in R. Currie *et al.* (1977) *Churches and Churchgoers*, Oxford, Clarendon Press, 226–9.

new industrial and mining communities in central Scotland and Fife; and since 1945 to new towns (notably East Kilbride, Cumbernauld and Livingston), but also more generally to most Lowland districts as a result of a centrifugal diffusion of the Catholic population of the Glasgow conurbation. This is particularly noticeable in east central Scotland where the proportion of Catholics in the total population stood in 1984 at 8.6 per cent for Edinburgh but 11.6 per cent for the surrounding Lothians. Even in the west the density of Catholics is now higher in Motherwell and Monklands (35.9 per cent) and Dumbartonshire (33.5 per cent) than in the city of Glasgow (30.7 per cent).

The spread of Catholicism throughout Scotland is essentially a product of Catholic population growth. Table 5 shows how the proportion of religious marriages solemnized by the Catholic Church has continued to grow whilst those of the next largest non-presbyterian denomination, the Episcopal Church, has declined since the First World War. The proportion of religious marriages conducted by the presbyterians has also diminished so that by 1970 almost a quarter of church weddings were Catholic. In part the Catholic Church has been able to solemnize the greater proportion of mixed marriages between Protestants and Catholics, but in a wider sense its constituency has continued to grow at a faster rate than that of the Protestant churches. The absence of a Catholic equivalent of Protestant church membership makes direct comparisons difficult, and the rise in the number of Catholics does not reveal much about adherence. To make comparisons it is necessary to look at patterns of churchgoing.

Churchgoing and the origins of religious decline

Statistics of religious activity should in theory be easier to collect than membership data, and should provide a more accurate guide to the social significance of religion. In practice the value of churchgoing censuses is much reduced because of the lack of consistency in manner of enumeration and the reliance placed on churchmen for counting. There is no census which can provide a reliable figure for the extent of church attendance in the population, and incompatibility between censuses limits the types of changes in patterns of religious observance which can be illustrated over time. None the less, 'snapshot' statistics can be used to draw out conclusions concerning the effects of social change.

The geographical patterns of churchgoing in 1851 and 1984 are shown in Figures 5 and 6. It must be emphasized that the two censuses are not directly compatible – in large part because the first shows *attendances* per head of population whilst the second is an estimate of *attenders* per head of population. However, the two maps suggest some interesting characteristics in churchgoing habits. In 1851 there was considerable variation within regions. In the Highlands and Hebrides churchgoing levels increased from south to north, being lowest in Argyll and highest in the northern counties of Ross and Cromarty, Sutherland and Caithness. In the north-east and the south-east levels varied considerably: high in Moray and Nairn but low in Banff and Kincardineshire, and high in Berwickshire but low in Selkirk. There was also considerable variation in the central belt with high figures in Dumbartonshire and low figures in West Lothian, but in the south-west there was a uniformly low attendance. By contrast, the 1984 map, despite its reduced detail, shows that firmer regional patterns had evolved by the later twentieth century. The Hebrides and the Lochalsh district in the West Highlands have an extraordinarily high level of Sunday worship compared to the rest of the country; 52 per cent of adults and children attend church or Sunday school in that area.

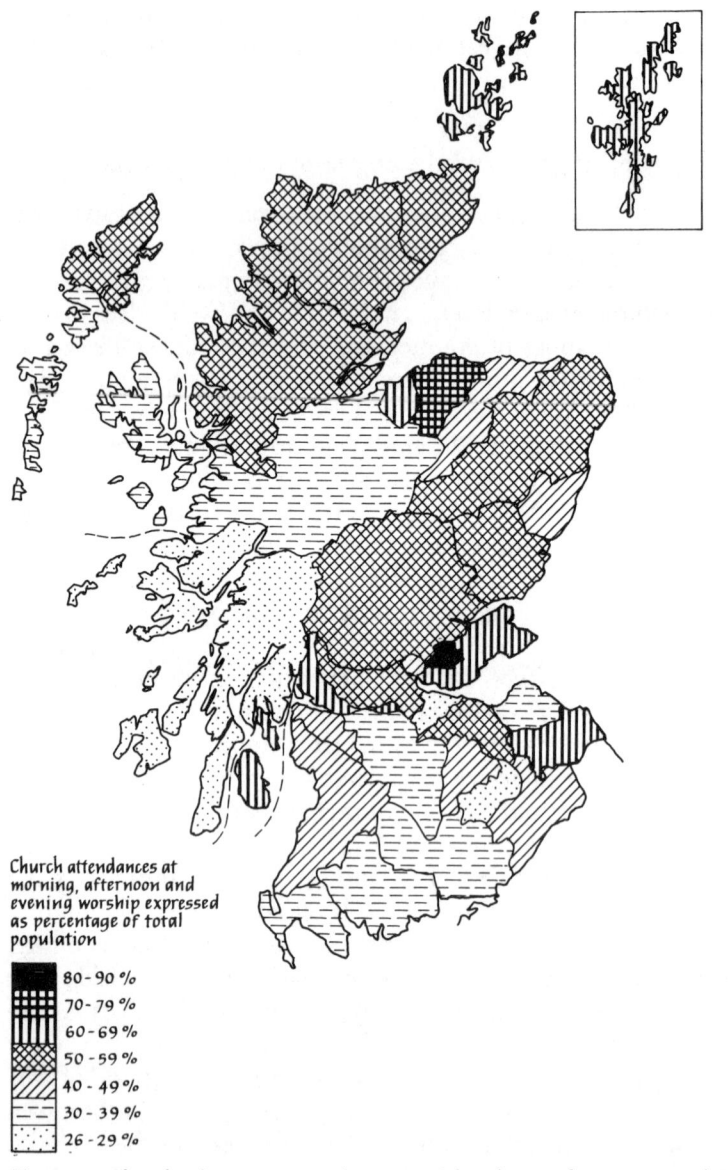

Figure 5 Churchgoing rates 1851, by county (church attendances at morning, afternoon and evening worship: % of total population)

Source: Figures based on data in Census of Religious Worship, 1851, *PP* (1854), lix.

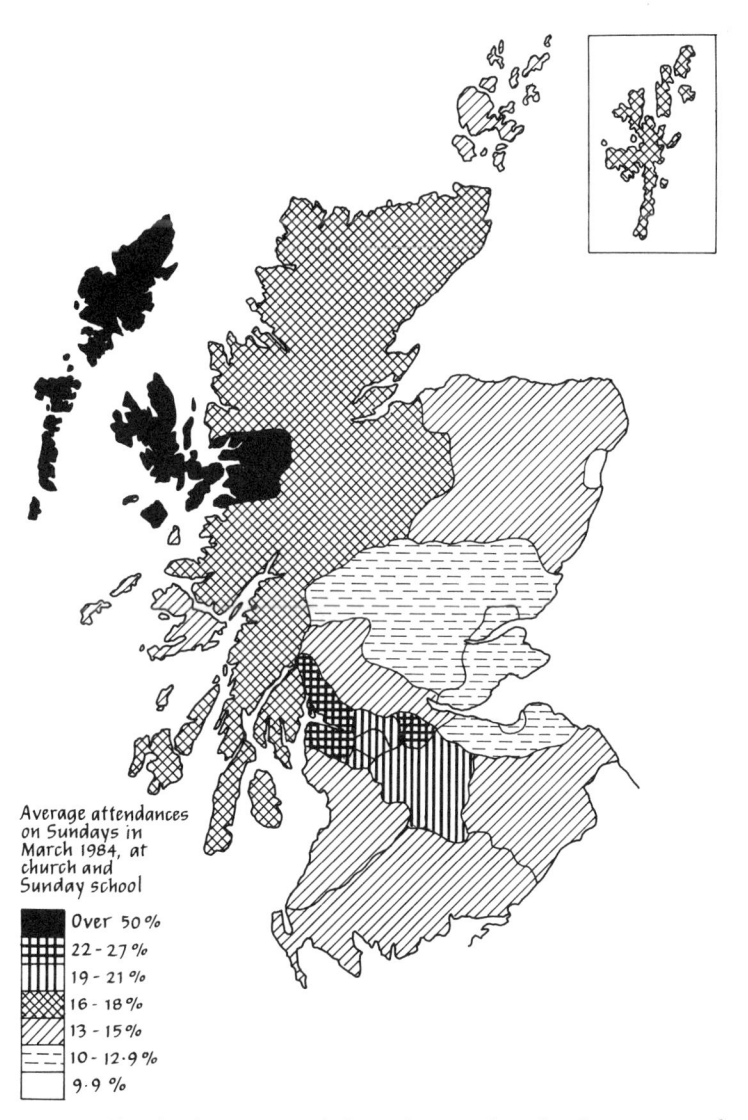

Figure 6 Churchgoing rates 1984, by region or sub-region (average attendances on Sundays in March 1984 at church and Sunday school)

Source: Based on data from P. Brierley and F. Macdonald (eds) (1985) *Prospects for Scotland: Report of the 1984 Census of the Churches*, Edinburgh, MARC/NBSS.

In the rest of the Highlands, Orkney and Shetland, Sunday turnout is reasonably high. But in the Lowlands there is interesting variation. The highest attendance rates are in the west central districts, and notably in those with a high Catholic population. The two districts with the highest proportions of Catholics also have the highest churchgoing rates outwith the Hebrides and Lochalsh: Dumbartonshire with a churchgoing rate of 23 per cent, and Motherwell and Monklands with 27 per cent. Edinburgh and surrounding Lothian have smaller Catholic populations and average churchgoing rates. At the other extreme from west central Scotland is Aberdeen city with a very small number of Catholics and the lowest churchgoing rate (9.9 per cent) in the country.

Despite the rather confused situation in the mid-nineteenth century, we can discern a major change by the 1980s in geographical patterns of churchgoing in the Lowlands. In 1851 levels of churchgoing were relatively low in all western Lowland counties with the exception of Dumbartonshire, whilst in the east, despite variation, the average level was significantly higher. By 1984 the position had been reversed with all western districts becoming areas of high attendance and eastern districts areas of low attendance; even the south-west (Dumfries and Galloway), where rates have generally been low throughout, has now overtaken Lothian, Fife and Tayside. There has been a spectacular falling away of churchgoing in eastern Scotland – especially in the cities (notably Edinburgh, Dundee and Aberdeen) and densely-populated areas (such as Lothian and Fife). Churchgoing in the later twentieth century is strongest in two different types of area in Scotland: the isolated Hebrides where puritanical presbyterianism is strong, and the urbanized districts of west central Scotland where Catholicism is most vigorous. As far as the latter area is concerned it is not sufficient to attribute high rates of Sunday worship to Catholics alone. Church of Scotland ministers have recorded that religious antagonisms sustain Protestant observance in some proletarian communities like Lennoxtown to the north of Glasgow, but it also seems that active religious connection is strong in the middle-class suburban areas around Glasgow: in Bearsden, Milngavie, Eastwood and Bishopbriggs. A sharp contrast in the

Patterns of religious adherence

religious habits of the people has developed between the Glasgow conurbation and east-coast cities.

An issue which arises from this is whether churchgoing was weakened by the growth of urban and industrial districts. It has commonly been observed, especially of England, that rates of church attendance seemed to diminish the larger a city, and especially an industrial city, became.[5] But these maps give some cause for doubting this proposition as far as Scotland is concerned. The 1851 census recorded churchgoing figures for fifty-three Scottish towns ranging in size from Dingwall with 2300 inhabitants to Glasgow with 340,600 inhabitants. An analysis of this data produces no statistically significant correlation between size of town and churchgoing rate; in other words church attendance was not lower for larger cities compared to smaller ones. As Table 6 shows, even amongst twenty of these towns there was a wide variation in church attendances between places of similar population – especially in towns of under 20,000 people. Much depended on whether small towns experienced an inflow or outflow of attenders for Sunday worship; this depended on whether churches which served populations drawn from wide areas were located within a town or outside its boundaries. In the larger cities where there was less likelihood of such Sunday 'migration' affecting the figures significantly, there was a reduced degree of variation in churchgoing rates. Still, there were appreciable differences. A lot depended here on the rate of population increase in the preceding ten years or so and on the ability of the churches to keep pace in the provision of places to worship. The Victorians argued at length about church accommodation as a factor in churchgoing rates, and particularly in relation to Glasgow where in 1851 there were church sittings for at most 35 per cent of the population – 20 per cent below the national average. Yet despite factors like low church accommodation and high pew rents (which afflicted certain localities more than others), the remarkable conclusion to be drawn from the cities is not how low church attendance was but how high it was. The habit of attending Sunday worship was not markedly greater in rural areas than cities in 1851, and though Glasgow's rate was lower than Scotland's as a whole it was on a par with many rural

Table 6 Churchgoing rates of Scottish towns, 1851

	Population	Church attendances at morning, afternoon and evening worship (% total population)
Dingwall	2,364	131.6
Selkirk	4,347	47.4
Banff	6,953	44.4
Brechin	8,210	113.2
Stirling	10,180	87.1
Forfar	11,000	56.8
Montrose	15,882	66.3
Falkirk	16,438	40.0
Inverness	16,496	70.9
Arbroath	19,829	33.6
Ayr	21,076	50.1
Kilmarnock	21,287	67.7
Dunfermline	21,687	49.2
Perth	25,585	81.7
Greenock	37,436	66.6
Paisley	60,333	49.6
Aberdeen	73,227	56.7
Dundee	81,494	58.1
Edinburgh and Leith	193,929	55.4
Glasgow	340,605	43.2

Source: Figures based on data in Census of Great Britain (1851): Religious Worship and Education, Scotland, *PP* (1854), lix.

counties and higher than a quarter of them. Low church attendance was not a characteristic confined to industrial areas. Indeed, amongst counties with low figures agricultural and Highland districts predominated: Argyll, Dumfriesshire, East Lothian, Invernesshire, Kirkudbrightshire, West Lothian, Selkirkshire and Wigtonshire.

The evidence of the 1851 Religious Census thus casts great doubt upon urbanization as a monocausal explanation for the decline of churchgoing. Using the 1851 census results and later urban censuses conducted by newspapers, it appears that urban churchgoing rates stayed quite buoyant during the second half of the nineteenth century. The figures in Table 7 would suggest that only two cities suffered dramatic falls in church attendance: Inverness between 1851 and 1881, and Dundee between 1881

Table 7 Churchgoing rates, 1835–1891 (% total population attending church)

	1835/6		1851			1876	1878	1881	1891
	Average attendance	'In habit of attending'	Morning	Afternoon	Evening				
Scotland			25.6	16.9	5.4				
Glasgow	24.9	40.3	20.7	18.2	3.8	19.3		18.8	
Edinburgh	23.1	46.1	25.2	24.4	5.8			21.7	
Dundee			24.2	27.0	6.9			21.9	15.9
Aberdeen			25.4	23.1	8.3		26.1		25.5
Paisley			19.6	24.7	4.9			19.5	
Greenock			27.5	32.7	6.4			19.7	
Brechin			43.6	39.4	30.1			33.1	
Montrose			23.7	24.9	17.7			27.2	
Ayr			24.2	22.9	3.0	26.0		18.1	
Inverness			35.4	21.4	14.1			19.9	

Sources: Figures based on data in Royal Commission on Religious Instruction, *PP* (1837), xxx, and (1837–8), xxxii; Census of Great Britain (1851); Religious Worship and Education, Scotland, *PP* (1854), lix; and R. Howie (1893) *The Churches and the Churchless in Scotland*, Glasgow, 92–108.

Note: The figures for years other than 1851 were not broken down by diet of worship (morning, afternoon and evening), but because of the nature of the figures and the widespread anecdotal evidence for the decline of 'twicing' after 1870, it is likely that they represent attendances at the largest diet, i.e. morning.

and 1891. We have no way of assessing the accuracy of the post-1851 censuses and we should not place too much reliance on the data they produced. None the less, what emerges is a steeper downward trend in church attendance amongst the smaller towns compared to the larger towns. In Glasgow, Edinburgh and Aberdeen the figures produced in the last quarter of the century were of similar proportions to those produced in 1851, whilst in the other places with the exception of Montrose there seems to have been a downturn in the rates of attendance in the thirty years after mid-century. The numerous censuses conducted in other Scottish towns are unfortunately not usable in this way, mainly because they failed to record Catholic attenders, but the general impression rendered by all of them is that the growth of non-churchgoing in Victorian Scotland was exaggerated by contemporary churchmen.

This leaves a real problem of identifying when churchgoing fell. That it did fall seems undeniable, though ironically we have fewer sets of statistics to demonstrate the twentieth-century position. The 1984 census was based on a questionnaire to clergy asking for the average attendance at Sunday worship during the month of March, and was thus prone to greater inaccuracy than those of the nineteenth century. Perhaps the most reliable recent census was conducted by Dr John Highet of the University of Glasgow in the mid-1950s. He showed that just over 10 per cent of the population of Glasgow attended morning worship in April 1954.[6] This was half the figure for 1851, and indicated a major fall in churchgoing habits in the city. But to locate the point within that hundred-year period when the decline originated we must revert to a variety of other statistics in order to construct circumstantial evidence.

It is clear that the fall in churchgoing has afflicted some churches more than others. We have already noted that church attendance has tended to be higher in districts with a strong Catholic population. This phenomenon is not confined to Scotland but has been observed in many countries; in England, for instance, attendance is high in Catholic counties like Lancashire. Whilst the Catholic Church has not been immune to declining attendances, especially since the early 1970s, the decay of churchgoing in the twentieth century has been most pronounced amongst Protestants. In Scotland this decay has not been solely, or even primarily, a product of non-adherence. We have seen how the proportion of the population in membership with presbyterian churches continued to rise until the 1950s, indicating that *adherence* remained strong. The explanation for declining *attendance* thus lies with the membership. Presbyterian churchgoing has fallen almost entirely because of the diminution of the habit amongst communicants. Between the 1850s and the 1950s the proportion of presbyterian church members attending Sunday worship fell from around three-quarters to one-quarter. Going to church has become less important as a criterion for maintaining church connection, and the Church of Scotland in particular has condoned the progressive laxity of its communicants. There is cause for suspecting that at certain times church

Patterns of religious adherence

membership has grown whilst attendance has been diminishing. One set of figures would indicate that between 1876 and 1891 Church of Scotland membership grew 23 per cent whilst attendance fell 30 per cent.[7] Similarly, the Church's high membership figures for the 1950s seem likely to conceal a downward trend in attendance, though purges on communicants' rolls from the 1960s make them a fairly realistic barometer of trends in active church connection since then.

Despite these problems the membership statistics go some way to revealing the origins of the presbyterian decline. Annual growth rates for presbyterian church membership were very high in the second half of the nineteenth century, varying from 1.9 per cent in the 1850s to 1.0 per cent in the 1890s. But in successive decades after 1900 the annual growth rate fell sharply: from 0.6 per cent in 1900–10 to 0.4 per cent in the decade of the First World War, reaching a mere 0.1 per cent in the 1920s.[8] Only part of this decline was due to the slowing down of population growth. By far the greater part was due to failing recruitment. This is best seen in the crisis that befell the Sunday school – the most important agency for recruiting church members. By the 1890s Sunday schools had attained an enormous significance in the religious life of the country, and especially in the urban and industrial districts. In 1891, 52 per cent of all children aged 5–15 years were enrolled at Sunday schools of the major presbyterian churches and average attendance was consistently around three-quarters of the enrolment. Given that many children also attended worship in churches, it is possible that more children than adults were active in religious observance. Be that as it may, there was a reversal of Sunday-school growth between 1890 and 1910, as Figure 7 shows. The proportion of Sunday-school scholars amongst 5–15 year olds fell to 46 per cent in 1911, 38 per cent in 1931 and 13 per cent in 1981, whilst the absolute decline in the numbers of scholars was accentuated after the First World War by the fall in the birth rate. The causes are examined in a later chapter, but the consequences were severe for church growth. Churches failed to recruit from all except children of church members, and even then their success was diminishing. The fall in Sunday-school enrolment after 1890 was followed by the

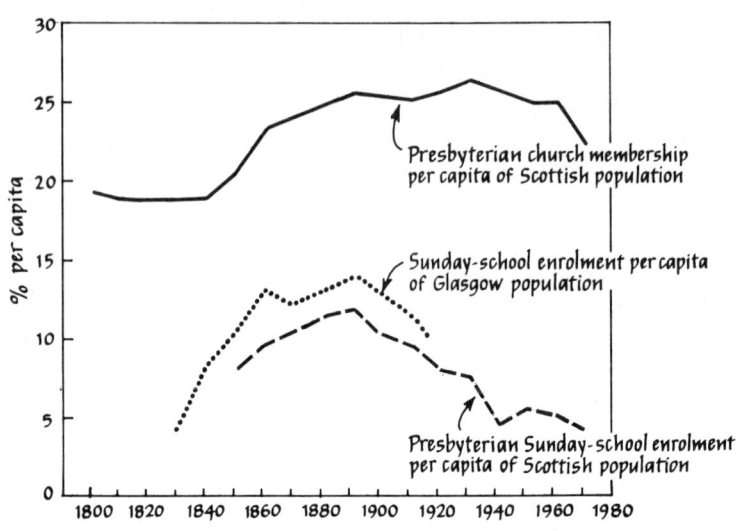

Figure 7 Church and Sunday-school membership per capita, Scotland and Glasgow 1800–1970

Sources: The data are from or derived from R. Currie *et al.* (1977) *Churches and Churchgoers: Patterns of Church Growth in the British Isles since 1700*, Oxford, Clarendon Press, pp. 25, 169–70, 172–4; Census of Religious Worship, 1851, *PP* (1854), lix: Glasgow Sabbath School Union, *Annual Reports* (1841–92); and Scottish National Sabbath School Union, *Annual Reports* (1902–17).

reduced growth in church membership after 1900. The presbyterian churches lost their most valuable outreach into the community, and through this failure in evangelization of the young were left vulnerable to losses thereafter.

Statistics of religion thus point to the period between 1890 and 1914 as crucial to the changing social significance of religion. It is as well to note, however, that churchgoing and recruitment to the churches through Sunday schools are not the only measures of religious observance. Religion intrudes into people's lives in a variety of ways, most of which are not quantifiable. But there is at least one statistical series which demonstrates a much more vigorous religious element in Scottish civil life in the twentieth century. Figure 8 shows that the religious solemnization of marriage has remained of considerable importance to Scots. A major factor in this was the non-availability of civil wedding in a registrar's office

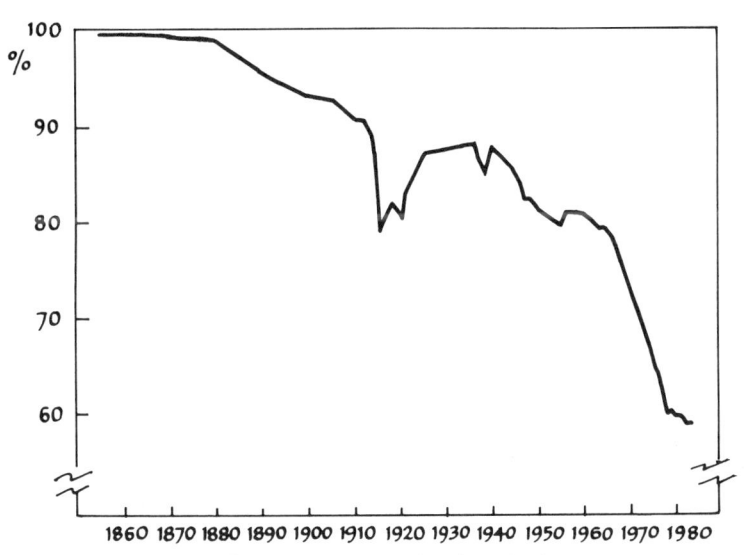

Figure 8 Proportion of marriages religiously solemnized, 1855–1984

Sources: Figures based on data in R. Currie *et al.* (1977) *Churches and Churchgoers: Patterns of Church Growth in the British Isles since 1700*, Oxford, Clarendon Press, pp. 226–9; Registrar General Scotland, *Annual Report* (1984), p. 107.

in Scotland until 1939. Instead, there were three forms of irregular marriage – by declaration, by promise, and by cohabitation and repute, the first two of which were abolished in 1940. In such circumstances, religious marriage was made by the force of law a firm part of Scottish tradition. In the early 1970s, 70 per cent of Scots were marrying according to religious rites compared to 55 per cent for England and Wales. The graph shows that though disaffection with church marriage emerged in the late nineteenth century, and increased temporarily during the First World War, it was not until 1961–78 that a sharp downward trend took place. Such statistics indicate that changes in religious custom occur at different rates and times, and do not altogether destroy the wider role of religion in people's lives.

Notes

1 R. Mudie-Smith (ed.) (1904) *The Religious Life of London*, London, 6–7.
2 Figures calculated from R. Currie, *et al.* (1977) *Churches and Churchgoers: Patterns of Church Growth in the British Isles since 1700*, Oxford, Clarendon

Press, 25; 1851 Religious Census, Scotland; and J. Highet (1960) *The Scottish Churches*, London, Skeffington, 60.
3 OSA, 2, p. 228.
4 Figures calculated from data in or derived by linear extrapolation from R. Currie, *et al.*, op. cit., 132-3; and R. Howie (1893) *The Churches and the Churchless in Scotland*, Glasgow, 38.
5 H. Perkin (1969) *The Origins of Modern English Society 1780-1880*, London and Henley, Routledge & Kegan Paul, 200-1.
6 The results of this census are given in J. Cunnison and J. B. S. Gilfillan (eds) (1958) *The Third Statistical Account of Scotland, Vol. 5, The City of Glasgow*, Glasgow, 956.
7 R. Howie, op. cit., xxiii-xxiv.
8 Figures calculated from R. Currie, *et al.*, op. cit., 25.

4
Religion in rural society, 1730–1890

By the middle decades of the eighteenth century Scottish rural society was in the midst of a long period of continuous change. The protracted transformation of the countryside was fuelled initially by agricultural improvements and a refashioning of the social structure – changes which were antecedent to industrialization and rapid urban growth. Between the 1660s and the 1770s agriculture and rural industry in the Lowlands were infused with commercial values and capitalist forms of organization, and similar processes in the Highlands and Hebrides caused the dismemberment of archaic clan society and impelled a confused and mostly hill peasantry either to emigrate or to settle in coastal townships where a sparse living was to be made from crofting and fishing. Whilst Highland crofting society remained relatively unchanged until the twentieth century, nestling on the margins of the national economy, rural society in the Lowlands came rapidly to feel the effects of proximity to industry and city culture. It was not until 1891 that Scotland's population became predominantly urban, but before then far-reaching changes had altered the fabric and tempo of country life.

The implications for rural religion were varied and not immediately resolved. On one level the advance of commercial organization and civil administration displaced the secular significance of the church. The proliferation of dissenting churches reduced the authority of the Established Kirk and weakened the role of religion as a force for parish unity and communal worship.

On the other hand the pace of change was slower in the countryside than in the larger towns. Agricultural work was bound more to the weather than to machinery, and the ambience of rural life remained one in which old customs and superstitions lingered in the folk memory. The style and significance of church life was not completely altered in this environment. Indeed the growth of dissent and rural puritanism can be seen in many ways as a restatement of traditional values and attitudes which were under threat from the new economic order. A traditional pre-industrial form of religion was able to survive into the nineteenth century, and whilst many of its features were under assault, its overall obsolescence was only becoming apparent in the second half of the nineteenth century.

The pre-industrial form of religion

Religion of pre-industrial and rural society presents a contrast to the religion of the manufacturing towns and cities which sprang up after 1780. By today's standards both government and the economy were underdeveloped and the functions and character of religion reflected this. At a constitutional level organized religion was central to issues of national politics and to the operation of the state. At the level of the local community the church played a pivotal role as the intermediary between the state and the family. Religion seemed more suited to the comparative stability and primitive science of rural society than to the more dynamic, rationalistic and technologically oriented character of industrial society. Yet there are severe limits to our ability to judge the extent of religious observance in the pre-industrial form of religion. We do not know what 'normal' levels of adherence were in the sixteenth and seventeenth centuries, and are unlikely to do so. The concern of the pre-industrial church and the government was not with apathy or indifference to religious ordinances but with rejection of church authority. This was particularly the case in Scotland where strong regionalism, the difficult terrain and distrust of monarchical power reduced the authority of the Crown. In the vacuum of secular government the Established Church was a vital instrument of civil power, having

Religion in rural society

in its parish churches, schools, officials and ethos of popular participation the most sophisticated machinery available to impose stability in society. To accomplish this, religion was an obligation on the people, not a choice as it became in the nineteenth and twentieth centuries. As a result, faith and belief were of secondary importance to overt obedience to ecclesiastical law.

From this obedience derived the distinctive character of the pre-industrial form of religion in Lowland Scotland. It was represented in four major relationships which bound the people to the Established Church: economic, judicial, devotional and educational. These relationships were developed in and for the agrarian society of the early-modern period, but their decline was a slow process. Rural religion of the late eighteenth and nineteenth centuries became a mixture of the traditional and the novel in which the religious heritage of the sixteenth and seventeenth centuries was fused with religious pluralism and the new social structure.

The economic relationship between church and people was of great significance. In principle the burden of maintaining church finances rested with the landowners who formed the board of heritors in each parish. The board was responsible for the construction and maintenance of a church capable of accommodating two-thirds of the population over the age of twelve, for the provision of a manse and a glebe of four acres arable or pasture for sixteen cattle, and for the payment of the minister's stipend from the teinds – an annual tax due to 'teind-holders', usually landowners, equal to one fifth of the agricultural rental value of the parish. For the kirk's educational work the heritors had to provide a school, pay a schoolmaster, and ensure that all children had access to schooling irrespective of means. The board was not an ecclesiastical court but a civil one, supervised by crown commissioners until 1707 and by the Court of Session thereafter until the commutation of teinds in the 1930s. By forcing landowners of whatever religious affiliation to meet their ecclesiastical obligations, the board symbolized the established status of the Church of Scotland.

In practice heritors ensured that costs were minimized and passed on to the lower social groups in the parish. Heritors challenged claims for expenditure, kept salaries low (especially schoolmasters'), and made tenants responsible for the payment of their proportion of the teinds. Landowners generally paid their portion in cash whilst tenants customarily paid in oatmeal, barley, butter, fish, kelp or other produce depending on the nature of the local economy. Tenants additionally undertook certain labour services, such as thatching the church and manse, and bringing in the harvest from the minister's glebe. These labour dues were in turn passed on to farm servants and the peasantry so that much of the work was carried out by those at the bottom end of the social spectrum. Heritors offset their expenses further by charging school fees and extracting rents for church pews. There were also charges for marriages and baptisms to be paid to the minister, the session clerk (who was invariably the schoolmaster) and the beadle, and the kirk session rented a mortcloth for covering coffins at funerals. Finally, parishioners were expected to contribute according to their means to the parochial fund for the relief of the poor. The poor's collections were made under the eagle eyes of the elders – whether on entering church for Sunday worship, by door-to-door visitation, or at a booth set up at a central point in the parish.

Those in receipt of poor relief were even more closely tied to the church. Applicants were subjected to lengthy and often humiliating investigation by the kirk session, and in order to qualify parishioners had to be free of scandal, had to attend church regularly, and had to bequeath all property to the church. But all parishioners were tied to the kirk economy. Farmers made their victual payments of teinds direct to the minister and obtained a receipt as proof for the landowner. In coastal communities teinds were collected every time fish was landed, and in selling his stipend produce the minister assumed a commercial function as a trading link between parishioners and outside markets. Non-commuted dues increased the drain upon the parish economy. Several days each year were given over by peasant communities to harvesting the glebe, and in the process grievance arose in having to bring in the minister's crops before any others from what was often the finest arable in the area. For the minister, agricultural and commercial concerns dominated his work: supervising his glebe farm and its servants, ensuring his stipend from farmers, and negotiating with heritors for maintenance of church property. By 1800 parish clergy were in constant dispute with landowners over the paucity of glebes and the ruinous condition of manses and churches, but as far as ordinary parishioners were concerned the minister and heritors were jointly the source of heavy financial burdens which placed the church at the centre of the local economy.

Equally important was the church's judicial role. The kirk session, presided over by the minister, administered the provision of communion and other purely ecclesiastical matters, but in the seventeenth and eighteenth centuries the vast bulk of its business was the supervision of parishioners' conduct. In this the session's role straddled ecclesiastical and civil law with at best a hazy division between the two. Until the 1740s secular justice was primitively organized in Scotland, resting in the hands of sheriffs and barons in private hereditary courts, and these law-enforcers relied upon kirk sessions to investigate and sit in judgement upon both criminal and religious offences. Despite the removal in 1712 of the session's authority to compel submission to its proceedings, and despite the formation after 1748 of a more coherent system of JPs, the church remained an important source of judicial authority in rural areas. The kirk session acted as the lowest court from which more serious cases could be referred to the civil system. Elders were often assigned portions of the parish to supervise, and they acted as 'searchers' or patrols on the lookout for instances of Sabbath desecration. But their work was not confined to moral or religious offences. They became in an *ad hoc* fashion general policemen enjoying the support of the civil courts. In one Borders district in the 1660s the baron made a blanket intervention to 'put into execution all acts and decrees of the kirk-session against all persons whomsoever'.[1] Some localities had 'session bailies' appointed to be representatives of civil justice and to add weight to kirk-session proceedings. More informally, elders were drawn from the same sections of society as officials of secular justice (burgh magistrates and rural baronbaillies) and often sat on kirk sessions consciously carrying out two functions. In a few cases the minister was also the JP, as at

Barras on the Isle of Lewis. A visitor there in 1802 remarked on the power thus concentrated in the minister, and on the parishioners' position: 'They submit, though sometimes reluctantly, to the decision of their pastor. From his court there are no appeals.'[2]

It is difficult to draw a clear line between what were considered civil and ecclesiastical offences. Some crimes such as adultery, fornication, witchcraft (an offence until 1736), drunkenness, swearing and Sabbath profanation were both, but in a more general sense there was no offence which sessions were unwilling to investigate. They heard cases such as theft, assault, wife-battering and even suspicious death. However, the overwhelming majority of cases in Established and dissenting kirk sessions before 1850 were for fornication and to a lesser extent adultery. Fornication was the bread and butter of session business with fines passing to the parochial fund for the poor: as one historian put it, 'the lascivious regularly providing for the needy'.[3] With fornication cases taking as long as a year to complete, many kirk sessions were continuously engrossed with the sexual exploits of parishioners. A case usually started when an elder reported the pregnancy of an unmarried woman. The woman and, if revealed, the father would appear to give evidence, and third parties would be summoned if guilt was not admitted. Session meetings sometimes became almost voyeuristic. A witness, his anonymity preserved, swore to an Antiburgher kirk session in 1776 that:

> in the beginning of winter 1774 a taylor returning from his work late at night, having left his master a little behind him, met with John [Miller] and his sister in law in a bank south from Crieff, and that some conversation took place between them, by which he understood it was them. That some time after the master coming up a little east from that place, and hearing some noise among the ridges, listened a little, heard a woman saying in a mournful tone 'O! Johnie dinna' do it'; – and after saw two persons rise up, and heard the woman say again 'you have given me foul cloths this night'; – and . . . that the persons he heard were guilty together.[4]

In cases where sessions had a choice of believing either a man or a woman, they uniformly believed the man. They often disbelieved the woman's evidence even when there was no contradictory account. During a sixteen-month investigation in 1795-6 neither the session of Aberfoyle Church of Scotland nor the Presbytery of Dunblane to which the case was sent up would believe Catherine Stewart's consistent story of being raped by Angus Kennedy, a married man, despite the fact that Kennedy told an elder during an interview that 'I cannot but say it was against her will.' Catherine was found guilty of adultery and fined 10/6d., a large sum for a weaver, whilst Kennedy, being a Catholic, was not summoned.[5] The session of Holyrood in Dumfriesshire believed none of the women in six cases of alleged rape in the eighteenth century, and the Stirling Presbytery of the Antiburgher Church rejected out of hand a woman's claim in 1773 that she had been raped at gunpoint and instead disciplined her for fornication. More barbarically, if a woman denied that she was pregnant the kirk session ordered that her breasts be milked for 'evidence' – a demonstration carried out in front of the session in the eighteenth century and by a doctor in private in the nineteenth. If a woman refused to reveal the father, the session ordered that she be interrogated during the pains of childbirth.

When it came to punishment women also suffered more severely. They were often fined more, and in the many instances of masters accused of fornicating with female servants kirk sessions demanded an increased burden of proof. Where the case was watertight the matter was usually passed up to the presbytery to avoid confrontation between session and local landowners. But not always. In 1792 at Gairloch in Wester Ross the major landowner, Sir Hector Mackenzie, was discovered to have lived in adultery with his maid for four years during which time he had fathered three bastard children. The local minister had accepted the donation of a mortcloth and cash in return for baptizing the children and keeping quiet about the laird's domestic arrangements. But an evangelical minister from another parish broke the scandal to a shocked presbytery and the repentant clergyman was ordered to fine Sir Hector sixty pounds. This was an unusually large sum. Masters were generally fined a pound or a guinea in the late eighteenth century, but in large numbers of cases they were not convicted. But those that were usually avoided the embarrassment of public rebuke which was the other part of kirk punishment. The social élites found sessions willing to administer private rebuke before the session whilst men and women from lower social groups had to submit in almost every instance before the 1820s to public rebuke or 'rant'. The minister ranted at the guilty for three Sundays or more from the pulpit with victims traditionally wearing sackcloth over their heads and standing on a repentance stool before the congregation. However, practice varied considerably. At Galston and Fenwick in Ayrshire penance was performed from parishioners' usual pews, and at Auchinleck in the same county the repentance stool was discreetly sited under a gallery. At the other extreme public humiliation could start before guilt had been established. In 1812 the Established Church Presbytery of Lochcarron in the West Highlands agreed to a request from an Applecross man that his wife's alleged lover be interrogated before the entire congregation.

Between them, Established and dissenting kirk sessions were still important to rural justice until at least the 1830s, sometimes investigating and punishing crimes like child murder, assault and theft, but above all fornication. But there were important changes taking place in kirk justice in the middle decades of the nineteenth century. Offences of drunkenness, imprudent 'dealing out of intoxicating drinks' and 'walking disorderly' became more common, especially in the rural United Presbyterian Church but also in the Free Church. Moreover, punishment changed. In urban congregations public rebuke was giving way to private rebuke around 1800, but in rural churches the traditional form was only receding in the 1850s. But significantly, suspension or ejection from the congregation became much more common between 1840 and 1870. Doune Free Church suspended a man in 1843 for telling his elder that 'if he did not get his Child baptised he would get it done by the Episcopal Church for one shilling'. Two men at Laurencekirk in the north-east were summarily struck off the roll of their United Presbyterian Church in 1849 for being seen in a drunken fight which 'made such an

Religion in rural society

exhibition as to draw a crowd around them, thereby bringing a scandal on the body'. The concern was no longer with the scandal of the individual but the standing of the congregation. From the 1840s the wayward were no longer tolerated and session justice, instead of purging their scandal, led to expulsion. This policy did not last long. By the 1870s kirk-session justice of the traditional sort had completely disintegrated, and even fornication cases virtually stopped. No longer did rural congregations countenance the 'rough' nor assume responsibility for the general conduct of parishioners. As a result, the all-inclusive, communal role of church justice which characterized pre-industrial religion was replaced by an urban-style theory of the church as a private and 'respectable' club.

The devotional and educational links between church and people in rural society were predicated upon the economic and judicial ones described above. This was not a libertarian society in which people had a choice as to whether they adhered to a church. In over a thousand parish theocracies kirk sessions imposed a compulsory culture of conformism. Parishioners were rarely forced to attend church. But in an environment in which the church represented a whole range of institutions and values – the Protestant state, law and order, the dutiful payment of church taxes, parochial education and correctness in sexual morality – neither the activity of going to church nor the passivity of not going indicated anything about the extent of religious observance generally. The communion season, for instance, was a highly popular event in seventeenth- and eighteenth-century Scotland, but it was more often an annual holiday than a holy event; thus, rarely more than 20 per cent of parishioners came forward to receive the sacraments. Truly 'religious' communions were infrequent and suppressed. The religious revivals at Cambuslang and Kilsyth in 1742 were deprecated by landowners for the loss of farm work which they caused. As a result, communions were held with decreasing regularity as the agricultural revolution proceeded. By the 1780s the lapsing of communion was the norm, and some parishes had not held the ceremony for sixteen years. As one recent historian concluded, 'active popular participation in religion was thus clearly not seen as socially desirable, but as socially dangerous'.[6]

Such evidence as exists suggests that religious observance at other times of the year was just as poor. There was exceedingly limited church accommodation in rural parishes before the arrival of dissenting meeting houses, yet there was little pressure upon it until late in the eighteenth century. Large numbers of churches, and probably the majority, were in very poor structural condition with rotting thatched roofs, rising damp and earthen floors through which it was not unknown for scraping feet to reveal corpses. Larger churches in towns were often disused or semi-derelict with worshippers meeting in cordoned-off naves or aisles; this was the case at churches in Aberdeen, Dornoch, Dunblane, Dunfermline, Dunkeld, Elgin, Haddington, Kirkwall, Perth, St Andrews and Stirling. Such conditions were in part the result of presbyterian irreverence for pre-Reformation Catholic churches, but were also both cause and consequence of low church attendance in pre-industrial Scotland. An Argyllshire minister echoed a common observation when he wrote in 1790 that 'with us of the church of Scotland, many of our country kirks are such dark, damp and dirty hovels, as chill and repress every sentiment of devotion'.[7] Neither the civil nor the ecclesiastical authorities were overly disturbed by this situation. They were quite content for the church to accommodate a representative congregation so long as its judicial authority was observed by the community as a whole.

The parish-school system should be seen in the same light. Education was regarded from John Knox onwards as an important means of inculcating acquiescence to the reformed kirk and its authority, and the church was undoubtedly important to the creation of a high standard of literacy in Scotland. But we should not exaggerate Scotland's educational prowess, and nor should the parish-school system be seen as the product of high-minded principles of open-access learning. Education was part and parcel of the control of the people exercised jointly by the state and the church. The schoolmaster was a key officer of the local church, customarily holding the posts of precentor and kirk-session clerk. He was paid by the heritors and his educational work was inspected by the presbytery. The curriculum depended heavily on the Bible and the catechism, and prepared children for a life of obedience to the kirk. Even the state take-over of parish schools in 1873 did not divert control from the local church and the landed classes. With elected school boards dominated by clergy and local élites, education like religious observance remained an adjunct to the wider relationship between church and people which maintained social order in rural communities.

This relationship was different in some respects in the pre-industrial towns of Scotland. Perhaps the most obvious differences lay in the economic and judicial functions of the urban kirk which were modified by the existence of powerful municipal corporations. Most town churches were managed by town councils who financed their ecclesiastical operations by charging seat rents or, as in Edinburgh and Montrose, by also imposing an annuity tax on property. The board of heritors was replaced by the town council which paid clerical stipends entirely in cash. In this way the urban clergy did not have a central role in the local economy in the way rural clergy had. Similarly, urban kirk sessions lost much of their power to burgh magistrates in the seventeenth and eighteenth centuries. Even the supervision of moral and religious law tended to be dealt with by the city authorities. In Glasgow in the 1780s Sabbath profanation by cattle drovers was countered by municipal decree, and the city's Sabbath 'searchers' were organized by the magistrates using volunteers drawn from the incorporated tradesmen. Moreover, there were no parish schools in most towns since royal burghs used their influence to be excluded from statutory educational provisions, and instead built their own and probably more exclusive high schools.

Despite this apparent 'secularization' of urban institutions, there is little evidence to suggest that church attendance was appreciably worse in towns. Church buildings were perhaps in better repair, though not always, and there was a growing economical use made of the large city churches. In each of the towns of Edinburgh, Glasgow, Dundee, Aberdeen, Perth and Stirling by 1780, multiple congregations assembled for worship in different sections of the principal kirk; in Glasgow Cathedral one congregation met in the choir, a second in the nave and a third in the crypt. Moreover, the greater wealth of the towns and the stronger presbyterianism of the councillors compared to rural heritors ensured a relatively high expenditure on the construction of new churches in the seventeenth and eighteenth centuries. In Glasgow the ratio of number of churches to number of inhabitants (indicated by rough censuses by the magistrates) improved from 1:2936 in 1660 to 1:2133 in 1708 to 1:1545 in 1740, and only fell again to 1:1712 in 1780 with the onset of rapid commercial expansion. Given that city churches tended to be larger than country ones, such figures seem to indicate that the population of Glasgow was just as well provided with pews as rural inhabitants. Still, it is evident that as in the countryside the entire population was not expected to attend church. Municipal authorities allocated pews to various organizations and social groups to create balanced congregations: pews were reserved for universities, incorporated trades, merchants' houses, councillors, inmates of charity hospitals and schools, and the poor. The middle ranks and others in the social élites rented more comfortable and expensive pews. In this way, municipal councils followed the same policy as rural landowners in using churches to symbolize social cohesion whilst at the same time discouraging religious enthusiasm.

In the pre-industrial form of religion the church was the primary focus for community identity. The rites and practices of popular religion were centred on a communal experience which enveloped all, including the casually apathetic and the non-churchgoer. With religious taxes and session justice as the fundamental ties between church and people, there was no need to enforce church attendance. In so far as it was measured at all, religiosity was gauged negatively by demanding avoidance of misdemeanour rather than positively by demanding evidence of enthusiasm or inner piety. But though dissenting churches created parallel church systems to that of the Established Church, ultimately the puritan presbyterians were undermining the basis of traditional religion. Whilst traditional values associated with communal worship and kirk discipline were re-stated by the dissenters, the role of religion was decreasingly one of uniting parishes. Increasingly religion became the focus for social division and the fracturing of rural communities.

The impact of economic and social change in the Lowlands

The agricultural and industrial revolutions created varied consequences for rural religion. Rapidly growing population from the 1740s had within five decades put great pressure upon church accommodation in most districts, and with this growth came an accelerating movement of people in search of industrial work or six-monthly contracts of farm service on enclosed and enlarged farms. Heritors felt little obligation to provide new churches for this expanding and shifting population, and a system of reserving pews for tenants and renting out the remainder to the more prosperous residents spread rapidly across the Lowlands between 1720 and 1800. Whilst general change in agricultural society was spread out over many decades, the sudden advent of these new arrangements in a parish church often ruptured the religious bonds of traditional rural paternalism.

Concomitant to this was increasing specialization in rural trades and manufacturing. Many small farmers and sub-tenants dispossessed by agricultural improvement found employment in the textile industries of linen, wool and, from the 1780s, cotton. This turned part-time cottage labour into full-time occupations as handloom weavers, spinners, dyers and bleachers. Loosening ties with the laird and the parish church, and subjection to the novel vagaries of the industrial labour market and the trade cycle, led these workers along with farm servants and country tradesmen to stand apart from established religion and to seek group identity in dissenting meeting houses. In more remote parishes, too, the binding fabric of the Established Church started to wither. The advance of large-scale sheep farming coupled with the enticement of work in industry induced rural depopulation in many hill-country districts, and left the remaining population with feelings of bitterness and alienation which drove many to reorganize old covenanting praying societies as congregations of the Secession, Relief or Reformed Presbyterian Churches. Improvement, whether agricultural or industrial, was giving birth to a commercially-oriented society in which social competitiveness and differentiation was weakening the communal inter-dependence upon which the agrarian parish church had been founded.

The effects of social change showed themselves quickly in the parish church. The increasing wealth of the landowning classes led to the erection of 'laird's lofts' in most rural churches in the eighteenth century. Some of these lofts were palatially furnished with external staircases, ante-rooms and fireplaces, creating a marked social segregation from the more spartan facilities enjoyed by the rest of the congregation. The separation of social groups was increased by the erection of 'common lofts' and by heritors requesting the local sheriff to sub-divide the ground floor of the church between them according to the valuation of each heritor's land in the parish. The legality of this process was never successfully contested, but it led to the erection of fixed pews in replacement of the stools which worshippers had formerly brought to church. The ostensible reason for 'pewing' was to aid the poor fund: capital in the fund paid for erection of pews which were then rented out to provide a steady income. But the system introduced a novel and acute separation of social ranks. In most parishes heritors reserved at least half and sometimes all the pews for their own tenants with the result that the increasing non-agricultural population had to compete for a small number of seats. The effects were rising seat rents and the intrusion of the free-market economy into the parish church. The number of the poor able to gain access to church diminished as more and more seats were allocated or sold by auction. Many could not afford to pay anything from sixpence to seven shillings for one seat for a year, and alienation from the Established Church started to emerge.

Poorer parishioners were those most obviously affected by pew-renting. As population grew in the eighteenth century increasing numbers were excluded from Sunday worship. A legal judgment of 1787 released heritors from any obligation to build new churches for 'a fluctuating population, which may be here to-day, and away to-morrow',[8] and ministers found themselves preaching increasingly to the prosperous and to the larger tenantry. But it was not just the poor who were excluded. In Sanquhar in the south-west there were 101 heritors in the late eighteenth century and the sheriff's division of the church gave many of them only one seat to accommodate an entire family whilst other inhabitants were totally excluded. For lower-income groups seat-renting was an invidious device which deprived them of the traditional right to 'hear sermon' from their parish minister. But others were also dissatisfied. Whilst tradesmen and tenants accepted the system as a source of status, promoting virtues of thrift and self-reliance, disquiet arose amongst them and amongst many heritors because they were paying directly to the church but having decreasing say in congregational government. As patrons started to exercise their right to choose the minister after 1730, it was amongst the independent small landowners, skilled artisans and merchants that pressure to dissent sprang up.

The starting point for dissent in rural parishes varied but was almost universally a product of conflict – either with aristocratic patrons or with the class of large landowners. In some parishes the cause was the abandonment in the parish church of 'reading the line' of psalms by a precentor for the benefit of the illiterate; this reason was prevalent on the east coast in parishes stretching from Berwickshire northwards to Aberdeenshire. In other places it was a simple lack of accommodation and the refusal of heritors to build extensions, lofts or new churches. Elsewhere the cause was increasing pew rents. Occasionally it was a failure of a patron to fill a ministerial vacancy – an act interpreted as an antipresbyterian way of saving money. But by far the most frequent reason was opposition, often violent, to the settlement of an unpopular minister chosen by an aristocratic patron. The act of opposing a presentation involved barring the minister and presbytery officials from entering the church. Often only the main door was nailed up or filled by a human barricade, leaving the minister, as with the Rev. Micah Balwhidder in John Galt's novel *Annals of the Parish*, to enter unceremoniously through a window. Kenneth Logue has argued that this partial obstruction demonstrated a belief on the part of the protesters that an induction was only valid if carried out after entry had been made through the correct door; any other entrance was symbolically and technically contrary to custom.[9] Protesters were defending the traditional right of the popular 'call' to a minister, and it was through ruling-class disregard for this right that cause was given for secession from the jurisdiction of an improper Established Church.

The spread of patronage disputes followed the diffusion of agricultural improvement. In the central Lowlands, the southeast, Fife and the Dundee area they reached their greatest frequency and violence between the 1750s and 1770s. In Perthshire, Easter Ross and the north-east they occurred mainly between the 1790s and 1850s. The passions were great and real, though there has long been a tendency to see the disputes in narrowly ecclesiastical terms. But whilst the Scottish peasantry were noted for the apparent passivity of their response to economic change, there lies in patronage disputes what must be regarded as the most significant Scottish equivalent to rural protest in the rest of the British Isles. For religious unrest was not directed at presbyterianism or even theocratic church government. Disputed control of the church was emerging from a wider social contest over religious and secular values in the new capitalist environment.

In rejecting a new parish minister and forming a dissenting church, rural protesters were snubbing the interlocked social and ecclesiastical élites: the aristocratic patron (or the Crown where it was patron), the board of heritors dominated by the large landowners or their factors, and often also the kirk session and its eldership of larger farmers. As early as the 1740s Thomas Gillespie, the founder of the Relief Church, was inveighing against 'patrons, heritors, town-councillors, tutors, factors, presbyteries' and those 'whose station or office afford them weight or influence in the matter of settlement of ministers'. 'Satan', he wrote, 'tempts legislators to invade the prerogative of the Lord Jesus.'[10] The protesters and dissenters were defending the theory of 'twa kingdoms' and the people's direct bond or covenant with God which conferred on them rights and privileges in the church. Thus, they were not revolutionaries. They unwaveringly supported the Hanoverian succession and the British constitution. Indeed, ramshackle battalions of Seceders assisted in 1745 in the military defence of Stirling and Edinburgh, and marched to the battlefield of Prestonpans to defend Protestantism from the 'popish' and episcopalian marauders of Bonnie Prince Charlie's Jacobite army. But the dissenters would not endorse the prevailing party in church and state – because it was 'unworthy' and because it was withdrawing from them traditional rights and customs.

The extent of this hostility varied amongst the dissenters. The Reformed Presbyterians, the direct descendants of the covenanters, were the most extreme, matching every new form of modern government with instructions to members on how to boycott it without actually breaking the law: thus paying taxes was permitted but becoming a tax collector was not. The Burghers and members of the Relief Church were relatively obliging, agreeing to take the burgess oath and confining non-cooperation to paying birth-registration dues to the parish minister without actually registering births. But the more rustic and numerous Antiburghers were less compromising. In most parishes they were in the vanguard of social and religious dissent from the rule of the gentry. John Ramsay, a Perthshire landowner, considered them the instigators of class antagonism in the early nineteenth century:

> Not many years ago, in walking upon the highroad, every bonnet and hat was lifted to the gentry whom the people met. It was an unmeaning expression of respect. The first who would not bow the knee to Baal were the Antiburghers when going to church on Sunday. No such thing now takes place, Sunday or Saturday, among our rustics, even when they are acquainted with gentlemen. It is connected with the spirit of the times.[11]

Ramsay here records the transformation of traditional Sabbatarianism into a display of social as well as religious dissent. In the new context of contracted farm service and waged labour, the Sabbath became not merely a day of rest but a day of freedom from the control of landowners, factors, farmers and the loom. By going to the parish church, with its serried ranks of authority figures, parishioners submitted to an extension of this control. John Younger, a Borders shoemaker of the early nineteenth century, heard his minister 'horse-rattling us into obedience to Pitt, Castlereagh and Peel Government as "ordained of God"'.[12] In some places the parish minister was the focus of the new economic order; at Alloa the minister was a major landowner and was the first in the neighbourhood to enclose fields. In this context the Sabbath, and especially the walk to worship in a dissenting meeting house, was central to the culture of the puritan presbyterians. The rigour of the walk, occasionally as long as thirty miles, expressed the intensity and meaning of dissent. As John Younger wrote, the Sabbath was 'the kindly interference of heaven with the stern conditions of our lot in the scale of humanity', and the walk to church was the free-will declaration of independence in a society where other freedoms were being circumscribed:

> There is no walk that a working man can take on the surface of his native earth like a walk to his place of worship. Here the harassments – the toils and anxieties of his everyday life, appear as if cleared away before his footfall. Here he feels more certainly than at other times the true dignity of his own existence and ultimate destination![13]

In the small Ayrshire weaving village of Fenwick in the 1840s the strongly Seceder community observed a strict Sabbath. Fenwick was a noted stronghold of Chartism and one of the local leaders – a radical republican and opponent of the Established Church – recorded in a handwritten pamphlet:

> At this hour, this hour of Sabbath evening quiet, it may be said that almost every dwelling has become a family sanctuary, every hearth an altar, every home a temple of praise. Pass along that long range of thatched dwellings, and your ear will often catch the evening song of devotion, as it rises from poor and humble men to the throne of the Eternal.[14]

As class consciousness developed, the Sabbath was incorporated into proletarian culture. Keeping its sanctity became not a test of civil conformism but a statement of class unity and independence.

A consequence of this was a rigid division between work and religious observance. The Burgher kirk session at Leslie in Fife held David Miller, a maltman by trade and a prospective elder, to be in scandal in 1742 for breaking a fast day by obeying his master's order to work and by selling a horse. A farmer in the same congregation three years later was found guilty of setting his non-Seceder servants to ploughing on a fast day. The fast day was an important institution in Seceder culture, generally not involving fasting but rather a harsher form of Sabbatarianism. Manifestos were issued to account for the occasion, and in these there was a bewailing of poor harvests, 'spoilt victuals' and 'injustices in matters of trade'. Such suffering was taken as 'the many evidences of the Lord's anger gone forth against us' for 'conformity to the world in sinful customs' such as drinking, dancing, swearing and selfishness. Seceders held roughly twice as many fast days as the Established Church: six per year compared to three in the late eighteenth century. Apart from New Year and occasions such as the monarch's birthday, Scotland has generally not observed national holidays until the twentieth century – in large measure because such holidays in other countries are usually 'popish' saints' days. In this situation the growth of dissenters' fast days represented a claim to time off from work. This was apparent between 1840 and 1880 in the transformation of fast days into Scotland's distinctive system of local holidays which still survive today.

The presbyterian dissenters saw economic struggle for survival as a unifying element in their faith. Through their kirk-session discipline, a supreme moral stature and dignity was striven for in the face of pressing circumstances. Commercial crime such as smuggling was sternly dealt with, as was sharp practice towards the poor. At Inverkip on the lower Clyde in 1814, the Antiburgher Church gathered a mass of evidence from housewives and traders to indict and finally convict a baker of selling underweight loaves of bread. Maintaining their congregations was a financial headache. Many in rural areas could not provide a glebe for the minister, and a considerable proportion were in persistent trouble with church authorities until the 1840s for failing to pay full stipends. Perhaps two-thirds of Antiburgher congregations in Stirlingshire and southern Perthshire in the late eighteenth century had no resident ministers but instead received 'sermon' when they could afford it. The Comrie congregation in the 1770s paid 9s. per sermon, and by 1800 there were so many congregations in Scotland 'paying-as-they-heard' that the national synod set a scale of charges: 12s. 6d. for a sermon to under 300 worshippers, and 15s. to over that number. Between 1800 and 1840 Secession presbyteries negotiated stipends with congregations before authorizing the appointment of a minister, and often insisted that pay rose *pro rata* with the membership.

But poverty was not always becoming. The practice of linking dissenting congregations in order to save money created widespread quarrelling between adjacent communities. The low level of ministerial stipends was more problematic, attracting men of low standard. The Antiburgher minister at Falkirk between 1774 and 1781 made free use of his sermons to rant at will at members of his flock, especially the elders, and was eventually forced to resign from the Church. Archibald Willison, also an Antiburgher minister, was accused by his brethren in 1806 of a catalogue of offences: habitually plagiarizing sermons, drunkenness, abandoning his congregation in Montrose, stealing eight notebooks from a fellow minister and using their contents in a sermon, and being 'in habit and repute an evil speaker, liar and tale-bearer'. But such was the shortage of clergy that he was permitted to move to Denny in Stirlingshire where eleven years later he was found guilty of fornication and deserting his post again, and was finally deposed.[15] Cases of fornication and drunkenness were quite common amongst dissenting clergy and elders – though this did not signify much more than a greater disregard for status than was common in the Established Church. But in a wider sense the Seceders of the eighteenth century did not enjoy high social status. The ministers preached in the broad Scots tongue for which they were ridiculed by the refined and anglicized ministers of the Established Church's Moderate Party. Dissenting clergy were poorly qualified before the 1840s. By 1800 the Burghers had no doctors of divinity; as one minister of that Church commented: 'their ministers have been too poor to purchase the title, and too illiterate to deserve it'.[16]

Religion in rural society

But the rustic image of the Seceders was never totally accurate. From the outset presbyterian dissenters were drawn from a wide cross-section of Lowland rural society. In West Calder parish in Midlothian in 1790 just over a third of parishioners adhered to dissent; out of a population of 968, 169 were Burghers, 142 Antiburghers, seven belonged to the Relief Church and three to the Reformed Presbyterian Church. As Table 8 shows, West Calder dissenters were spread throughout the social structure. They had a higher than average representation amongst groups 1 and 2, but lower amongst groups 3 and 4. Expressing the data another way, dissenters made up 37 per cent of the eleven landowning families, 40 per cent of the tenant farmers and portioners, but only 21 per cent of cottagers and day labourers. The same social spread is also evident in Jedburgh and Strathaven Burgher congregations. What is noticeable, though, is the high proportion of farmers in the eighteenth century; but in Jedburgh by 1825–35 this class had disappeared from the congregation to be replaced by increased numbers of tradesmen and by the new group of hinds, or married servants who lived on enlarged farms. As the society was becoming increasingly polarized, so dissent grew stronger amongst farm workers rather than tenants or small landowners.

At the same time tradesmen were a major occupational group in dissent. Particularly numerous in both country and town districts were wrights, smiths, coopers, masons, bakers, butchers, carpenters and shoemakers. In one sense they shared with farm servants an hostility towards the landed classes and their trammelling of popular rights in the Established Church and the agricultural system. Yet tradesmen were the small entrepreneurs and respectable artisans who supported the new ethos of commercial capitalism and the virtues of hard work and independence it encouraged. Their standards of living were generally rising and it was they who led the shift away from dissent's rustic image. They adopted 'New Licht' theology in the 1790s and religious voluntaryism in the 1830s, thus adapting their culture to the social opportunities of the modern age and complementing economic individualism with the religious individualism of the disestablishment movement.

Table 8 Social composition of rural dissent in the Lowlands (%)

	Jedburgh Burgher Church (Fathers' occupations, baptismal register)		Strathaven Burgher Church (Fathers' occupations, baptismal register) 1767–1789	West Calder Parish, 1790 (Occupations of heads of households)	
	1737–1745	1825–1835		Social structure of total population	Social structure of presbyterian dissent
(Numbers)	(40)	(72)	(88)	(968)	(321)
1 Landed and professional	40	15	63	52	59
(a) Landowners				7	8
(b) Merchants, proprietors	7.5	1	3		
(c) Ministers, schoolmasters		3		1	
(d) Tenants, farmers, portioners	20		58	42	51
(e) Stewards, shopkeepers, innkeepers, and millers	12.5	11	2	2	
2 Skilled tradesmen	37.5	59	30	14	17
(a) Metal trades	15	17	9	5	8
(b) Building trades		3	2		
(c) Bakers, butchers		13			
(d) Textile trades	12.5	13	14	4	2
(e) Shoemakers, tailors, etc.	10	13	5	5	7

(continued)

Table 8—continued

	Jedburgh Burgher Church (Fathers' occupations, baptismal register)		Strathaven Burgher Church (Fathers' occupations, baptismal register) 1767–1789	West Calder Parish, 1790 (Occupations of heads of households)	
	1737–1745	1825–1835		Social structure of total population	Social structure of presbyterian dissent
(Numbers)	(40)	(72)	(88)	(968)	(321)
3 Farm and related workers and unskilled	22.5	26	2	24	18
(a) Shepherds, gardeners, thatchers	10	11			
(b) Hinds		11			
(c) Carriers				2	3
(d) Cottagers	2.5			11	8
(e) Day labourers	10	4	2	11	7
(f) Herdsmen					
4 Others			5	11	4
(a) Indwellers			5		
(b) Widows				7	2
(c) Unspecified				4	2
	100	100	100	101	98

Sources: Figures based on data in Jedburgh Burgher/United Secession Church, Baptismal Register, SRO CH3/350/3; Strathaven Burgher Church, Baptismal Register, SRO CH3/289/1; OSA, vol. 18, 190–5.

But the social and cultural transition within rural dissent was promoted also by the influence of textile workers, and especially weavers. Located in hundreds of planned villages set up by landowners to absorb dispossessed small tenant farmers, the weavers became strong adherents of dissent and notably the Antiburgher Church. But by the early nineteenth century these textile villages – whether based on handloom weaving in the home or on cotton mills – were centres also for the Methodists, Burghers, Baptists and Relievers. Individual villages and towns acquired their own religious complexions: the Burghers and Relief Church at Inveresk, Antiburghers and Relievers at Blairgowrie, the Antiburghers at Buchlyvie and so on. At Alva the Established Church minister owned the mill and his weavers walked out of his church in 1842 to form a Secession congregation. The larger factory villages often bred feverish religious enthusiasm; Deanston and Doune in Perthshire had by 1866 seven churches representing six denominations – the Established, Free, United Presbyterian, Wesleyan Methodist, Episcopal and Roman Catholic churches not to mention small groups of Brethren and Mormons. Parishes specializing in bleaching and calico printing were strongly Seceder; this applied to Slateford near Edinburgh, Cardross, Balfron, Renton, Tibbermuir and Scone. Mining and metallurgical villages like Lochgelly and Dysart in Fife, Cambusnethan, Inveresk, West Calder, Saltcoats and Ardrossan were also strongly Seceder, though the strength of presbyterian dissent amongst colliers and metal workers was dramatically weakened between 1830 and 1860 by the influx of Irish Catholics as strike-breakers. The significance of the industrial villages to rural society is twofold. Firstly, they helped to foster dissent amongst agricultural workers and rural tradesmen. The presence of more numerous and often well-paid textile workers enabled churches to be erected and ministers employed when small numbers of dissenting farm servants, for instance, could not afford to do so. In the second place these villages promoted urban-style culture and social divisions in the countryside, allowing the ambience of industrial society to permeate Lowland rural life.

In addition to formal religious dissent, folk religion could serve a similar purpose as agricultural society adapted to the new social order. This was perhaps particularly relevant in the landward parts of the north-east where presbyterian dissent arrived relatively late and was weaker than in most other parts of the Lowlands. The secret Society of the Horseman's Word, derived from older societies of ploughmen and millers, emerged in the early nineteenth century in Aberdeenshire, Banffshire and the Mearns as semi-satanic ritualism which seems to have embraced a large proportion of the farmhands, and to have spread out during the next hundred years as far as Orkney in the north and Lanarkshire in the south. A 'minister of the Word' used a parody of the catechism to introduce initiates to a supposed secret language for controlling plough horses, and 'Made Horsemen' had to shake hands with the 'devil' (a hoof held by a man) and undertake assorted anti-Christian tasks such as reciting passages from the Bible backwards. The Society's development appears to have coincided with agricultural improvement and increasing specialization amongst farm servants, drawing upon masonic and guild influences to act as a kind of proto-trades union. For highly mobile farm servants, working on six-monthly or yearly contracts, the Society may have contributed a sense of religious brotherhood in place of church fellowship. Interestingly, it started to wither at the same time as presbyterian dissent virtually disappeared at the beginning of this century, though it was not the hostility of the churches that killed it, but the tractor.

The decay of dissenting presbyterianism was under way by the mid-nineteenth century. The first major impulse was the decline of handloom weaving – a progressive but swift process starting in the 1830s – which dramatically reduced the strength of rural dissent. The decline was not just in terms of numbers but also in terms of vitality, for the weavers were often the most vibrant members of dissenting congregations. The virtual disappearance of the handloom weavers constituted a major loss to the United Presbyterian Church and also to the Methodists and the Baptists. Their ethos of an oppressed yet proud occupation withered and with it went the last major vestige of covenanting culture in the Lowlands. The United Presbyterians became increasingly the rural bourgeoisie, growing intolerant of intemperance and the 'rough' culture of the emerging rural proletariat. Though we know little about the social composition of the Free Church in Lowland country districts, there is some evidence that in the middle of the century it replaced the United Presbyterian Church as the focus of religious culture in rural plebeian society. It attracted considerable support from the peasantry in Aberdeenshire during a wave of agricultural improvements in the 1850s, and its position in other regions would bear further research.

More important than shifts within rural dissent was the steadily improving position of the Established Church in the second half of the nineteenth century. Despite the popular passions aroused by and centred on patronage, pew-renting and the other sparks to dissent in earlier decades, the 'Auld Kirk' in most country parishes retained the adherence of about one-third of the population even at the peak of disaffection in 1850. The parish church enjoyed a permanent place in the social landscape, its enduring status connected by law and custom with the perpetual elements in country life: land-ownership and the heritors' board, the harvest and the teinds, education in the parish school, and burial in the parish churchyard. It had retained the loyalties particularly of landowners (even when they might live in England and frequent the Anglican Church), their retainers and their tenant farmers, but circumstances were by the 1870s and 1880s enhancing its appeal. Agricultural advance was precipitating rural depopulation, easing pressure on pews in the parish church; moreover, much had been done during the course of the century to relocate Established kirks from sites in remote corners of parishes, selected for the convenience of the largest heritor, to spots in the largest village or town. More fundamentally, the Church of Scotland's brand of presbyterianism – less evangelical, less emotional, bland even in comparison to the older Seceders – was coming into favour in the Scottish church generally in the later nineteenth century. The revivalism of Moody and Sankey, which became very popular in the cities, never really caught on in rural Scotland. The 'lukewarmness' of the Established Church became a positive virtue, broadening its social appeal. In any event by 1874 the system of patronage, the cause of so much of the schism in presbyterianism, had been abolished by parliament.

Religion in rural society

At root, though, there was a greater transformation underway: the decay of pre-industrial-style religion and the importation of urban religion. Non-churchgoing was emerging as an identifiable rural 'problem' and was countered by a battery of city agencies: mutual improvement societies, prayer groups, Bands of Hope, Sunday schools and home missionary societies. By 1890 the major denominations were noting a loss of energy in country kirks: church-building was past and many parishes were clearly 'over-churched'. The elements of growth and social fragmentation which had focused religious energy and enthusiasm were now gone and were replaced in many parts by decline and congregational insolvency. Even in rural Aberdeenshire, where the established status of the Church of Scotland had been used in mid-century as 'a stick with which to beat landlords and capitalist farmers',[17] the Free Church lost its identification with anti-landlordism as the issue was moved into the political and trades-union spheres. The secular significance of the Establishment–dissent split was dissolving, and the arrival of modern occupations (in the post office, banks and shops) and rural local government (county councils in 1889 and burgh councils in many small towns around that period) were realigning the Lowland countryside to city culture and city ways. Even town halls in rural burghs were built to look like churches, challenging the institutional significance of the kirk. The countryside was breeding civic ways, and in the process the stature of rural religion was altered and brought within an urban framework.

The Highlands, Hebrides and Northern Isles

In 1760 this vast and diverse area of western and northern Scotland held over a quarter of the country's population. By 1890 it held less than a tenth and by 1940 under seven per cent. This dramatic decline was one reflection of the distinctive fortunes experienced in this half of the kingdom. Rapid population growth in the eighteenth century went into reverse after 1860 as the streams of emigrants forced to abandon homes and livelihoods exceeded natural increase. As in the Lowlands religion became the focus of an oppressed culture of puritanical and semi-millenarian presbyterianism. But whilst the English-speakers in the northern isles of Orkney and Shetland as well as in some coastal communities on the adjacent mainland came strongly under the influence of Lowland churches, the Gaelic-speakers of the Highlands and Hebrides maintained cultural and religious isolation. The landowning class looked to the south and to England for the social identity conferred by the Episcopal Church, but the crofters appropriated imported presbyterianism and turned it into the vehicle for sustaining introverted Gaelic culture during the economic transformation of the 'Clearances'. The result was a society estranged from the Lowlands. Puritanical religion offered insularity and remarkable resilience to a crofting community divorced from an increasingly alien ruling class and from the modern capitalism which was none the less transforming their lives.

The Highlands and Hebrides were the last parts of the British Isles to be properly Christianized. The efforts of missionaries before AD 1000 were dissipated by successive waves of settlements, and by 1700 there was a varied culture of Celtic, Norse and pagan customs. A lengthy and unsystematic liturgy of pagan and neo-Christian rituals prevailed: the worship of saints like St Bride and St Maelrubha; magical practices involving sacrifice of bulls and tampering with milk; tales of fairies, beasts and 'water-kelpies'; and reverence for the poetry, song and second sight of seers. The Reformation had had only a localized effect in the Highlands because of shortage of clergy and lack of enthusiasm, and whilst Franciscan missionaries from Ireland had initiated a Catholic revival in a few isolated districts after 1619, and whilst episcopalian clergy served nobles' houses, the Lowland Established Church had made little headway by the beginning of the eighteenth century.

Jacobitism and the need to impose civil order on the turbulent clan society led to a prolonged effort by church and state to presbyterianize the north-west after 1715. But the problems were immense. The presbyterian form of church government seemed unsuited to both the clan system and the crofter-landlord society which replaced it after 1770. Highland terrain was unsuited to parochial supervision by ministers and elders. Parishes were generally devoid of roads and bridges, in many cases until the 1840s, and they were of colossal proportions: Lismore and Appin was sixty-three miles by sixteen; Kilmalie (Fort William) sixty miles by thirty; Harris, covering seven inhabited islands, was forty-eight miles by twenty-four; and the parish of Applecross was so large and inaccessible that its proportions were still unknown by the minister in 1790. There were few Highland parishes under 400 square miles in area, and to compound the Church's problem they had little civil significance. Boards of heritors rarely existed in the early eighteenth century; payment of teinds and parish schools were uncommon; and as ecclesiastical units parishes were of purely token significance, bearing little relevance to the realities of parochial supervision and church attendance. In addition the Church had few Gaelic-speaking clergy and came to rely in the seventeenth and eighteenth centuries upon itinerant missionaries and teacher–catechists. This brought its own peculiar problems. Tacksmen or middle-ranking farmers applied for such posts for extra income, and many were of dubious character. One catechist was accused in 1792 of magical practices including 'recourse to certain herbs and an Iron key which were thrown into another's milk in order to restore the fruit of it'; to confound his inquisitors, the catechist defended himself by claiming 'that he did actually restore the fruit of the milk'.[18] It was difficult to counter such 'abominable and heathenishe' practices without a permanent local church. Elders were in short supply, some parishes having none in the second quarter of the century, and others recruiting women. But the Gaelic language seemed to harbour many of the problems. It was seen as underpinning pagan culture and as the principal obstacle to the absorption of the Highlands into the British state. From 1709 to 1810 the largest agency tackling the 'problem' was the Edinburgh-based Scottish Society for the Propagation of Christian Knowledge (SSPCK). Through its schools and its pro-English policy, it sought to induce literacy, Lowland manners and customs, and the cult of work in Highland society. The heaviest concentration of its schools were along the Highland line separating the north from the Lowlands, and in these areas between 1730 and 1800 industrial villages offered employment to its scholars. In this way Highlanders were drained off for industrial labour in the south and the Gaelic-speaking area started its long process of contraction towards the west Highlands and Hebrides.

It is not surprising, perhaps, that presbyterianism was looked upon initially by Highlanders as an alien intrusion. Parish churches and SSPCK schools were supported by the government Commissioners for Forfeited Estates who until 1784 tried to suppress Jacobitism, paganism, episcopacy and the clans in almost equal measure. There was a vigorous government-backed drive to force heritors to erect churches and manses between the 1740s and 1770s, but communities disliked the new demands for teinds and labour services and the confiscation of excessive amounts of good arable to form enticing glebes for incoming Lowland clergy. Presbyterian ministers were left in no doubt that they were unwelcome intruders. The minister of Gairloch in the 1710s, having no church, manse or glebe, was forced to rent land to farm but had to leave through poverty when Jacobite rebels stole his cattle. Aeneas Sage of Lochcarron had his house set alight four days before his induction in 1727 as the first presbyterian minister in the parish, and he carried arms thereafter, narrowly avoiding at least one further assassination attempt.

The process of presbyterianizing was a long one. Ministers' methods varied, but they invariably focused on Sabbatarianism as it was, as John MacInnes has observed, 'a simple, general and easily understood test of religious observance'.[19] The eldership developed into a prestigious office which ministers held out to loyal supporters who, as the so-called 'Men', became the first lay leaders of the new crofting communities. Venerated for godliness and given privileges of speaking at communion 'enquiry' meetings and of discussing Scripture at fellowship meetings, 'the Men' combined the traditional and the modern by uttering magical sayings and allegories. The power of 'the Men' first emerged in Easter Ross in the 1740s and spread across the Highlands and Hebrides in the next fifty years. Their coming signified a wider puritanization of Highland presbyterianism in which Episcopal and Moderate clergy were branded as 'the ungodly' and the less numerous evangelical ministers were accorded the status of prophets. One such was Lachlan Mackenzie of Lochcarron who between the 1780s and 1820s came to identify in lifestyle with the crofter–fishers of his area. He wrote of himself:

> *The Parson has no horse nor farm,*
> *No goat, nor watch, nor wife,*
> *Without an augmentation* too,*
> *He leads a happy life.*[20]

Mackenzie and his predecessor Aeneas Sage represented a growing trend of evangelical hostility to the 'lukewarmness', immorality and wealth of Moderate ministers. During the time when these two men were members of the Presbytery of Gairloch, they actively pursued 'unworthy' colleagues: Sage accused the neighbouring minister at Applecross of rum-smuggling in 1754; the minister of Lochbroom was disciplined in 1798 for drunkenness and embezzling kirk session fines and the poor fund; and Mackenzie had his own schoolmaster deposed for fornication in 1821. In the Presbytery of Argyll to the south, according to one account, five ministers were deposed for various offences in the space of four years in the first decade of the nineteenth century. The crusade of fearless evangelical pastors unseated many patently idle ministers from their parish sinecures.

Such changes within the Highland church were but reflections of rapid social transformation. Improving landowners cleared estates in some areas to make way for mixed farming and in others for large-scale sheep farming. In the latter, the population was moved to coastal townships where inhabitants turned to crofting, fishing and the collection of seaweed to make kelp. In both instances the collapse of the old traditional order of the Highlands and the sense of betrayal thrust a wedge between lairds and people, driving the latter to evangelicalism. Religious revivals were reported with increasing frequency after 1790; Moulin in 1799, Skye and Arran in 1812, Breadalbane in Perthshire in 1816, and almost continuously in Lewis between 1824

---

* augmentation–increase of stipend

and 1833. Accounts spoke of crofters who 'see visions, dream dreams, revel in the wildest hallucinations', and Lewis folk in the 1820s were said to be 'seized with spasms, convulsions, fits, and screaming aloud'.[21] But these were merely peaks in a prolonged heightening of popular religious experience. Those affected, certainly before 1810, were not merely the poor but also the prospering. Indeed, Lachlan Mackenzie was quite explicit that it was amongst the improving tenants, those granted extended twenty-five year leases, that religious enthusiasm was greatest; more generally, he reported, the good herring fishing of the early 1790s and 'the spirit of industry' made for 'a great appearance of religion in Lochcarron'.

The socio-religious division that was emerging after 1770 was between on the one hand the landowners, their servants, estate factors and shepherds, whom the Moderate clergy served, and on the other hand the middle and lower ranks of the crofters and tradesmen. The poet James Hogg acutely observed the split on a visit to Lochalsh parish in the west Highlands during the communion season of 1802. The ordinary people of the parish and surrounding areas thronged in the fields to hear two visiting Gaelic-speaking ministers preaching whilst 'the more genteel people' met in the parish church to listen to the minister Alexander Downie. Downie was representative of the wealth and leaning of the Moderate clergy in the Highlands. He spoke little Gaelic, was 'a good shot but a wretched preacher', and was often absent from his parish, allegedly residing sixty miles away, probably on one of his large farms on the island of Skye. He owned several properties in the west Highlands on which he was a noted improver in sheep and cattle breeding, and in addition had a large stipend, a glebe, a lucrative army chaplaincy, and was on a par with the social élites of Highland society. The social split at Downie's communion celebration was apparent in tension between him and the visiting evangelical clergy who, as custom dictated, were entertained in the manse. The evangelicals were young, serious-minded, and quick to take offence from the jovial banter at their host's sumptuous table.

But whilst Moderate and Evangelical clergy were forced to mix both socially and at presbytery meetings, disaffection amongst

Religion in rural society 121

the laity turned into an informal dissent. From the ranks of 'the Men' emerged a few lay preachers who encouraged parishioners to open-air Sunday worship outside the doors of the parish church. The extent of this 'Separatist' movement is difficult to gauge as it was highly localized and often temporary, but it was sufficiently widespread in the Highlands and Hebrides in the early decades of the nineteenth century to indicate that presbyterianism was seriously divided. The 'Separatist' leaders, like Highland emigrants, were not the poor but the alienated élites within the lower ranks. The emigrants displayed the same predilection for puritanism, becoming strongly attached to Secession and Relief ministers sent over to America in the late eighteenth and early nineteenth centuries. As in the Lowlands, the real social composition of the puritans belied their culture of an oppressed and wasted peasantry suffering as a result of economic change forced upon them by landowners. But the sense of oppression, of deprived rights and privileges, was powerful and crucial to their mythology, and religion provided the focus for their grievances and for their new identity.

A vital and often underrated factor in exciting Highland puritanism was the work of Lowland missionaries. They came from a variety of denominations and movements, and all found a ready response amongst both the middle and lower ranks of the north and north-west. Between 1797 and 1808 the Haldane brothers' Society for the Propagation of the Gospel at Home sent dozens of lay preachers, divinity students and visiting English evangelicals like Charles Simeon and Rowland Hill into the Highlands preaching an open evangelical gospel tinged with Painite ideas about the dignity of man. On the first tour alone, James Haldane and two companions delivered 308 sermons and distributed 20,000 tracts to over 200,000 hearers. The results were rarely the founding of permanent congregations, although Baptist and Congregationalist churches were established in Thurso and Wick in the extreme north, Tiree in the Inner Hebrides and in some other coastal towns and townships. Similarly, extensive missionary work by the Secession and Relief Churches produced only a small number of congregations: in Thurso, Wick, Easter Ross, Nairn and the Mull of Kintyre. But the influence of these southern evangelists should not be measured in terms of denominational recruitment. Vast expanses of the north could be covered by itinerant preachers, and popular religious enthusiasm was easily ignited. A pair of missionaries sponsored by Relief congregations in Glasgow got large audiences in the late 1790s from amongst prosperous slate-quarry workers at Easdale in Argyll. Without solicitation, revivalist symptoms appeared: crying, wailing and self-remonstration. Between the 1790s and 1830s the lower and middle ranks of Highland society welcomed any and all evangelical preaching, and the role of the Seceders was particularly important. Two of their missionaries reported in 1819:

> A spirit of religious inquiry has been excited, chiefly by the labours of pious and zealous individuals, who have been in the habit of itinerating from place to place; so that the people, having got a tasting of doctrine, with which they were formerly unacquainted, are ardently longing for more. Provided they can only be permitted to enjoy it, they care not from what quarter it comes, or by what instrumentality it is conveyed. When a preacher goes amongst them, who has the character of being an evangelical preacher (no matter to what denomination he may belong), the people flock to hear him, and listen with gladness to the message he delivers.[22]

Some of these southern dissenters stayed on in the Highlands, but more generally native preachers emerged to spread the puritan gospel and to appropriate it to native Gaelic culture.

The missionary explosion in the Highlands and Hebrides after the 1790s extended also to the Orkneys and Shetlands. The people here were culturally different from the rest of the north, being English-speakers drawing heavily upon Scandinavian customs and religious practices. None the less, the economies of these islands were a mixture of the Highland and the Lowland, combining crofting and fishing with more sophisticated commercialism and craft industry in the ports of Kirkwall, Stromness and Lerwick where there were strong associations with, amongst others, the Hudson's Bay Company. Like the crofter–fishers of the Highlands and the Moray Firth coast, the islanders of Orkney and Shetland proved to be receptive to the millennialist gospel brought by southern missionaries. The Haldanite movement enjoyed considerable success after 1798, leading to the foundation of strong Baptist and Congregationalist churches in some of the smaller islands and isolated parishes. In the Shetlands the Methodist Church had its most successful appeal anywhere in Scotland, and a separate synod was founded there. With the arrival of commercial herring fishing from the late 1870s, these evangelistic churches boomed amongst both fishers and the larger groups employed at the curing stations. But the most striking success of all fell to the Seceders who swept through Kirkwall and adjacent parishes in the south-east of Orkney around 1800, and later spread out to some other parishes. Their support in outlying districts was, like that of the Haldanites, amongst crofter–fishers, but in the Kirkwall area it was predominantly amongst artisans and townsfolk. The dissenting churches appealed to similar groups, and recruitment depended on missionaries being in the right place at the right time. On the small Orkney island of Burray, for instance, dissent first arose in a significant form in 1832 when the heritors refused permission to 250 parishioners to erect themselves a loft in the parish church. An itinerant Baptist missionary was on hand and gave sufficient preaching for a congregation to be formed. In this respect both the Orkneys and the Shetlands were more like the Lowlands in that formal dissent emerged quickly, but there were many isolated islands and parishes in which crofting–fishing communities with low incomes sustained a staunch puritanism akin to that of the Gaelic-speaking areas of the Highlands and Hebrides.

The growth of commercial herring fishing and the continuation of older trading links created a modernizing economy in the Northern Isles. But in the Highlands and Hebrides the benefits of modern capitalism were spread less amongst the population. The increase in evictions in the first half of the nineteenth century, and the collapse of the lucrative kelp industry after 1810 threw the crofting community into a prolonged depression in which continued population growth put extra pressure upon the scarce farming land in coastal townships. Evangelical puritanism, instead of being associated with 'the spirit of industry', as noted by Lachlan Mackenzie in the 1790s, soon became associated instead with declining living standards and mounting hostility to landlords and factors. An unsympathetic Edinburgh magazine reported in 1814:

> Many of the converts became emaciated and unsociable. The duties of life were abandoned. Sullen, morose, and discontented, some of them began to talk of their high privileges and of their right, as the elect few, to possess the earth. . . . The landlord was pronounced unchristian because he insisted on his dues.[23]

Evangelicals became increasingly associated with discontent. On the Atholl estates in northern Perthshire in 1800-04 Haldanite preachers organized an emigrant scheme for tenants disturbed by agricultural improvements. In the Great Glen it was reported in 1806 that the evangelical movement had been started

> by certain religious itinerants who addressed the people by interpreters and distributed numerous pamphlets calculated, as they said, to excite a serious soul concern. The consequences were that men who could not read began to preach, and to influence the people against their lawful pastors. . . . They next adopted a notion that all who were superior to them in wealth or rank were oppressors whom they would enjoy the consolation of seeing damned.[24]

In Assynt parish in Sutherland in the early 1810s, the clearance of peasants from their traditional farms and houses was marked by violent opposition to the induction of a Moderate minister, leading to the dispatch of troops from Edinburgh and the prosecution of several parishioners for mobbing and rioting. Emigration increased, drawing off many of the formerly prosperous small tenants from Protestant areas. By contrast most of the Catholic emigrants were labourers and the poor. Protestant landowners in Catholic areas combined agricultural improvement with anti-Catholic purges, attracting evangelical ministers and teachers from the Gaelic schools societies of Edinburgh and Glasgow to preach an overpowering Protestantism. One teacher noted that even 'the Protestants were almost papists at heart', and those who could not accept it emigrated to be replaced in some cases by presbyterians from neighbouring districts.

Amongst the more numerous presbyterians however, the teachers from the Gaelic schools societies contributed to revivalist passions in the 1810s and 1820s. The erection of extension churches under a government-sponsored General Assembly scheme increased the number of parishes in which social segregation of worshippers was taking place. These new churches attracted evangelical clergy who served the crofting population, and the split was reinforced in the 1830s by visits from southern clergy canvassing support for the Evangelical Party in its struggle with the Moderates during the Ten Years' Conflict. Religious tensions rose markedly. The number of patronage disputes in the Highlands and Islands increased during this decade and religious revivals erupted in Easter Ross in 1839, spreading as far as Skye, Harris, Mull and Kintyre. When the Disruption took place in May 1843, it was no surprise to find the crofters being swept *en masse* into the Free Church.

The significance of the Disruption in the Highlands was enormous. On the island of Lewis 98 per cent of the people left the Established Church, in Sutherland reportedly 99.8 per cent, and in all but the Catholic areas and a few of the larger towns like Inverness the figure was rarely less than 90 per cent. Practically everyone seceded except landowners' families, their domestic servants, factors and estate workers, together with some of the small number in the professions: or, as a Free Church publicist put it, 'all who are not the creatures of the proprietor, and have not stifled their convictions for a piece of bread'.[25] Rarely can such a cataclysm have befallen a major Christian church. Sixty years of proselytizing by a mixed band of evangelicals had resulted in a people for whom puritanical presbyterianism was, in the words of the Free Church General Assembly, 'riveted in their souls'.[26]

But the significance lay not just in the denominational polarization of Highland society. For the Disruption's impact was dramatically heightened by mounting evictions of tenants and the potato blight. Throughout the late 1840s and early 1850s the economic position of the crofters worsened as their source of livelihood was threatened alternately by landowners and failure of the potato crop. Hugh Miller, a prominent Free Church journalist, witnessed an impoverished congregation of his fellow brethren meeting for worship a few weeks after the Disruption near Helmsdale in Sutherland. They met near the crowded cottages and small patches of cultivation to which they had been recently cleared by the Duke of Sutherland. The 700 people, he wrote, 'were expelled from their inland holdings, and left to squat upon the coast [and] occupy the selvage of discontent and poverty that fringes its shores'; he commented that he had 'rarely seen a more deeply serious assemblage; never certainly one that bore an air of such deep dejection'.[27] In an effort to stifle organized peasant opposition, the Duke of Sutherland and other landowners refused sites for Free Church buildings and threatened crofters who sheltered seceding clergy with eviction. Within five months of the Disruption the Free Church General Assembly described a 'conspiracy against the Free Church on the part of the landed proprietors', and four years later a House of Commons Select Committee was appointed to investigate. Disturbances were reported, especially in Ross-shire, and alleged 'rioters' were charged when factors tried to prevent open-air preaching. Free Church congregations were driven to extraordinary lengths to find meeting places because of the concentration of landholding with the large estates. At Sunart on the west Highland peninsula of Ardnamurchan, Sir James Riddell's refusal of a site forced the Free Church congregation to the novel solution of using a moored ship as a church for many years. Elsewhere sites were generally negotiated in the 1850s and churches built, but the landowners' obstruction imprinted the Disruption in crofter mythology as a great social as well as ecclesiastical revolution.

The Free Church alignment with the lower ranks in Highland society was of an intensity unmatched elsewhere in Scotland. The Lowland Church, more wealthy and bourgeois, was conscious of its responsibilities to the oppressed crofters. In 1846 it organized a philanthropic venture which raised £15,000 to send a ship with food supplies up the west coast, and in a wider sense Free Church ministers became severe critics of evictions and the landowners' treatment of their poorer tenants. But the puritanism of the crofters was not opposed to the new social order created by the Clearances. It welcomed the new values of hard work and self-reliance that improvement implied, and opposed old Highland customs and the clan system. As James Hunter, the historian of the crofting community, has put it, there was in the puritanism of 'the Men' 'a more or less conscious attempt to come to terms with the realities of a social and economic system dominated by landlordism rather than by clanship'.[28] Throughout the presbyterianizing of the north and north-west, the key element had been the southern influence. The gospel brought was a Lowland one, carried by missionaries steeped in covenanting history and the dissenting struggles of the Secession, Relief and independent churches. The process was one in which the Highlands were absorbed into the denominational system of the Lowlands. Whilst the Gaelic language survived, the process involved the suppression of traditional clan customs, superstition, dance, song and poetry, and the acceptance of the dissenting culture of religious and economic individualism which had emerged from capitalist society.

Although accepting the modernization of society and its values, the crofting population of the north did not reap immediate benefits. The anti-landlord stance adopted by the Free Church in the late 1840s and 1850s quickly dissipated and when the next great crofters' struggle emerged in the 1880s it was a motley crew of Established Church Christian socialists, labour activists and Liberals which won the Crofters' Act of 1886 and some measure of security of tenure for Highlanders. Support from the southern Free Church was muted, indicative of the widening gap between Lowland and Highland sections in the Church. The Church in the Lowland cities and towns was moving swiftly towards a liberal, middle-class theology, breaking its by now token adherence to hell-fire preaching and aggressive puritanism. In 1892 the Free Church formally abandoned Calvinist doctrine, and in 1900 combined with the United Presbyterian Church. To the crofters these developments were the abandonment of traditional presbyterianism, and the result was the formation of essentially Highland churches; the Free Presbyterian Church, formed in 1893, and the larger Free Church which refused to join the 1900 union. Once again, these ecclesiastical events reflected a wider situation. Whilst Lowland economy and society had grown considerably in sophistication and prosperity, the Highlands were becoming increasingly tied to a static system of large estates on the one hand and small-scale crofting and fishing on the other. The Crofters' Act, for all the benefits it brought, cemented the society to an unchanging economic structure, and the ecclesiastical breaches of 1893 and 1900 merely welded the crofting community to a similar fixed religious tradition. There had clearly been an enormous anomaly in the Lowland–Highland union within the Victorian Free Church and its dissolution around 1900 was perhaps inevitable. But the irony was that after a century and a half of converting the Highlands to puritanical presbyterianism, the south abandoned Calvinist and covenanting culture and left the Gaelic-speakers of the north as the last upholders of the religious heritage of the seventeenth-century Lowlands.

Notes

1 Quoted in T. C. Smout (1972) *A History of the Scottish People, 1560–1830*, Glasgow, Fontana/Collins, 116.
2 J. Hogg, *Highland Tours*, ed. W. F. Laughlan (1981), Hawick, Byways, 111.
3 C. Larner (1981) *Enemies of God: The Witch-Hunt in Scotland*, London, Chatto and Windus, 56.
4 Stirling Antiburgher Presbytery, MS minutes 9 April 1776, CRA, CH3/286/1.
5 Aberfoyle Church of Scotland, Punishment Book, 5 January 1794 to 19 April 1795, CRA, CH2/704/4.
6 T. C. Smout (1982) 'Born again at Cambuslang: new evidence on popular religion and literacy in eighteenth-century Scotland', *Past and Present*, 97, 118.
7 OSA, 8, p. 352.
8 Quoted in *Statement of Facts and Case for the Heritors of Neilston relative to Church Accommodation in the Parish* (1826), Glasgow, 18.
9 K. J. Logue (1979) *Popular Disturbances in Scotland, 1780–1815*, Edinburgh, John Donald, 169.
10 T. Gillespie (1774) *A Treatise on Temptation*, Edinburgh, 145, 202.

Religion in rural society

11 J. Ramsay (1888) *Scotland and Scotsmen in the Eighteenth Century*, Edinburgh and London, II, 557.
12 *Autobiography of John Younger, Shoemaker, St. Boswells* (1881), Kelso, 354.
13 John Younger (1849) *The Light of the Week: or the Temporal Advantages of the Sabbath Considered in Relation to the Working Classes*, London, 19, 26.
14 James Taylor quoted in T. D. Taylor (ed.) (1970) *The Annals of Fenwick*, Ayrshire Archaeological and Natural History Society, 12.
15 Stirling Antiburgher Presbytery, MS minutes 30 July 1806, CRA, CH3/286/3; D. Scott (1866) *Annals and Statistics of the Original Secession Church*, Edinburgh, 267-70.
16 J. Peddie (1800) *A Defence of the Associate Synod against the Charge of Sedition*, Edinburgh, 7.
17 I. Carter (1979) *Farmlife in Northeast Scotland 1840-1914*, Edinburgh, John Donald, 160 *et seq*.
18 Church of Scotland Presbytery of Lochcarron, MS minutes 3 and 5 April 1792, SRO, CH2/567/3.
19 J. MacInnes (1951) *The Evangelical Movement in the Highlands of Scotland 1688 to 1800*, Aberdeen University Press, 45.
20 OSA, 13, p. 561.
21 Quoted in J. Hunter (1974) 'The Emergence of the Crofting Community: The Religious Contribution 1798-1843', *Scottish Studies*, 18, 106.
22 Quoted in J. McKerrow (1841) *History of the Secession Church*, Glasgow, 639-40.
23 Quoted in J. Hunter (1976) *The Making of the Crofting Community*, Edinburgh, John Donald, 97.
24 Quoted in ibid., 97.
25 H. Miller (1843) *Sutherland: as it was and is; or How a Country May be Ruined*, Edinburgh, 11.
26 Convener of the Gaelic Committee quoted in *Discussion in the General Assembly of the Free Church of Scotland on the State of Sutherland and Ross Shires* (1843), Glasgow, 8.
27 H. Miller, op. cit., 11.
28 J. Hunter, op. cit., 101.

5
The challenge of the cities, 1780–1890

The Impact of urbanization

The growth of cities had a dramatic impact upon religion. The urbanization of the British population which fell mainly between 1780 and 1900 has long been identified with the secularization of habits and popular philosophy, turning attention from the God-made countryside to the man-made industrial centres, and has been associated more directly with the forces which undermined the role of the churches. More than anything, the crucial innovation seemed to be social segregation. The new industrial proletariat became for the Protestant churches the 'lapsed masses' and 'home heathens' of slum tenements, out of the reach of all agencies of civil society. 'For them', wrote a Free Church minister in Glasgow in 1870, 'the hundred spires of our City's churches suggest no bright thoughts of heaven.'[1] In Scotland as in the rest of Britain urban society became the greatest headache to the churches as their traditional authority and community function became fundamentally challenged by an entirely new context.

Urbanization brought immediate changes to the nature of the churches' role. These changes were not merely the product of growth of city populations – that is quantitative leaps in the need for churches and clergy – but were qualitative. For example, the employment of children in the new cotton-spinning factories, and the general growth of child labour which this encouraged, led to the older weekday-education provided by charity schools being unsuited to the needs of the working-class young. In 1785 the Rev. William Porteous of the Established Church moved the city fathers of Glasgow to expand charity schools, but two years later he reacted within five days to the city's first and very violent cotton strike by proposing to the council that Sunday schools were needed to educate 'apprentices' on their one day of rest. Sunday schools were the first of the many forms of religious voluntary organization to emerge in Scottish cities over the next hundred years. The original one in Aberdeen in 1787 was set up 'for the instruction of poor children in reading English, learning the principles of the Christian religion, and psalmody', and by keeping children at 'exercises' virtually continuously from 8 a.m. to 7 p.m. it was hoped that Sunday games and burglary of residents' homes during divine service would be eliminated.[2]

It is noteworthy how the early attempts to adapt urban religion to the industrial age were co-ordinated by town councils. Since they owned most burgh churches and had since the Reformation taken responsibility for the religious life of the citizens, town councillors and magistrates continued for several decades to manage Established Church responses to the new society. Practically all the Sunday schools set up in Scottish cities in the 1780s were municipally patronized; the 'Society for Managing the Sunday schools in Glasgow' became an incorporated institution of the city in 1790, preventing nearly 800 boys and girls from becoming 'useless or pernicious members of society'.[3] Councils continued to manage older city-centre Established Churches until the 1920s and sanctioned the efforts of religious voluntary organizations. Certainly town councils had secular matters of pressing concern. Insanitation, poor housing, the provision of public utilities like water and gas, and the suppression of disorder and crime took up an ever increasing amount of council time and expenditure. But interestingly, the improvement of the urban environment became a matter to which councillors applied a religious perspective. The municipal response to proletarian unrest, as in Glasgow in 1811–13, tended to be the planning of 'large plain churches' for working-class districts. As church elders, town councillors tended to see the advancement of slum clearance and sanitary regulations as deriving from a religious vision of how urban society could be improved. Evangelical councillors in particular grouped together, sometimes across party lines, to press for city improvement acts and municipal take-over of private water and gas companies. The Glasgow City Improvement Act of 1866, which set about the demolition of city-centre slums, originated in a secret philanthropic scheme run by twenty-two wealthy citizens and councillors and financed by the Clydesdale Bank under the inspiration of a Free Church minister, Dr Robert Buchanan. His missionary work in the wynds of the Tron parish convinced him in the 1850s that improvement in the working classes' religion and morals was dependent in some measure on 'breaking up the denser quarters of the city, [and] of letting in upon them the light and air of heaven'.[4] In 1857 and 1858 Buchanan led the Glasgow presbytery of the Free Church into staving off a ratepayers' reaction against the costs of a mammoth project to bring clear Highland water from Loch Katrine, and, as the unofficial chaplain to civic improvement, gave the teetotal toast at the celebration banquet to the joint stream of water and the gospel: 'Let that living water be made to circulate through all the dwellings of the city.'[5]

This conjunction of religious and municipal designs produced other co-operative activity. In the 1850s and 1860s municipal sanitary departments turned to congregational parish missionary societies to distribute leaflets on hygiene and sanitation during the fever epidemics of typhus and cholera, and Sunday-school teachers were used by councils to provide the best information on the extent of literacy and attendance figures at day, evening and Sunday schools. Perhaps most commonly, though, was the way in which the churches and religious organizations turned to the councils for enforcement of moral and religious laws. In 1850 the Sunday-school teachers of Glasgow inundated the council with petitions to close public houses on the Sabbath and to restrict the number of licences issued. The council acceded and, like Edinburgh at the same time, adopted a restrictive licensing policy which was engrossed in Scottish legislation in 1853. Municipal licensing courts were from the early 1840s dominated by evangelicals who were hostile to the drinks trade and were invariably teetotallers. In this field, and in a number of others, municipal administration became increasingly puritanical in the second half of the nineteenth century. The Sunday running of trains became a *cause célèbre*, creating a national rumpus in the 1840s which largely prevented it and another in the 1860s which, much to the chagrin of the dissenters, permitted it. Even so, Sabbath trains remained limited in Scotland until the mid-twentieth century. From the 1830s onwards municipal authorities pressurized many industries and employers to reduce Sunday labour; as their own contribution art galleries and museums were closed on the Sabbath to reduce 'profanation'. By 1904 a university research student was noting that Glasgow councillors used their powers 'in a narrow and puritanical manner', going so far as to censor pictures from art exhibitions in the city.[6] In this way the civil magistrates were increasingly called upon to act for the benefit of the churches' moral and religious code.

But the role of the public authorities in relation to religion was narrowed after 1830, in the main because of the electoral power of the presbyterian dissenters who objected to municipal ownership of Established churches. In the 1830s seven Glasgow councillors on the Evangelical wing of the Established Church, led by the publisher William Collins, started a scheme to build twenty churches in the city with the aim of putting 'the city rulers under the necessity of lowering the seat rents of the present churches, in order to meet the competition; and thus so far impair the city revenue from these churches'. The scheme was successful in this objective because the number of paying worshippers in the council's kirks fell from nearly 9000 in 1832-3 to 7000 in 1842-3, with average rents falling from 11s. 4d. to 9s. 8d. The Disruption of 1843 accelerated the process with over 3000 worshippers leaving and unlet seats being rented for half price. The city-centre location of the ten council churches in Glasgow proved progressively unpopular with congregations, and there was a steady drift of paying worshippers to suburban churches in more pleasant surroundings. A similar trend occurred in Edinburgh. Congregations objected between 1810 and 1835 to increases in seat rents imposed by the town council, and extension churches built in the late 1830s caused an outflow of worshippers and a fall in seat rents.

For all practical purposes, councils abdicated attempts to control urban religion in the 1820s as dissenters and ratepayers successfully stopped ecclesiastical schemes which would increase taxation. But despite this decay in municipal control of religion, town councils played a crucial role in the early stages of rapid urban growth and industrialization. They brought together ecclesiastical, educational, philanthropic and medical agencies to develop and adapt civil administration to the rapidly changing environment. Rural parishes and small towns with no burgh administration were less fortunate. In textile, mining and metallurgical communities which sprang up between 1785 and 1830 ecclesiastical and civil administration was often chaotic. The parish church, the parish school and parochial poor relief were utterly inadequate to cope with rapid growth of population. In such places the only civil authority was the heritors' board and the kirk session, both of which were quickly trammelled by the advent of industrialism. The parish of Old Monklands to the east of Glasgow grew rapidly in the 1830s with the expansion of coal and iron mining and smelting, its population rising from 9580 to 19,709. Its one parish church, which attracted mostly older agricultural families, was quite insufficient, and in desperation for church accommodation a Relief congregation was formed in 1837 renting the top floor of a new tenement where around 350 sittings were made available. The consequences were evident in the results of the religious census in 1851 which showed that the neighbouring community of Airdrie, which was in exactly the same predicament, had a church attendance rate of 23 per cent – the second lowest amongst the fifty-three Scottish burghs. Inadequate civil government and poor church provisions tended to go hand-in-hand. Heritors could not afford to build new churches or schools, and the inhabitants had often to struggle for many years or decades to provide for themselves.

The adverse effects of rapid urbanization were widely reported. The Edinburgh bookseller William Creech noted changes in the religious habits of the capital's residents:

In 1763 – It was fashionable to go to church, and people were interested about religion. Sunday was observed by all ranks as a day of devotion; and it was disgraceful to be seen on the streets during the time of public worship. . . . In 1783 – Attendance on church was greatly neglected, and particularly by men; Sunday was made by many a day of relaxation; . . . The streets were far from being void of people in the time of public worship; and, in the evenings were frequently loose and riotous; particularly owing to bands of apprentice boys and young lads.[7]

A minister in Stirling noted the same thing in 1790: 'There is generally no room in churches for the accommodation of the poor', he recorded, causing them to 'loiter away the days of public solemnity, in sloth and vicious indulgence at home'.[8] A Glasgow contributor to the *Statistical Account* of the 1790s spoke of a recent decline in the 'strict severity and apparent sanctity of manners': 'There is now a great deal more industry on six days of the week, and a great deal more dissipation and licentiousness on the seventh.'[9] Most Established Church ministers welcomed the coming of industry, and in rural and Highland areas they were positively longing for its arrival. But there was general agreement amongst clergy of the Established Church between the 1780s and 1840s that the beneficial effects of industrial employment could not develop in a vacuum of moral and religious influence. Most crucially, they noted that the cities generated social distance: in work, in place of residence, in income, and in religion. In pre-industrial society, religion had been a binding cord in the community. In the nineteenth-century city, it became increasingly a line of social demarcation.

Evangelicalism and the rise of the middle classes

An immediate effect of the growth of industrial cities was to widen the gap between urban and rural sections in the presbyterian churches. In the Established Church, for instance, the numerical growth in the number of city-based clergy and elders challenged the traditional gentry control of the general assembly and resulted in various moves to forestall an urban take-over: notably by denying ministers from chapels-of-ease access to seats in church courts. But in a more general way the cultural and religious interests of urban and rural élites increasingly diverged. For the landed classes the Church embodied the principles upon which the country had been managed for generations: patronage (in church and state), deference, and the power and stability vested in heritable property. The burgeoning cities of the late eighteenth and early nineteenth centuries, on the other hand, nurtured a new and contrasting social system and culture based on independent values: competition, self-reliance and status through hard work rather than inheritance. The urban middle classes, products of city prosperity and opportunity, demanded recognition: the extension of the franchise, the reform of government policy on the basis of *laissez faire*, and equality with the landed classes in matters of religion. More than that, the middle classes brought to the churches an aggressive and enthusiastic commitment which conflicted with the rural élites' stress on religion as a sedate instrument of civil government. The cities were transforming ideas about what religion should be.

The distinguishing feature in the social identity of the new middle classes was evangelicalism. It was not so much a theological system as a framework of response to the emergence of modern urban society. It was not limited to any one denomination, nor even to Protestantism. Nor was it the sole preserve of the middle classes, for it enveloped the values which governed the urban social system. But the middle classes, as a broad yet remarkably united social élite, were the masters of its development. From its initial emergence as an identifiably urban phenomenon in the last two decades of the eighteenth century, it continued to dominate middle-class attitudes to urban civilization until the 1880s. Spurning theological debate, it called citizens to action in the name of God, the economy and the individual.

The doctrinal complexion of Scottish evangelicalism is a matter of some confusion, and there is particular uncertainty as to how it relates to the Calvinist heritage of presbyterianism. There is no doubt that by 1890 the distinctive theological emphasis of Scottish presbyterianism had been emasculated in the main denominations, but it is problematic to ascertain when and how this had

The challenge of the cities 137

occurred. There is a strong school of thought that Calvinism was a vital ingredient in the economic transformation of Scotland after 1750. The most vigorous contribution has been made by Gordon Marshall who argues that between 1560 and 1707 Calvinist theology played an instrumental role in the evolution of the secular ethic of modern Scottish capitalism.[10] He identifies the doctrine of predestination as crucial to the inculcation of entrepreneurial attitudes: because salvation is already decided yet is unknown for certain, the individual strives in life for the assurance of redemption which comes from worldly success. Historians of the eighteenth and nineteenth centuries have asserted the relevance of this doctrinal impulse to industrialization and the emergence of the middle classes. Roy Campbell in his history of modern Scottish industry attributes presbyterian theology with encouraging a social action by the individual in partnership with God which produced 'the utter self-confidence and assurance of his actions . . . necessary for a successful entrepreneur'.[11] Historians of the left as much as of the right have tended to agree on the fundamental influence of Calvinism on Scottish development, albeit with sometimes different stresses. Keith Burgess has seen it as 'an ideology ready-made for a comparatively backward society embarking on a course of capitalist development', and argues that predestination 'tended to justify social mobility and personal wealth as proof of being one of the "elect"'.[12] Allan MacLaren has been the most expansive on this issue, arguing that Calvinism and the doctrine of predestination spread through most of the Scottish Protestant churches – including the Methodists, the Baptists and the Congregationalists. The Disruption he regards as a restatement of concepts of the Elect and Non-elect by the dominant middle-class membership of the Free Church, creating in the evangelizing schemes promoted by that denomination a policy 'to regulate society on Calvinist principles'. He has attributed other consequences to the Calvinist heritage – notably a fatalistic Scottish reaction to nineteenth-century cholera epidemics, which elicited the institution of extra fast days by some church courts.[13] Some ecclesiastical historians have seen in heresy trials in the presbyterian churches a sustained attachment to Calvinist precepts: such trials took place in the

Established Church in the 1820s and 1830s, in the Secession Church in the 1840s, and in the Free Church in the 1870s. In a more casual way, other historians have identified Calvinism in the industrial discipline imposed by Scottish manufacturers upon their workers, in the heavy-handedness with which civil authorities imposed the law, and in the ferocity of teaching methods in Scottish schools. More generally, the tenor of Scottish life well into the nineteenth century is often portrayed as doom-laden with hell-fire-and-damnation preaching the mark of the society.

But the tone of presbyterian worship can mislead as to content. For one thing Scottish congregations were noted for their irreverence during the one-hour sermon; the passing round of sweets was standard, talking not uncommon, and there were sometimes reports of business being conducted between the pews. In the 1800s and 1810s heating appliances, modern lighting, curtains, and decoration swept into urban churches. Between the 1850s and 1870s presbyterian services were revolutionized by the shortening of sermons, the displacement of hell-fire preaching by the joyful offer of salvation, and by the introduction of hymns and organs. The emphasis of urban presbyterianism from the 1790s was on religious opportunity. In the context of an expanding economy generated in large measure by entrepreneurial zeal and skill, evangelicalism became readily associated with the holistic advance of the individual. In this way, evangelicalism complemented economic individualism. Between 1780 and 1850, the stress of presbyterian preaching and policy was on what Ian Muirhead described as the 'individualism of conversion':[14] on rebirth through education, reading the Bible, private prayer and contemplation. After 1850 this gave way in middle-class circles to a restrained revivalism as the route to salvation. In 1874 this trend reached its zenith during the visit of the American evangelists Dwight Moody and Ira Sankey. First in Edinburgh and then in Glasgow, they preached to hundreds of meetings, notably lunchtime assemblies in the business quarters and in the evenings in suburban middle-class churches. The visit culminated in April at the Kibble Palace in Glasgow's Botanic Gardens where 7000 of the city's well-dressed and well-heeled crowded in for the final meeting leaving thousands more outside. They marvelled at

The challenge of the cities 139

Sankey's joyous singing and his playing of the 'Kist o' Whistles' (or harmonium), and listened with mounting anticipation to Moody's short sermon calling forth people to the new life. Clearly, the Scotland of the covenanters and Calvinism was much transformed.

These developments were both the cause and the symptom of declining Calvinist doctrine. Initially, the dilution of traditional standards was most marked in the Moderate faction in the Established Church. Thus, it is possible to regard the dissenters of the Secession and Reformed Presbyterian Churches as reacting to this liberalizing tendency amongst the effete landed classes. In the late 1780s the synod of the Antiburgher Church complained that 'Arminianism is become the too fashionable doctrine of the day',[15] and predestination theology was certainly still taught to dissenting divinity students until the middle decades of the nineteenth century. But the dissenters were from the start torn apart by internal conflict over predestination versus Arminianism – that is, over the extent of the Atonement given by Christ on the cross. Preachers in the extremely puritanical and Calvinist sect of Scotch Baptists, which was popular in parts of Fife in the second half of the eighteenth century, held to the doctrine of predestination, 'yet they think it dangerous to comfort people by those considerations when they are in a backsliding state'.[16] The desire of the dissenters to offer the gospel, to win recruits and to maintain allegiance amongst a shifting population, created great anxiety that people should be motivated to search for the Scriptural message.

As a result, the preaching of predestination and of the Elect was relegated to the background. In many cases, it was entirely substituted by an Arminian offer of Christ. In this way dissenting clergy got into trouble with hard-liners in their denominations. Nearly half of the Reformed Presbyterian Church, the direct and most Calvinistic descendant of the covenanters, adopted universal salvation in the 1750s and were forced to leave the Church. Many ministers in the Burgher and Antiburgher Churches were preaching Arminianism from the 1790s and remarkably few were brought to book for it. Church leaders were aware of the divisions amongst clergy and members, and chose wherever possible to ignore the demands for heresy trials emanating from predominantly rural ministers. Every major decree of the Secession Church on doctrinal issues involved accommodation between predestination and Arminianism. An Act of that Church in 1742 stated: 'For the record of God being such a thing as warrants *all* to believe in the son of God, it is evident that it can be no such warrant to tell men that God hath given eternal life to the elect', and added that 'our faith and good works . . . are the cause of our *eternal salvation*'.[17] In 1828 the Church issued a 'balancing formula' which decreed that whilst 'Christ died for the elect', yet 'His death has also a relation to mankind sinners, being suitable to all and sufficient to the salvation of all'.[18] Even the puritanical presbyterians in the Highlands were in the eighteenth century avoiding predestination. Lachlan Mackenzie of Lochcarron preached a typical evangelical gospel: 'The rock gave water not for one or two only, but for all the congregation'; 'And if a man wait on the means of grace, shall his labour be in vain? God forbid.'[19] The offer of salvation, if it was to be attractive in a rapidly changing society, had to be wide and achievable within a reasonably short time.

Differences of emphasis were infinite, and it could be observed in any case that the preaching of an evangelical predestinarian might not be so different from that of a salvationist. The issue only surfaced when a minister under examination by a church court openly avowed the doctrine of universal salvation. James Morison did this in the Secession Church in the early 1840s, and his ejection from it is often cited as evidence of the Calvinistic leanings of the Seceders. But his going fomented a vigorous debate which concluded in 1845 with a formula which conceded to the rampant anti-Calvinists 'a full, sincere, and consistent offer of the Gospel to all mankind'.[20] There was obfuscation of the issue, but the trend was clear. Whilst the doctrine of predestination was rarely denied formally, it was equally rarely preached in the main presbyterian churches of the nineteenth century. In the Free Church, for instance, the Calvinist group was a small and vocal minority which through its unbending claim to be the upholder of 'true presbyterianism' exerted an influence beyond its size. But even with the backing of the Highland Free

The challenge of the cities 141

Church, this minority could not stem evangelical innovation: the singing of hymns and the use of organs, the admission of the English evangelist Brownlow North as a lay preacher in 1859, and the rapid drift of the urban Church towards a policy of disestablishment. 'Bare old Calvinism', as Thomas Carlyle observed in 1844, was 'under sentence of death'.[21]

Much of what is regarded as distinctive in Scottish presbyterianism of the industrial period was in fact a product of evangelicalism of the style and doctrine which took a hold amongst the English Methodists and other nonconformists. English evangelists found a ready welcome in the pulpits of many Scottish kirks, and they reinforced the call to action issued to middle-class congregations of Glasgow, Edinburgh and other towns. The call was an evangelical summons: to individual enquiry and to evangelization. The urban church became unlike the rural one in that it became decreasingly 'laid on' by the state and by the élites. Building a church and inculcating the gospel truths had to be undertaken by voluntary effort and 'Christian liberality'. The effect was to turn the cities into the vibrant focus of aggressive Christianity with endless and very successful appeals for money for building churches, manses and mission stations, for mounting foreign missions, and for the publication of tracts. Equally, though, urban evangelicalism demanded personal commitment through voluntary effort in Sunday schools, Bible classes, tract distribution, home visiting, the temperance soirée, and hundreds of other related activities. Voluntary organizations became overwhelmingly religious in tenor and objective, providing the outlet for 'respectable' and 'useful' middle-class leisure. And the centre of this activity was Glasgow, dubbed by one evangelical in the 1830s as 'Gospel City'.[22]

The most obvious product of the evangelical call to action was the construction of churches. The dramatic growth of population in cities like Glasgow necessitated church extension at a fast rate, but town councils could not find the funds with which to build sufficient numbers. A few municipal kirks were erected in the larger cities between 1780 and 1820, and a few thereafter were enlarged. Very quickly the shortage became evident in Glasgow when demand for pews forced the council in 1782 to raise seat rents to keep pace with prices in other kirks. Further seat-rent rises followed, as in 1796 when councillors were confident that congregations 'would cheerfully pay, seeing it to be applied to so good a purpose'.[23] Their confidence was not misplaced as demand continued to rise until 1806 when every seat in the eight council churches was rented and many paying applicants were refused. The council, acting in part as an entrepreneur and in part on congregational demand, relocated the Wynd Church from its position in city-centre slums to a prominent west-end site. The outcome was an 'extraordinary' increase in seat-rent income, and as a result the rents in all the churches were raised in 1807. To continue meeting the demand, the council removed seats reserved for the poor and discontinued the practice of allocating sections of low-rent seats for the use of the working classes. Consequently, the middle classes came to dominate in these congregations whilst the working classes were only allocated two new churches erected in the east end in 1819–20.

But the most spectacular aspect of bourgeois religion was the growth of dissenting churches in which aspiring social groups could practice self-determination. The Relief Church was initially the most popular denomination for dissent in Scottish towns; it had already claimed a firm control of middle-class groups in some small towns like Jedburgh and Campbeltown, and in Glasgow it opened five churches between 1792 and 1806. But in Dundee the largest religious group at the end of the eighteenth century was the Glasites, whilst in Stirling and Edinburgh the Seceders were proving the most popular amongst a range of evangelical denominations. In Glasgow after 1815 the Secession Church took over from the Relief as the leading dissenting denomination. The Seceders built four churches there between 1817 and 1823 and remained until the 1830s the fastest-growing Protestant group. From the mid-1830s, the growth of urban dissent was obscured by the erection of some 200 extension churches under an Established Church scheme organized by Thomas Chalmers and relying on the subscriptions of evangelical supporters. When the Free Church was formed in 1843, these congregations 'came out' virtually *en masse*, and whilst they lost their churches in a House of Lords ruling, they hardly blinked before raising money all over again to provide replacements.

The challenge of the cities 143

After 1850 the provision of new churches became increasingly a product of missionary enterprise conducted by middle-class congregations and directed at the working classes. Church extension was only one part of a much wider evangelical social policy, providing an overarching moral and religious interpretation of the cities' social problems which, from the evangelical point of view, were all interrelated products of spiritual failure of the individual. The failure to strive for and gain the assured salvation awaiting everyone who 'came to Christ' induced idleness, lack of worldly success, and a whole host of moral shortcomings. Starting in the 1780s, evangelicals progressively isolated the moral shortcomings and developed agencies to tackle them: Sunday and mission schools to attack illiteracy which prevented reading of the Bible; tract distribution to provide moral and Scriptural guidance; temperance and teetotal societies to turn the working classes from drink; penny savings banks to encourage thrift and reduce improvidence; sanitary benevolent societies to distribute advice on hygiene; model lodging houses to improve morality and sanitation, and co-operative building societies to promote the spirit of self-improvement. The agencies became progressively refined according to occupation, sex and age: railwaymen's missions, mill-girl prayer groups, mothers' kitchen meetings, the Bands of Hope, the Glasgow Foundry Boys' Religious Society and its imitator the Boys' Brigade, the YMCA and the YWCA, the Girls' Guildry and so on. In this work, the voluntary helper was crucial. And the middle classes were attracted to the work in great numbers, especially after 1840. It provided an active response to fear of revolution, acting as insurance against the day when, as Thomas Chalmers put it, 'the mighty mass of a city population . . . may lift against the authorities of the land its brawny vigour'.[24] It provided social identity and accounted for worldly success, and more importantly the manifest degeneracy of urbanism and industrialism was analysed in a manner which did not disturb middle-class ideology. 'It is a righteous and irreversible law of Divine providence', the Free Church's Robert Buchanan told an assembly of Glasgow's merchants in 1850, 'that the *moral* rules the *economic* condition of society. We must begin at the right end.'[25] Amongst a social class who were often hostile to state intervention in the rescue of social casualties, the moral and religious crusades of evangelicalism were an attractive solution to the urban condition.

Such was the influence of evangelical thinking on social policy that it can be argued that evangelicals dictated when and in what manner state intervention was necessary. Though not united on such 'political' matters, evangelical ministers and leading laity were frequently influential in promoting social reform and civic improvement: for instance, in the provision of free access to public parks in Edinburgh and Glasgow; in slum clearance and sanitary legislation in the 1850s and 1860s; in the formation of a state system of education in 1872; in licensing of public houses; and in the organization and administration of public works schemes for the unemployed, especially in the 1840s. Concomitantly, evangelicals were influential in directing attention away from certain activities. The generosity of the rich through handouts of charity and poor relief was, as the minister of Irvine in Ayrshire saw it in 1790, the cause of 'the streets being so infested with vagrant poor', and the minister of the industrializing parish of Eastwood to the south of Glasgow felt that it 'encourages idleness, drunkenness, and debauchery'.[26] In St John's parish in the east end of Glasgow in 1819, Thomas Chalmers started a celebrated scheme to re-create the rural parish of pre-industrial Scotland with parochial relief relying solely on voluntary donations and on close scrutiny of parishioners. Although the St John's experiment made Chalmers a famous figure in the evangelical world, it was largely a failure: in part because of the shortage of lay helpers and in part because it did not reduce poverty. The experiment collapsed some time after Chalmers left in the 1820s, but he tried a similar scheme of parochial supervision in the West Port district of Edinburgh twenty years later, and other partial imitations were tried elsewhere. A national campaign by Chalmers in the 1840s against the poor-relief system was finally unsuccessful, but the ideas behind it were very popular amongst middle- and lower-middle-class groups who not only found rates a heavy burden but who believed strongly that worth and status in modern urban society were to be gained by financial self-reliance.

The challenge of the cities

Removing the unhealthy influence of indiscriminate charity was combined in the evangelical scheme with the development of legitimate agencies of social improvement. Sunday schools became after 1796 largely the preserve of evangelicals in the dissenting churches and grew with great speed after 1814 to be the largest religious voluntary organization of nineteenth-century Scotland. By 1850 more city children were at Sunday school than day school and the scholars were almost exclusively working-class. Until the 1840s Sunday-school teachers were generally organized in inter-denominational district societies, but thereafter congregations took over the management of Sunday schools and made them the central institution of home-missionary and evangelization activities. Sunday-school teachers were the backbone of evangelicalism. In the 1810s and 1820s they distributed tracts which inundated working-class districts. They found this enterprise had its shortcomings because, as the Glasgow Religious Tract Society noted in 1815, 'It is extremely difficult for such a Society to determine what measure of success may have attended their exertions, as Tracts are in general circulated in quarters, from which no future information concerning the result is received.'[27] To facilitate contact with working-class adults, city missions were established – the first in Glasgow in 1826 – to send divinity students into the slums to visit the working classes in their houses between once and twice every four months with the aim of 'diffusing and increasing amongst them a knowledge of evangelical truth'. These inter-denominational organizations were joined from the 1840s by congregational missionaries attached to the Free, United Presbyterian, Congregationalist and Evangelical Union Churches, and from this point lay helpers took an increasingly greater part in evangelization. Sunday-school teachers, some 3000 of them in Glasgow alone in 1850 and over 10,000 by 1890, were the mainstay of district visitation. They more than any other group displayed the vigour of Victorian evangelicalism, and were instrumental in enlarging the scope and extent of religious organization. To give one instance of the energy and commitment of evangelical churches, St Peter's Free Church in Glasgow 'came out' from the Established Church in 1843 with a church built by subscription a few years before, but lost it in 1849 under a House of Lords ruling that it belonged to the state church. They started raising funds to build a new one, but at the same time began a home-mission scheme which by March 1849 included a day school, a ragged school, a female school of industry, an evening school, various Sunday schools with over 500 children, and an Association for Missionary Visitors to maintain attendances at the various activities. A year later the congregation was running five day schools with 600 pupils and had started a young men's association. With the addition in the 1850s of teetotal societies for children and adults, and the development of other agencies such as medical missions, evangelicalism provided the principal outlet for middle-class energy and created a religious dominance of 'respectable' urban culture in the mid-Victorian decades.

The unifying feature of this home-mission work was the 'aggressive' system. One agent of the Glasgow City Mission, working in the east end of the city in the early 1850s, recalled 'starting out at six o'clock every Sunday morning, running from street to street, knocking at the doors and rousing the careless, and thus getting together, and keeping together, their Bible Class. . .'.[28] The working classes became increasingly badgered by such missionaries. Parents were constantly the target of pressure to send children to Sunday school, and by 1850, when Free Church congregational missions were operating in the central slum areas of the major cities, home visitation was occurring at least once a month and sometimes more often. By the 1870s the 'aggressive' system was the norm, with every middle-class congregation having an evangelization association and usually a mission station where the working classes were encouraged to strive for financial independence and full congregational status. As increasing numbers of full congregations were sanctioned in the 1860s and 1870s, they too commenced evangelization work and duplication of effort became a major problem. Inter-denominational rivalry arose and in Glasgow, the biggest mission centre, a Home Mission Union was formed in 1885 which allocated small districts with as few as 180 families to each subscribing congregation which then carried out monthly visitation. In this way the whole city was covered,

The challenge of the cities

and problems of 'poaching' by one congregation on another's mission district were ironed out.

This mammoth panoply of religious voluntary organizations became the vehicle for implementing social reform amongst the working classes and the poor, and for improving the quality of urban life generally. Individual agencies tackled specific problems or obstacles to social and religious salvation. Until 1850 agencies were predominantly educational, but thereafter teetotalism and revivalism heightened the emotional character of redemption. Urban revivalism first emerged on a large scale in New York in 1858 and enthusiasts in the Free and United Presbyterian Churches immediately anticipated and worked for its arrival in Scotland. It came in 1859–62 after a trade depression, and in the major industrial districts of Scotland religious prayer meetings were conducted in factories and offices and in the wynds and closes of Edinburgh and Glasgow. The revival was to some, especially in the Established Church, 'rude' and threatening, causing high absenteeism from work. There were opponents even within the dissenting churches; there were 'good people' in the Free Church who felt that if prayer meetings continued until midnight 'all the arrangements of society would come to an end'. But there were reports of 'the appearance of greater earnestness and prayerfulness throughout our churches' and it was noted that the revival was 'most conspicuous among those classes of society who hitherto have been the least accessible to any religious influences whatever'.[29] Over the next thirty years the stress of evangelization was to re-create this revivalism, and to link it with the taking of the 'pledge' of total abstinence. Middle-class involvement in the Moody–Sankey revival of 1873–5, especially amongst office-workers and students, reinforced the focus on the conversion experience, and diverted enthusiasm from 'secular' social reform.

By the 1890s the range and variety of church activities was enormous. St Mary's Free Church in Govan had Sunday schools with 1137 children, Bible classes with 493 scholars, 155 Sunday-school teachers, an average of 469 children attending 'Sabbath Forenoon Meetings' watched over by 77 monitors, a Literary Society with 185 members, male and female fellowship associations with

213 members, Christian Endeavour societies with 251 members, a Company of the Boys Brigade with 58 officers and boys, Gospel Temperance Meetings with 420 members, a Penny Savings Bank with 19,000 transactions annually, and branches of the YMCA. And to watch over, recruit and maintain working-class members, the congregation provided 292 Home Mission workers to undertake door-to-door visitation on a monthly basis. Few congregations by 1890 were offering a less varied range of activities, and many encouraged more. In these the evangelical call to action was answered by the Victorian middle classes, and with the 'soirée' (born out of the temperance movement), middle-class leisure became a commitment to the evangelization of the cities.

This shift towards greater lay involvement in evangelization reflected changes in the composition of the middle classes within the presbyterian churches and especially the dissenting denominations. Between the 1730s and the 1780s the dissenters came from a wide range of urban occupations. In Stirling, where dissent became in the 1730s a temporary vehicle for an anti-government political movement, the Secession Church attracted about half the population including many in the trades incorporations. In other towns where dissent accounted for more than 40 per cent of adherents – such as Jedburgh and Dundee – the local élites were well represented amongst those who left the Established Church. The tendency in the eighteenth century was for urban dissent to be characterized by extremes of wealth: on the one hand the breed of new entrepreneurs like David Dale from Glasgow and the Sandeman family from Perth, and on the other hand their servants and many of their employees. Table 9 shows for the Glasite congregations of Dundee and Perth in the early 1770s the numerical significance of the new commercial élites and of the weavers and spinners who were for the most part employees of senior lay members in the churches.

With such a membership, lay participation in evangelization tended to be restricted to the upper social groups; those who were working-class themselves, or were striving for higher social status, tended not to conduct home-mission work. The same was true of the tradesmen who were by the early nineteenth century dominating many dissenting congregations in the cities.

The challenge of the cities

Table 9 Social composition of Dundee and Perth Glasite Congregations, 1771/2 (%)

(Numbers)	Dundee Glasite Church: male members 1771 (82)		Perth Glasite Church: male members 1772 (50)	
1 Professional, commercial, etc.	20		32	
(a) Manufacturers		10		10
(b) Merchants and shopkeepers		7		10
(c) Professional		3		12
2 Skilled tradesmen, etc.	49		48	
(a) Metal, wood and building		6		4
(b) Textiles		38		26
(c) Apprentices				6
(d) Clerks, messengers at arms		1		4
(e) Others		4		8
3 Unskilled and others	27		10	
(a) Servants		23		10
(b) Chapmen		3		
(c) Gardeners		1		
4 Unspecified	4		10	
	100		100	

Source: Table compiled from data in D. B. Murray (1977) 'The Social and Religious Origins of Scottish Non-Presbyterian Protestant Dissent from 1730–1800', unpublished Ph.D. thesis, University of St Andrews, 83–4, 88–9.

Table 10 indicates the dominance of skilled working men in John Street Relief Church in Glasgow in the 1820s; two-thirds of occupations on the baptismal roll were from this group. But within thirty years a significant shift had occurred. Skilled tradesmen fell to 45 per cent whilst middle-class groups rose from 17 to 37 per cent. One result was the creation of a mission congregation under the superintendence of the John Street kirk session. The growth of both the higher- and lower-middle classes in the John Street congregation was indicative of the tendency for newer congregations to rise in status as their members moved up the social scale in terms of occupation and prosperity. As a result dissenting churches, as edifices, developed rapidly between 1780 and 1890 in size, style and cost as congregations built new churches in progressively more suburban districts. The Secession congregation in

Table 10 Social composition of John Street Relief/United Presbyterian, Church Glasgow: based on fathers' occupations in baptismal roll (%)

(Numbers)	1822–32 (161)		1853–57 (148)	
1 Professional, commercial and manufacturing	6		10	
2 Lower middle class (clerks, shopkeepers, factors, spiritdealers, etc.)	11		27	
3 Skilled working class (except major textiles)	66		45	
(a) Metal, wood, furniture and building		29		27
(b) Butchers, bakers, fishmongers, millers		21		7
(c) Engineers, engine-drivers, printers, shoemakers		9		10
(d) Clothiers, tailors		7		1
4 Major textiles	9		5	
(a) Foremen				1
(b) Weavers, spinners, calico printers, etc.		9		4
5 Unskilled	9		13	
	101		100	

Source: Figures based on data in Baptismal Register, John Street Relief/United Presbyterian Church, Glasgow, SRO, CH3/806/12.

Irvine in Ayrshire first assembled in 1807 in a back-street malt kiln, then moved in 1845 to a more pretentious church with a vestry and a hall, and after paying off the debts within a few years moved to another new church in 1862. In this way the United Presbyterian Church, which the bulk of the Secession and Relief Churches became in 1847, had in the later nineteenth century an overpowering air of commercial prosperity vastly different to the more puritanical and petit-bourgeois character of the urban Seceders at the start of the century. As one reflection of this, the highest rates of literacy amongst brides and grooms in 1871 were to be found with those marrying in United Presbyterian churches (see Table 11).

In an important study of Aberdeen, Allan MacLaren has demonstrated how increasing differentiation and social mobility within the middle classes was an instrumental factor in the formation of the Free Church in the city in the mid-nineteenth century. His analysis of the elders who left the Established

The challenge of the cities

Table 11 Proportion of brides and grooms unable to sign marriage books in religious ceremonies, 1871 (%)

	Men	Women
United Presbyterian Church	3.8	11.8
Free Church	6.7	15.7
Church of Scotland	7.0	16.5
Episcopal Church	9.8	20.9
Roman Catholic Church	46.0	61.7

Source: Figures based on data in Census 1871 (Scotland), 1, xlii–xliii.

Church at the Disruption of 1843 shows that an aspiring and socially dynamic breed of commission agents and merchants was crucial, for they were far more numerous amongst those who 'went out' than amongst those who stayed in. At the period of the Disruption this group was challenging the established middle classes of the city and the Established Church which they controlled. These 'insolent social upstarts' displayed their entrepreneurial vigour and recently acquired wealth by changing house and business very rapidly, moving westward within the city to new developments at some distance from the older and more staid middle-class streets. Their walkout at the Disruption was an integral feature of their emergence, their new Free churches being located beside their new residences. In the Victorian period, according to a local comment in 1902, 'the height of a merchant's ambition in Aberdeen was a house in Crown Street and a seat in the Free West Church'.[30]

A study of nine presbyterian congregations in Glasgow at the same period provides much support for MacLaren's analysis.[31] Peter Hillis found that lower-middle-class groups were more common amongst the dissenting churches (making up 19 per cent of the membership) than the Established churches (9 per cent). As in Aberdeen, Hillis found the kirk sessions of all the Glasgow congregations he studied dominated by the higher social groups in the congregations. In the Established churches 71 per cent of elders were high-status middle class, 14 per cent low-status, and only just over 2 per cent working class; in the dissenting churches 78 per cent of elders were high status, 19 per cent low status and 4 per cent working class. The eldership was in the nineteenth century, as it perhaps has always been in the cities, a preserve of those who had attained success in business and with it the standing and financial means with which to lead congregations.

But the authors of these two studies disagree fundamentally about the extent of middle-class dominance in the churches as a whole. MacLaren identifies kirk-session discipline as the key. It was concerned especially with moral offences amongst the lower classes, and notably fornication and drunkenness. Whilst elders were liable to censure for business irregularities, few of the middle-class membership were disciplined or even investigated for moral offences. Hillis on the other hand sees church discipline as applied equally to middle- and working-class members, and more generally discounts the notion of working-class exclusion from the churches. Part of the explanation for such divergent views rests on differing perceptions of class relations in society as a whole. But in any event, individual congregations varied enormously in social composition, even within the same denomination. Variations resulted from the predominance of certain occupations in some districts, and from the level of church accommodation available. But in addition, it was suggested earlier that the social make-up of a congregation tended with time to rise. Such upward mobility could be quite swift, reflecting the social dynamism of urban life generally. In such circumstances, it would be unwise to see the social composition of presbyterianism as static or uniform.

Religion and the making of the Scottish working classes

Allan MacLaren has argued from his research in Aberdeen that working-class church membership was low. He notes aspects of congregational management which deterred working-class admission: pew rents, the need for fine clothes, segregation of social classes between pews, and more generally a patronizing and offensive bourgeois attitude towards lower-income groups evident in kirk-session discipline and elders' supervision of

The challenge of the cities 153

working-class members. He cites the case of a Free Church kirk session which denied communion to a member who had 'accommodated in her house, for a short time, a female of disreputable character'; in another instance an hotel waiter was told 'to abstain from such an objectionable occupation in future'.[32] MacLaren's work stresses both the repugnance of middle-class churchmen for working-class life and culture, and the role of the churches as a primary agency for extending bourgeois control over the proletariat outwith the employer–employee relationship.

Contemporary evidence from the period is not hard to find in support of MacLaren's general argument. The working classes tended to be progressively excluded from many city congregations as the building of new churches fell behind the rise in population between 1780 and 1850. In Edinburgh in the 1790s the Church of Scotland initiated separate evening services for servants and 'the common people', whilst in Glasgow between 1780 and 1820 special diets of worship were arranged for the working classes on Thursday and Sunday evenings. Even this division did not satisfy ministers and middle-class congregations who continuously asked Glasgow town council to discontinue the special services – mostly on grounds of hygiene. In the 1830s, many Established Church ministers identified rising seat rents as the cause of diminishing working-class adherence, and the inter-denominational Glasgow City Mission in 1826 observed that high seat rents could be the only explanation for the fact that one-quarter of all pews in the city were unoccupied. The apparent decline of working-class members was perhaps more marked in industrializing rural parishes. The minister of the cotton-spinning community of Lochwinnoch reported in the 1830s that free seats for the poor had practically disappeared and that 'the other seats are let so dear as to be a very heavy burden upon poor persons; . . . if a family be large their sittings in church are almost equal to their [house] rent'.[33] The process of social segregation was continuous throughout the century as new congregations were established and as the wealthier members moved on within a few decades to finer and more opulent churches. When, in the 1860s, the minister of Cambridge Street United Presbyterian Church in Glasgow led wealthy merchants and manufacturers to a more palatial church in the west end, a scribe chalked on the door of the new building on its opening day:

> *This Church is not built for the poor and needy,*
> *But for the rich and Dr. Eadie.*
> *The rich may come in and take their seat,*
> *But the poor must go to Cambridge Street.*[34]

But there is also considerable evidence of large working-class sections in city congregations. Peter Hillis's analysis of seven Glasgow congregations between 1845 and 1865 indicates an average working-class membership of 61 per cent. Established Church congregations had the highest proportion, averaging 79 per cent in three of the older parish churches in city and long-settled suburbs; in four newer dissenting congregations the proportion was 54 per cent. Further division of the working-class membership into the skilled and unskilled showed that the former were more prominent in dissenting congregations (making up 80 per cent of the working-class communicants) than in Established Church congregations (where the figure was 69 per cent). One congregation which left the Established Church at the Disruption of 1843 showed a notable change in social composition. In 1838, 68 per cent of the working-class members at St Stephen's Church were skilled artisans, but by the early 1850s the figure for the reconstituted St Stephen's Free Church had risen to 83 per cent.

The Royal Commission on Religious Instruction noted of Edinburgh in the mid-1830s that dissenting congregations were 'generally composed of the poor and working classes'.[35] Similarly in Glasgow the commissioners found that in all but the Episcopal churches and the older parish churches of the Establishment the city's congregations were 'composed, in great measure, of the poor and working classes, the proportion of these being in few cases below one-half, while in the congregations of the Dissenting denominations, it is, for the most part, above two-thirds'.[36] Yet by the 1860s and 1870s, many of these congregations – especially of the Secession and Relief Churches – were to have a

The challenge of the cities 155

reputation for wealth and solid middle-class status. Clearly, a significant social transformation occurred in many urban congregations during the first three-quarters of the nineteenth century. The seeds for this change were evident in the Royal Commission's report in the 1830s. The commissioners found that all but the Baptist churches charged seat rents. In Edinburgh they noted that 'although 9-10ths of the Dissenters' seat-rents are above 5s. a-year, yet their Congregations are generally composed of the poor and working classes, and that the rate of seat-rent is in most cases fixed by vote of the congregation.' Furthermore, the Royal Commission remarked on a standard feature of seat-renting: namely, that lower-priced seats had a low occupancy rate compared to higher-priced seats. There was a 'dislike of the people to occupy low-priced or gratuitous sittings, avowedly set apart for the poor'. In part this was because these seats were of an 'inferior nature', being invariably located in the awkward back pews at the rear of the gallery; and in part because of reluctance of people to take seats which were given 'on sufferance, from which they are liable to be displaced at pleasure'. In Edinburgh's churches in 1836, 88 per cent of expensive pews priced between twenty and forty shillings were let; but this occupancy rate fell to 76 per cent for mid-priced seats between nine and eighteen shillings, and to 60 per cent for cheaper seats at between two and eight shillings. In the ten council churches of Glasgow between 1813 and 1886, lower-priced seats were always less popular – except in the 1870s in Blackfriars' Church which the staff and students of the University had recently left. A stigma attached to occupying low-priced and free seats, with the result that those amongst the lower-income groups who were drawn to church-going in the presbyterian churches tended to have strong economic aspirations and to be upwardly mobile in the social structure. The ability to pay for pew rents, and perhaps to forgo other expenditure, became a mark of those who wished to distance themselves from the 'rough' working class and to lay claim to social respectability.

The dissenting denominations appealed to artisans for two reasons. In the first place church accommodation was offered at a price they could afford and, as the Royal Commission pointed out, one that could often be decided by congregational democracy.

In the 1830s, this meant that the more evangelical congregations had lower seat rents. In Edinburgh the older and more wealthy parish churches had 30 per cent of seats priced at over fifteen shillings with a top price of forty-two shillings. By comparison, in the newer Established churches built mostly by subscription, and from which there was a higher-than-average defection to the Free Church in 1843, only 5 per cent of seats cost over fifteen shillings with a top price of eighteen shillings. And in the Secession churches a mere 4 per cent of seats were offered in the high-price range with the highest rent being twenty-one shillings. As a result, dissent was strong in working-class districts. In the parish of St John's in the east end of Glasgow in the early 1820s, over three-quarters of the overwhelmingly proletarian community who held seats in a church did so in dissenting congregations. This was interesting and perhaps ironic, because the parish and its Established church had been specifically created by the town council for the better accommodation of working-class worshippers; but the popularity of the first incumbent Thomas Chalmers attracted middle-class worshippers in large numbers from other districts and led to the church having the highest average seat rent (10s. 8d.) in the city. The same was true elsewhere. One commentator observed that 'the working men of Edinburgh and its neighbourhood . . . were in large part either non-religious, or included within the Secession pale'.[37]

In the second place, the pricing system for seats was the mechanism by which the lower working classes were excluded from self-managing dissenting congregations and for giving those congregations, before 1850 at least, a socially homogeneous composition and identity. In the Established churches in Edinburgh in the 1830s, 7 per cent of sittings were offered at the very low price of three shillings or less, whilst the Secession churches offered less than 1 per cent; more revealing is the fact that the occupancy rates for these cheap seats was over 50 per cent in the Establishment but only 3 per cent in the Secession. Dissenting culture in the cities was designed to demarcate between 'rough' and 'respectable', and the narrow range of seat prices reflected the high degree of social uniformity achieved in the first half of the nineteenth century.

The challenge of the cities 157

This social homogeneity was evident in the appeal of dissent to certain occupational groups. As in rural parishes, tradesmen like wrights, smiths, shoemakers and butchers were prominent, but so also were shopkeepers, miners and metallurgical workers. Two large occupational groups in dissent before 1850 were the weavers and spinners. They were attracted not only to the Secession and Relief Churches but also to the Methodist Church (as in Kilsyth), the Baptist Church, and Irish immigrants to the Catholic Church. Weavers were also prominent in the short-lived Chartist Church of the early 1840s. About thirty congregations were formed, mostly in the textile communities, and recruiting overwhelmingly from the Seceders. This ecclesiastical experiment was one product of the changing fortunes of the handloom weavers. After 1815 their wages almost continuously declined and led to a mood of depression in the occupation. Some commentators have seen this as the cause of declining working-class church adherence as weavers could not keep pace with rising seat rents and demands for increased contributions to church funds: church-going was associated with prosperity and the weavers' living standards were falling.[38] Under threat from power looms in the 1830s and 1840s, they turned increasingly to political movements and lost the sympathy of the dissenting churches' leaders.

Yet it would be wrong to overlook the sustained popularity of religious attitudes amongst depressed working-class occupations. Covenanting and predestinarian theology often mixed in a volatile cocktail with salvationist evangelicalism (sometimes promoted by American evangelists) to produce strong religious feelings and outbursts of revivalism. As early as 1807 a clergyman wrote: 'In Scotland weavers in Glasgow, Paisley, Perth, Dundee, etc., are among the first to join any new sect set up, the effect no doubt of their sedentary life and the melancholy monotony of their occupation.'[39] Thus, he went on, 'where a great number of weavers are gathered, there new and gloomy notions of religion prevail'. The forlorn and self-remonstrating attitude of some working-class congregations produced a reverence for covenanting history and at least a partial adherence to predestinarianism. Belief in the Elect became a compensation for perceived oppression and economic distress, especially amongst occupations prone to cyclical or seasonal depression. A Glasgow weaver's poem of 1838 went: 'Religion cheers the weaver in his cot/ . . . And charms with heavenly hope our humble lot.'[40] Christian Watt, a fisherwoman from a village near Fraserburgh in the north-east, went through a 'crisis of life' in the 1850s as catastrophe piled upon catastrophe: she lost five brothers at sea, open fields were enclosed by large landowners, fish prices plummeted, and she became pregnant out of wedlock with the likely prospect of being summoned before the Established kirk session on a charge of fornication. Her memoirs recall her anger. She told the landowner and his wife: 'How any of the wealthy . . . have the sheer hard neck to enter any church and call themselves christians! God will spew them out of his mouth.' Though a Congregationalist, she planned to 'wreck the session' by demanding to appear 'in the body of the kirk not the vestry', and then 'start on one elder, a Fraserburgh businessman who had in the past been known to frequent bawdy houses in Aberdeen'. Writing later in her life, it was her view that 'The kirk had become an organisation to suppress the working class', and her faith in redemption was placed in a proletarian predestinarianism: 'Many are called but few are chosen; before your first sark [shirt] gets over your head God knows who are going to be his.'[41]

At the same time, however, the differences between Arminianism and predestinarianism could become blurred – in depressed communities and occupations as in prospering ones. Conversion experiences – Christian Watt had two – became increasingly of a salvationist variety. Mostly in small towns before 1859, revivals attracted weavers, miners and ironworkers to gospel services, especially in the late 1830s and 1840s. In Christian Watt's Congregationalist denomination the debate on the extent of the Atonement came into the open in the mid 1840s with the Arminians defecting in large numbers to the newly-formed Evangelical Union. But in a more general sense, predestinarianism waned in urbanized and industrialized districts. In Ayrshire, for instance, the evangelical 'new views' won over the 'rugged old men' of the Secession clergy in the 1840s. This trend accelerated in the next thirty years as religious revivalism appeared in the large urban centres and as the churches instituted widespread

The challenge of the cities 159

evangelization of working-class districts. The revival of 1859-62 was particularly important in this respect, attracting mass assemblies of the working classes: allegedly 15,000 to a rally at the mining village of Dreghorn in Ayrshire and 10,000 to another at Huntly in the north. Workers started prayer meetings in factories: notably amongst female powerloom weavers at Bridgeton and Pollokshaws in Glasgow but also amongst railwaymen, policemen and others. Revivalist preaching quickly became a norm for evangelical ministers, though the quality of the methods was highly variable. A Church of Scotland minister, not unsympathetic towards revivalism, was critical of the style of a Free Church colleague at work in Lauder in Berwickshire in 1859:

> Instead of preaching the Gospel he indulged in realistic descriptions of revival scenes where people were 'struck down', and strong men 'felled to the ground like oxen'. Following on this, he asked all to engage in prayer. For a few minutes he remained silent, until one felt the tension of suppressed excitement, and then he began, 'O Lord, *do it* – do it now.'[42]

Mission stations mushroomed in working-class districts of the larger cities: the most famous perhaps were the Wynd Mission in Glasgow and the Carrubber's Close Mission in Edinburgh. But these were merely the frontrunners in a missionary explosion amongst the Scottish industrial classes with which the evangelical churches – mainly the Free, United Presbyterian, Methodist and Congregationalist Churches – tried to keep abreast.

From church reports in the 1860s and 1870s, it is difficult to avoid the conclusion that working-class interest in organized presbyterianism was growing and, moreover, that it was overwhelmingly of an Arminian character. American evangelists such as Charles Finney and Edward Payson Hammond introduced the distinctive revival service: short sermon, joyous hymns, and the call to the 'anxious' to come forward. The stress in working-class presbyterianism shifted markedly to the sureness of salvation and the joyousness of the conversion experience, and away from an older emphasis on prolonged and serious contemplation of sin. Preaching of hell-fire and damnation diminished, giving way to the American-style offer of the open gospel exemplified in the preaching of Dwight Moody in the 1870s, 1880s and early 1890s. Between 1873 and 1880, working-class mission congregations urged the kirk sessions of their parent middle-class churches to 'sanction the introduction of instrumental music' in the form of the harmonium popularized by Ira Sankey. Those kirk sessions, especially in the Established Church, which refused such demands caused the decline and sometimes the collapse of mission churches, but kirk sessions in the Free and United Presbyterian Churches were more obliging and their missionary efforts flourished.

Religious voluntary organizations for the working classes also grew enormously from the 1870s. The Bands of Hope for instance offered a new and partially secularized version of the Sunday school which attracted a mostly proletarian membership, whilst Sunday-school scholars were, between 1870 and 1890, more and more the children of middle-class church members. The Bands provided not only a teetotal religion but 'respectable' leisure. In Dundee the Band of Hope organized a whole range of pursuits including marches, parades, rambles and river excursions, and through such secular attractions continued to grow: the number of Bands in Scotland rose from seven in 1871 to 570 in 1887 and to over 700 in 1908 with 147,000 members. The Catholic Church had its own League of the Cross which, despite a much smaller juvenile section, had a membership of over 30,000 in the Archdiocese of Glasgow by the end of the century. In all denominations, the trend in the last quarter of the nineteenth century was towards meeting all the leisure needs of young and old alike: through respectable activities in temperance pubs and hotels; Christian reading-rooms and libraries; football competitions organized by denominations, Sunday-school unions, the Boys' Brigade and temperance organizations; outings and picnics for the under-twelves; militaristic and jingoistic uniformed organizations for youths both male and female; and for older youths and adults prayer meetings, gospel assemblies (both temperance and ordinary), games rooms (in Catholic churches) and women's guilds. Though caused by the revivalism of the 1860s and 1870s, the explosion of religious leisure harmonized working-class religion to an increasingly secular world of shorter working hours,

The challenge of the cities

the half-day and then full-day Saturday off. By combining the offer of sport and pastime with an evangelization effort unmatched before or since, the Scottish working classes were subjected between 1870 and 1890 to the peak of the 'aggressive' system.

The growth in the churches' outreach to the working classes included the Catholic community. The essence of the Catholic Church's problem was keeping pace with Irish immigration to the new industrial districts of west central Scotland, and there was a distinct shortage of chapels and priests in the early decades of the nineteenth century. But in the second half of the century enormous strides were made in building chapels and in recruiting priests, of whom an increasing proportion were from Ireland or the Irish community rather than from the Catholic areas of the Highlands and the north-east. The result was a substantial rise in religious observance amongst Catholics leading to, by the middle of the twentieth century, their predominance in most Lowland districts with high rates of churchgoing.

It is commonly observed that the Catholic immigrants were uniformly poor and that they joined the lower echelons of the Scottish working classes. There were certainly high proportions of Catholics in unskilled and low-status skilled occupations like navvying, labouring, spinning, weaving and mining. Perhaps a quarter of weavers were Catholic after 1815, and there were large numbers in unskilled metal-working. Whilst upward social mobility by Irish Catholics has probably been underestimated in Victorian Scotland, it remains likely that they were more uniformly proletarian in character than any other religious group. In the twenty-three Scottish towns in 1851 from which census returns were made by priests, only 45 per cent of Catholic church seats were set apart for private renting compared to 69 per cent in Established churches, 73 per cent in Free churches and 77 per cent in United Presbyterian churches. If we take into account the fact that the vast majority of gratuitous pews were unoccupied in presbyterian churches whilst Catholic city chapels were very full (certainly in 1851), it seems that the lower working class were much more in evidence in Catholic than in Protestant congregations. This certainly seems to be the conclusion from Table 11 (p. 151) which shows that shortly before the introduction of compulsory education Catholic brides and grooms had significantly higher rates of illiteracy than those in the main Protestant churches.

But it would be wrong to regard the Irish Catholic community as uniformly poor, and equally wrong to overlook the extent to which the Church induced a social (and ethnic) hierarchy amongst its active worshippers. Many thousands of Catholics paid seat rents, in some cases substantial sums on a par with presbyterians. A decade after its opening in 1816, St Andrew's Church (now Cathedral) in Glasgow was raising £600 a year from seat rents. Native recusant Catholics of aristocratic pedigree were paying as much as £5 for a seat in an Edinburgh chapel in 1815, but even ordinary worshippers at Glenlivet in the north-east were in 1829 paying between four and twelve shillings a year – an identical range of prices to that found in most Seceder congregations. Pew-renting spread quickly amongst Catholic chapels in the 1810s and 1820s, and was used by many Scots-born priests to segregate the 'respectable' from the 'rough'. Christine Johnson reports that a priest in Paisley was so strict over non-payment of rents in the early 1810s that many worshippers stopped attending, and in response to the problem Bishop Scott of Glasgow suggested in 1812 that 'seat-minders' be appointed to regulate the immigrants: 'The Irish must be treated in a different manner from our Scots people, or they never can be helped on the way to salvation.'[43] Friction between Irish and Scots, both laity and clergy, persisted until at least the 1860s, but in industrial districts the Irish character of the Church came to dominate leaving only northern dioceses with a strong tradition of native Scottish Catholicism.

But assimilation to urban and industrial society brought increasing attunement to the ideals and values of self-help and 'improvement', and created in the Catholic Church virtues and institutions very similar to those in the presbyterian churches. Churchgoing was increasingly associated with prosperity, fomenting the practices of pew-renting and of wearing 'Sunday best'. An Ayrshire priest noted in the 1830s: 'The Irish will not come out on Sunday and go to chapel unless they can be clothed and appear like natives. They will not go in ragged clothes as they went in Ireland.'⁴⁴ In 1842 the Catholic teetotal pioneer Father Mathew administered the pledge on Glasgow Green to a mixed assembly of Protestants and Catholics, reputedly 40,000 in number. But the temperance cause seems to have languished in the Scottish Catholic Church during the mid-Victorian decades. In the large Archdiocese of Glasgow in 1887, there were only twenty-two branches of the Church's temperance organization, the League of the Cross, with a membership probably in the region of 1000. But in that year Archbishop Eyre became a strong promoter, organizing an executive committee of laity and clergy which within four years had created an extra 106 branches and a total membership of 30,000. Games rooms were a common feature of chapel rectories by the 1870s, providing 'respectable' alternatives to the public house and street gambling; in many cases, though, gambling (especially cards) and boisterousness were merely switched to church premises, and, as one priest noted, the men 'would play at their games even if Benediction was given in the Church, near them'.⁴⁵

Whilst promoting the ideals of urban society and thus Irish integration into the industrial milieu, the Church came to represent a wider segregation of Catholics from Scottish presbyterian life and culture. Chapels formed the core of a set of distinctively Catholic cultural associations and practices. Separate Catholic schools developed during the century, and the Church provided its own versions of Protestant organizations like the Boys' Brigade. Observance of saints' days became in the presbyterian environment an act which marked out Catholics in Scotland in a much more prominent way than it did in Anglican England. Irish nationalism, though discouraged by Church authorities, was promoted by some priests and in a more general fashion could not fail to be associated with Catholicism. High degrees of Catholic inter-marriage (80 per cent in Greenock in 1855) and residential segregation in 'wee Dublins' slowed down social assimilation. Economic assimilation was restrained by concentration in certain occupations, factories and pits. In 1851, 52 per cent of unskilled workers in Greenock were Irish-born, and amongst dock labourers this rose to 65 per cent; even forty years later nearly half the unskilled in the town were Irish-born, which taken with second and third-generation immigrants probably created an occupation dominated by Catholics. In Coatbridge in 1861, 60 per cent of unskilled metal workers were Irish. Moreover, partly through the use of immigrants as strike-breakers and partly through sectarianism, Catholics were generally isolated from the trades-union and Labour movements before 1890.

The hostility of both middle- and working-class presbyterians, and discrimination in employment, lay at the root of Catholic isolation. Antagonism between 'Proddie' and 'Pape' was not new to Scotland; government proposals in 1778–9 to repeal the penal laws against Catholics produced severe Protestant riots in Edinburgh and Glasgow supported by many churchmen and incorporations of the two cities – and this at a time when there were barely a few dozen Catholics in those places. The needs of industrial manufacturing had by 1792 produced a remarkable change, with the Protestant cotton-spinning masters of Glasgow underwriting the costs of a chapel and encouraging a priest to settle in order to instil order and discipline amongst Catholic workers from the Highlands. In the 1810s, Protestant manufacturers financed the setting up of Catholic schools in the city. But the arrival of Catholic and Protestant Irish after 1800 brought an enlivened culture of sectarianism. Working-class Protestant missionaries such as the inimical Harry Long of Glasgow agitated for resistance against the attempts 'to bring this land under the sway of the Romish Pontiff, and wrest from us the dear bought and invaluable liberties which we possess'.[46] Many presbyterian ministers, prominent laity and manufacturing companies subscribed to sectarian missions in the second half of the nineteenth century, and employers like the firm of William Baird & Co., ironmasters of Coatbridge, used patronage of the Orange Lodge as a form of company paternalism with which to create Protestant worker-identification with management and thus undermine trades-union organization. Sectarianism developed into an intrinsic element of the industrial culture of Scotland, not only institutionalized by, for instance, the exclusion of Catholic schools from the state system of education established in 1872, and by the deliberate siting of some presbyterian mission churches in predominantly Catholic districts of Glasgow, but also perpetuated in popular custom which created segregated public houses. This culture was not to diminish after the 1880s but rather harden, and whilst it was not entirely unique within mainland Britain, it had none the less an unmatched muscularity and transcendence of social class.

The discussion thus far leaves a major problem of interpreting the extent of working-class 'irreligion'. This section has stressed the ways in which the working classes participated in religion, but the Victorian churches, mainly the presbyterian ones, were obsessed with the 'unchurched', the 'lapsed masses', the 'sunken portion'. It is still axiomatic of many historians' analysis of nineteenth-century religion that the vast majority of the working classes did not go to church and that the vast majority of the churchgoers were not working-class. The first statement is probably true; the second is becoming decreasingly likely. There is clear evidence that many congregations – arguably the majority – were dominated by the working classes, and specifically by skilled workers. Perhaps Victorian churchmen perceived them as 'middle-class' since they strove to dress appropriately, to pay their seat rents and contributions to church funds, and more generally to uphold the values and ideals which sanctioned elevation in the society. It is unskilled occupations like 'labourer' which tend to be grossly under-represented in lists of presbyterian church members. Church adherence was undoubtedly low amongst the lower working class, most notably in slum districts of the large cities, and early in the century in new satellite industrial villages as yet unreached by organized religion. It was noted of one such community outside Edinburgh in the 1820s: 'Demand and supply were admirably well-balanced in the village of Niddry: there was no religious instruction, and no wish or desire for it.'[47] But even here we should not succumb to a static image. Social mobility, especially from one generation to the next, and increasing evangelization and church-building in the period from 1850 to 1890 meant that opportunities to gain admission to a church were widening rather than diminishing.

The first hundred years of industrialization and urbanization had produced remarkable changes in the role of religion. In both town and country the advent of dynamic social capitalism had dissolved the communal bonds which held the people within the ambit of the Established Church, and local élites had to acknowledge that their measured manipulation of popular religion through the board of heritors, the kirk session and pew-control was redundant. It was redundant not because religion had become less popular but because, arguably, of the reverse. The social significance of religion had been heightened by the interaction between social fragmentation and denominational pluralization, and by the rise of a network of socio-religious values which through a variety of socially- and culturally-divergent versions attuned the outlook of the people to the new society.

On the surface these values constituted unifying ties between churches and social classes, but their relevance lay in adaptability to different work and life experiences. Adherence to sabbatarianism, teetotalism and self-help might be shared by miners, millworkers and wealthy merchants, but such virtues were as much statements of group independence and solidarity as of inter-class discourse and unity. Thus, it is quite legitimate to regard religion as providing an ideology of social uniformity and as offering a venue for social contest. Teetotalism, for instance, first emerged within a tradition of working-class radicalism in the 1830s and 1840s, but in the following decade it was absorbed – perhaps 'appropriated' – by the lower middle class and the evangelical churches. But this elevation, in part a product of upward social mobility amongst artisan groups, did not lead to a withering of proletarian attachment to teetotalism and other congruent values. Those rejected as not 'respectable' by churches, and even by peers as was Christian Watt, did not then reject the values by which they had been adjudged failures. The judges became in Christian's words 'that bunch of hypocrites' and were the unworthy purveyors of a stolen heritage and culture. 'You missionaries tell us that carters and factory lassies hae souls as well as ither folk', said one Glasgow slum-dweller to an evangelizer in the 1850s: 'For my pairt I aye thocht they had, – why is it, man, you canna tell us something we dinna ken?'[48] For those of the lower working class and the poor, with little or no access to economic and social 'improvement', resentment bred fierce alienation from patronizing proselytization. Small efforts to offer church

The challenge of the cities

services for those in working clothes often brought massive responses, but the impermanence of congregations thus gathered led the churches into continuing to regard attenders at mission stations as the 'unreformed'. But the 'double rejection' thus created did not destroy popular religious belief and attitudes amongst the 'sunken portion'. The 'lapsed masses' may have been non-churchgoers, but they were not necessarily non-believers.

Notes

1. J. Johnston (1870) *Religious Destitution in Glasgow*, Glasgow, 10.
2. *Scots Magazine*, February 1787, 99.
3. R. Renwick (ed.) (1913) *Extracts from the Records of the Burgh of Glasgow*, Glasgow, viii, 388.
4. R. Buchanan (1871) *The City's Spiritual Wants*, Glasgow, 6.
5. Quoted in N. L. Walker (1877) *Robert Buchanan D.D. An Ecclesiastical Biography*, London, 511–3.
6. M. Atkinson (1904) *Local Government in Scotland*, Edinburgh, 160–1.
7. OSA, 6, p. 609.
8. ibid., 8, p. 292.
9. ibid., 5, p. 535.
10. G. Marshall (1980) *Presbyteries and Profits: Calvinism and the Development of Capitalism in Scotland, 1560–1707*, Oxford, Clarendon Press.
11. R. Campbell (1980) *The Rise and Fall of Scottish Industry, 1707–1939*, Edinburgh, John Donald, 28.
12. T. Dickson (ed.) (1980) *Scottish Capitalism: Class, State and Nation from before the Union to the Present*, London, Lawrence & Wishart, 114, 214.
13. A. A. MacLaren (1974) *Religion and Social Class: The Disruption Years in Aberdeen*, London and Boston, Routledge & Kegan Paul, 28. See also A. A. MacLaren (ed.) (n.d.) *Social Class in Scotland: Past and Present*, Edinburgh, John Donald, 3–5, 36–54.
14. I. A. Muirhead (1980) 'The revival as a dimension of Scottish church history', RSCHS, xx, 191.
15. Quoted in J. McKerrow (1841) *History of the Secession Church*, Glasgow, 371.
16. Quoted in D. B. Murray (1977) 'The Social and Religious Origins of Scottish Non-Presbyterian Protestant Dissent from 1730–1800', unpublished Ph.D. thesis, University of St Andrews, 111.
17. Quoted in McKerrow, op. cit., 180.
18. Quoted in J. R. Fleming (1927) *A History of the Church of Scotland 1843–1874*, Edinburgh, T. & T. Clark, 10.
19. Quoted in J. MacInnes (1951) *The Evangelical Movement in the Highlands of Scotland 1688 to 1800*, Aberdeen University Press, 184–5.

20 Quoted in Fleming, op. cit., 45-7.
21 Quoted in W. Ferguson (1968) *Scotland 1689 to the Present*, Edinburgh and London, Oliver & Boyd, 336.
22 *Autobiography of a Scotch Lad* (1887), Glasgow, 30.
23 MS Report of Glasgow Town Council Committee on Ministers' Stipends, 5 May 1796, SRA.
24 Quoted in R. Buchanan (1850) *The Schoolmaster in the Wynds*, Glasgow & Edinburgh, 4.
25 ibid., 32.
26 *OSA*, 7, p. 177; 18, p. 208.
27 *Glasgow Religious Tract Society. Annual Report 1815*, 5.
28 J. G. Paton (1889) *Missionary to the Hebrides: An Autobiography*, London, 60-1.
29 *Wynd Journal*, 22 October 1859; United Presbyterian Church, Presbytery of Glasgow MS minutes 26 September 1859, SRO, CH3/146/52; R. Buchanan (1860) *Assembly Addresses*, Edinburgh, 13.
30 Quoted in A. A. MacLaren, *Religion and Social Class*, 82.
31 P. Hillis (1981) 'Presbyterianism and social class in mid-nineteenth century Glasgow: a study of nine churches', *Journal of Ecclesiastical History*, 32, 47-64.
32 Quoted in MacLaren, op. cit., 129.
33 *NSA*, 7, Renfrew, 105-6.
34 Quoted in Hillis, op. cit., 54.
35 Royal Commission on Religious Instruction, Scotland, First Report, *PP* (1837), xxi, 29.
36 ibid., Second Report, *PP* (1837-8), xxxii, 17.
37 Hugh Miller (1856) *My Schools and Schoolmasters*, Edinburgh, 309.
38 G. Struthers (1843) *The History of the Rise, Progress and Principles of the Relief Church*, Glasgow, 446-9; N. Murray (1978) *The Scottish Hand Loom Weavers 1790-1850: A Social History*, Edinburgh, John Donald, 165-78.
39 James Hall, quoted in D. B. Murray, op. cit., 214.
40 Quoted in N. Murray, op. cit., 165.
41 D. Fraser (ed.) (1983) *The Christian Watt Papers*, Edinburgh, Paul Harris, 24, 56, 68, 93.
42 Quoted in S. Smith (1926) *Donald Macleod of Glasgow*, London, 76.
43 C. Johnson (1983) *Developments in the Roman Catholic Church in Scotland, 1789-1829*, Edinburgh, John Donald, 142-5.
44 Quoted in A. Ross (1978) 'The development of the Scottish Catholic community 1878-1978', *Innes Review*, xxiv, 33.
45 Questionnaire completed by M. I. Dempsey, 1887, Roman Catholic Archdiocese of Glasgow Archive, Temperance box.
46 *Glasgow Protestant Missionary Society, Annual Report* (1880), 5.
47 H. Miller, op. cit., 312.
48 J. McCaffrey (ed.) (1976) *Glasgow 1858: Shadow's Midnight Scenes and Social Photographs*, Glasgow University Press, 14.

6
The 'social question' and the crisis for religion, 1890-1929

Towards the end of the 1880s signs began to emerge of serious changes in the status of organized religion and in the acceptance of the evangelical analysis of industrial society. It was noted in Glasgow that church attendances decreased in 1888 because of the counter-attraction of the International Exhibition; the city's United Evangelistic Association found that it was 'fostering a worldly spirit, antagonistic to earnest spiritual life'. Moreover, despite massive presbyterian opposition, alcohol was sold at the Exhibition. In the early 1890s, Labour Churches and Socialist Sunday schools appeared in industrial towns preaching a semi-secular gospel of universal brotherhood. A revival campaign led by an American evangelist, George Pentecost of Brooklyn, failed to get much response from the well-to-do in the Free Church congregations of the city's west end in 1888, but a lecture by the medical officer of health to the literary society of Park Established Church on the subject of 'Life in One Room', being an account of the overcrowding and squalor in which over a quarter of Glasgow's population lived, instigated commissions of inquiry into the links between housing, poverty and non-churchgoing. Four years earlier, a Conservative MP speculated to a meeting of Church of Scotland elders that 'there must have been some great fault — some gross neglect of duty — on the part of ourselves and others who have comfortable surroundings and live in the enjoyment of Christian civilisation'.[1] For Established churchmen, evangelical palliatives seemed to have failed to improve the urban condition. The assistant minister at Edinburgh's Tron Church discounted the ability of either missionary work or charity to 'raise such of the masses as are in no condition either to be reasoned with or preached to'.[2] Received evangelical wisdom was under challenge.

The issues under discussion from the 1880s were not new. Drawing attention to non-churchgoing, to apparent retreats from Sabbath sanctity and to the adverse effects of insanitary housing upon morality were inherent features of evangelical campaigning for funds and voluntary effort throughout the century. But the churches discovered very quickly that a complex series of changes were under way which constituted a crisis for organized religion. This crisis was not unique to Scotland. Its urban shape found in Glasgow, Edinburgh and Dundee has been documented in London, Reading, Sheffield and other cities south of the border, and many of the themes – such as changing leisure habits, the rise of socialism and the labour movement, and ecumenical reunion within Protestantism – had international bearings. There were many ramifications, and they were felt most acutely in the powerhouse of nineteenth-century religion – the dissenting evangelical churches.

The decay of evangelicalism and the church crisis

The crisis for the churches took a number of forms. There was the start of a downturn in the numbers of people participating in religious organizations: whether as churchgoers, helpers in voluntary organizations, or as 'clients' of evangelizing schemes. At the same time there were changes in the nature of the activities and objectives of church organizations with popularity shifting from the more 'religious' activities to the more 'secular' ones. Demographic movements, particularly within cities, produced financial difficulties for many congregations as members left and created pressure for denominational unification to permit weakened adjacent congregations to amalgamate. But perhaps the first manifestation of crisis, certainly in the presbyterian churches, was the contraction in evangelization. To put it bluntly, the middle-class mission to the unchurched working

The 'social question' and the crisis for religion 171

classes lost both bourgeois lay assistance and proletarian acceptance. In 1886 the Evangelistic Association of Queen's Park Free Church in the growing middle-class suburbs on the south side of Glasgow was setting about with enthusiasm the task newly assigned to it by the city's Home Mission Union of visiting every family in its small mission district at least once a month. The Association had a good band of over forty visitors drawn from the church membership, and they worked in tandem with other agencies of the congregation: Sunday schools, Band of Hope, Penny Savings Bank and tract distribution service. But by 1892 attendances by visitors were well down, threatening the whole operation, and in order to preserve its work the Association amalgamated its mission district with that of a neighbouring congregation. Three years later the tract distributors of the congregation had all but given up, and the Association took over the service to prevent it from collapsing. But the Association itself was in a bad way. It had no funds to buy hymn books for poorer worshippers at mission services, and in 1896 there was such a desperate shortage of voluntary workers that the Association did not even bother to meet for over ten months to plan its activities. By 1900 the organization was in tatters. The secretary was accused of not doing his job, the treasurer had no idea of the income and expenditure for the year, and the annual subscription to the Home Mission Union had not been paid. The missionary stated openly that there was much to discourage the volunteers, and in apparent acknowledgement of decay, the Association's minutes petered out ten months later.

The decline in middle-class participation in mission work directed at the working classes was an important aspect of the decay of evangelicalism, but it was only one. At different levels the role of evangelical precepts and activities was diminishing in bourgeois circles, undermining faith in the religious ideology which had dominated urban society for a century. There was an outward preservation of the evangelical values of self-help, thrift and 'respectability', and if pressed on the point there would probably have been few in the middle orders in society who would have openly disavowed evangelical orthodoxy. But the manner and extent of its social transmission, its place in the middle-class firmament, and the goals it was expected to achieve in the society of late Victorian and Edwardian Scotland did change very significantly. At the root of this lay a transformation in the middle classes' relationship with the city and with urban problems, but a variety of circumstances contributed to a much larger evangelical crisis amongst the urban élites.

One manifestation of this crisis was a shaking of the intellectual, ecclesiastical and psychological foundations of religious certainty in Scotland in the 1890s and 1900s. One aspect was ecumenicalism – the prospects of presbyterian reunion – which from 1895 onwards weakened the role of denominational identity as a factor promoting Scottish church adherence. But there was a wider perspective. The dominance of evangelical enterprise in the early and mid-Victorian years had been founded on certainty not only in the social relevance of evangelical visions but in their uniqueness for reforming society and removing social ills. Evangelicalism had operated, and could only operate with any real power, as a single hegemonic ideology unchallenged by contesting ideologies. Because of this, it had been able to incorporate methods of social reform like the municipalization of public utilities, the compulsory purchase of slum property, and increased state spending generally which in the mid and later twentieth century came to be considered quite alien and socialistic to the right-wing fundamentalism characteristic of modern evangelicalism. Even at their most conservative in 'religious' matters, pre-1880 evangelicals were radicals and innovators in social policy. The Rev. James Begg, severe Calvinist and scourge of worship reformers in the Free Church, was yet the leading Scottish advocate, lay or clerical, of municipal and philanthropic housing improvement. He wrote in 1866:

> The noble breadth of the commentary of our wise ancestors on the Decalogue, – the universal and perpetual standards of moral obligation, – cannot fail to command our admiration: 'The sixth commandment requireth all lawful endeavours to preserve our own life and the life of others;' 'The eighth commandment requireth the lawful procuring and furthering of

the wealth and outward estate of ourselves and others:' thus placing, in effect, our obligation to promote sanitary and social reform on the strongest foundation on which they can rest, viz., the direct commandment of God.[3]

Not only did this type of *evangelical* call to 'secular' reform tend to disappear after 1880, but the certainty of the biblical imprimatur for it withered. In part evangelical conviction decayed because the call to this type of action was coming from Christian socialists, socialists and those motivated by non-religious concerns, but it was also dissolving from within the churches because of the cumulative effect of liberalization of presbyterian standards, the modernization of worship, and most crucially because of the inexorable advance of biblical criticism.

Although Darwinism had been perceived as a threat to evangelical Christianity by Dwight Moody who had preached and written against it during his Scottish tour of 1873-4, Scottish popular opinion was little affected by evolutionism until the 1890s. In the same way, secularism was comparatively weak in Scotland, being as far as presbyterians were concerned not a rational and ordered 'unbelief' but rather a pragmatic opposition to Sabbatarianism and to the propagation of traditional religious values. For example, those branded as 'secularists' in Glasgow in the 1870s and 1880s were not Scottish Bradlaughs, but a Unitarian minister and a Mormon minister who stood (and were elected) as candidates for the school board advocating the exclusion of religious instruction from state schools. The religious issues thrown up by evolution theory and by secularism did come to have a bearing in Scotland, but the irony for Scotland is that the publicizers of those issues, and *de facto* the propagandists of religious doubt, were not initially scientists or rationalists but presbyterian ministers. It was the 'Higher Critics' of the theological colleges, perhaps especially in the evangelical Free and United Presbyterian Churches, who absorbed Darwinist ideas and tried to adapt biblical interpretation to the scientific circumstances. It was the creation of doubt within the churches between 1890 and 1910 which fomented public debate, press commentary, and a popular literature of 'atheistical sixpenny books at railway stalls'.

Responding to this, one book dating from 1906, entitled *The Religious Doubts of Common Men*, takes the form of a correspondence between a poorly-educated Aberdeenshire farmer of sixty-five years of age and an educated lawyer conversant with recent publications in Bible research. The farmer wrote to his old school chum in the hope that he would not 'flee up in a panic like oor meenister when I touch him up on the Higher Creeticism':

> My reading has been limited to the daily newspaper, an agricultural periodical, and a Sunday magazine. But I have read enough and I have heard enough to satisfy myself how great a change has taken place since I was a boy in the view which all educated people, and even the ministers of the Gospel, take with reference to the Bible, and the very foundations of the Christian religion. I am indeed in sore perplexity. My faith in the truth of all that I was taught in childhood and youth, as to the history of the world, as to the five books of Moses, as to the inspiration of the sacred writings, and even as to the New Testament and our blessed Lord and Master Himself, has been so shaken that I do not know what to believe. . . . I long for a simple faith, which I can hold firmly by when death approaches me. It maddens me to think that I may be taken away surrounded by doubt and darkness. I get no help whatever from the minister of this parish . . . all that he can say is that we are passing through a transition period, as he calls it, that we at present see darkly and imperfectly, and that by and by the light will break in upon us and faith revive.[4]

Such unease did not necessarily create widespread unbelief, but tended rather during a period when the public mind was charged with doubt to undermine faith in the church (and perhaps the minister), and in the propriety of propagating that faith and encouraging others (through proselytization) to adopt it as an agent of social and individual improvement. The first casualty was not churchgoing but the spreading of the Word. Between the 1850s and the 1880s middle-class 'pastimes' had been centred on the promotion of 'improving' agencies − on propagandization rather than passive pursuits, with what Stephen Yeo[5] has described as the 'vice-presidential class' of evangelical entrepreneurs acting as patrons and benefactors, and the lower ranks of the middle classes acting as Sunday-school teachers, Band of Hope leaders and mission-district visitors. What occurred between the 1880s and the outbreak of the First World War was the withdrawal of both these groups from evangelization.

The withdrawal of the 'vice-presidential class' was caused by the changing nature of industrial organization in the late nineteenth century in which family firms outgrew the single factory where the owner had combined business management with patronage of community and church organizations. Industry was tending to concentrate in larger, often limited-liability firms with impersonal management, shareholders and an increasingly national rather local organization. The leaders of industry were not only becoming wealthier but more estranged from their employees, and were withdrawing from their role as patrons in organizations as diverse as church missions, Orange lodges and temperance clubs. Family firms, if they survived, were moving in the same direction with the owners living in country mansions and delegating management to others. A celebrated example was John Campbell White, Lord Overtoun (1834–1908), who in the 1860s inherited from his father and his uncle a booming chrome manufacturing concern at Shawfield near Glasgow. He built up and broadened his business interests, as well as his philanthropic and religious undertakings, becoming amongst other things a major benefactor of the Free Church (paying for the erection of churches and the stipends of ministers and missionaries) and of religious organizations like the Glasgow United Evangelistic Association, the Bible Training Institute and the Glasgow Medical Missionary Society, of each of which he was president, and the National Bible Society, the Colportage Society and the Boys' Brigade, of each of which he was vice-president. During a strike at the chrome factory in 1899, Keir Hardie lambasted Lord Overtoun for the poor health conditions there, the low wages and long hours worked by his employees, and for the hypocrisy of a self-proclaimed Sabbatarian making Sunday a day of labour. Overtoun and the Free Church were severely embarrassed by the publicity aroused, especially since the charges were substantially true. But Overtoun's defence was that he no longer took an active part in management, having moved to distant Dumbartonshire and devolved responsibility to two nephews. His many interests consumed his time, and increasingly at a national level. This happened as much in church affairs as in business. As the first-named trustee of the United Free Church formed in 1900, he was called upon to contest a legal case brought by the remnant Free Church which briefly deprived the United Free Church of all its property. Overtoun was actually an evangelical of the old breed, a man who conducted his own Bible class for many years until the later nineteenth century, and who took a close interest in the mission work he financed. But the nature of business, church and philanthropic organization was changing, becoming larger and more centralized, and as the hierarchy of management in all three spheres became ever more remote, active control was abdicated in favour of professional managers and missionaries. He intervened to rectify conditions at the factory, but that merely confirmed the nature of the problem which intensified as evangelical entrepreneurs died out.

Another example illustrates the effects of other aspects of the 'social question' on the work of the 'vice-presidential' class. Sir Michael Connal (1817–93) was a Glasgow merchant and head of a shipping company and he, like Overtoun, was a prominent member of the Free Church with a particular interest in education. At the height of working-class riots in 1848 he established the Spoutmouth Bible Institute, a modest reading-room and Bible-class hall off the Gallowgate in Glasgow's east end. He conducted classes for the religious education of older boys until 1865 when others were brought in to assist, and in other activities he displayed the willingness of the Victorian middle classes to mix with the industrial classes, to confront and attempt to reform what he described as 'the roughness' and the 'low domestic state' of those he met at a 'Miners' Mission Conversazione' in 1873. He represented the tradition of the committed young evangelical entrepreneur who regarded it as 'wholesome but not always pleasing to visit the poor'. His education work led him and several like-minded businessmen to become members and controllers of the Glasgow School Board after it was set up in 1873,

The 'social question' and the crisis for religion

seeing the work of the state schools as part of the same paternalistic design as missions. But in the early 1890s, near the end of his life, he perceived the fundamental collapse of the design: on the school boards, where, as we shall see shortly, educational ideology shifted towards welfarism under socialist and Christian socialist influence; and in his Bible Institute which was failing to attract working-class lads. In a mood of depression in 1892 he wrote in his diary: 'The "Spout" in a state of transition – the future is very dark – I believe it has done good.'[6]

The decay and abdication of the 'vice-presidential' governors was matched further down the social scale amongst the middle-middle and lower-middle classes. This section in society was growing enormously in the late nineteenth century with the expansion of white-collar occupations in both public and private sectors: local government, state education, and administration in business and commerce. Members of these groups were 'natural' dissenters in the tradition established over the previous hundred years; they were upwardly mobile, aggressively 'respectable', and were often the children of the skilled working classes who, as we have seen, were particularly likely to belong to one of the dissenting presbyterian churches. But unlike their parents, and unlike the previous generations of the middle classes who had found self-identity in, especially, the Disruption and the Free Church, the emerging lower-middle classes of the late Victorian period found little with which to identify in fading ecclesiastical disputes, and as a *lower*-middle class were more keen to distance themselves from proletarian society than to reform it. In this way the numerical dominance of these nascent bourgeois within the middle classes transformed the culture and religious ambience of the urban élites as a whole, fomenting a mutiny amongst the evangelical troops.

The most obvious impact of the new middle classes was on the logistical operations of the presbyterian churches: on the management, size and location of congregations. The Free and United Presbyterian Churches had a tradition of being highly responsive to population movements, social restructuring and evangelizing opportunities. But between 1850 and 1879 the dissenters built churches faster than they gained adherents, with the result that the average number of members per congregation fell. In response, church extension virtually stopped in the 1880s, but new difficulties emerged. In rural areas depopulation was exacerbating the effects of over-ambitious church-building in earlier decades and of falling attendances amongst dissenting agricultural workers; by the early 1890s, a Free Church statistician considered the countryside to be grossly 'over-churched'. In the cities the problem was different but no less acute. Starting in the late 1870s, there was a large-scale movement of the urban middle classes to new suburban estates of spacious terraced housing and elegant tenement flats: suburbs like Edinburgh's Marchmont and Morningside, and Glasgow's Hyndland, Jordanhill, Cathcart, Pollokshields and Bearsden. The dissenting churches, and especially the Free Church, responded initially by erecting the characteristic 'iron churches' of the period – some built to individual and highly ornate designs, and others available 'off the shelf' from a specialist Glasgow firm. But the rapid growth of population in these middle- and lower-middle-class suburbs necessitated the erection of permanent churches. In Glasgow between 1895 and 1900, the Free Church built thirteen new churches and the United Presbyterians six. The result was a sharp fall in the average size of dissenting congregations, which translated in real terms into burgeoning suburban churches and ailing inner-city ones. The middle-class exodus left many churches in central urban districts in a parlous state by the late 1890s, and forced the presbyterian denominations to watch migratory movements more closely and to increase co-operation between them in 'church planting'.

These developments severely weakened the Free and United Presbyterian Churches and strengthened the relative position of the Established Church. The Church of Scotland has always been more sluggish in responding to demographic change and in the 1860s and 1870s it had built relatively few new churches in response to revivalist campaigns. But this sluggishness turned into a positive benefit in the late nineteenth century. Because of its parish system, it had churches already in place to serve at least some of the suburbanizing population of the large cities. In Glasgow, for instance, there was actually a net loss of one church

The 'social question' and the crisis for religion 179

during the 1890s whilst the dissenters built upwards of twenty-five. As a result, the average size of Established Church congregations was growing whilst those of the Free and United Presbyterian Churches were falling. The result for many dissenting congregations was the threat of insolvency: inability to pay contributions to denominational funds and to pay ministerial stipends. Pressure built up very rapidly in the 1890s for denominational union between the Free and United Presbyterian Churches to permit congregational amalgamations. With similar pressure coming from rural congregations, it was no accident that the formation of the United Free Church occurred in 1900. It was the cue for a wave of rationalization. Within months of the union, fourteen congregations in Glasgow were involved in amalgamations and a further set of closures ensued two years later.

The move to outlying suburbs altered the middle classes' relationship with urban society. As commuters on trams, the inner-city areas were places of work from which to retreat at evening time and weekends to more pleasant houses and gardens. Their new churches came to symbolize their prosperity and their cultural concerns, with the church hall developing as a busy recreation centre with an intensive programme of daily events. The range of pursuits and organizations catered for all ages and tastes; as well as Sunday schools and Bands of Hope, there were women's guilds, girls' guilds, fellowships and young men's and women's societies providing activities like literary and drama clubs, rambling, summer retreats, golf clubs and curling clubs. The minister of St Matthew's Free Church in the comfortable Edinburgh suburb of Morningside regarded such activities in 1895 'as links in the chain of full Church membership',[7] and there was general acknowledgement that middle-class youth were at last benefiting from the kind of group activity long provided through home-missionary work for the working classes. Yet it was evident that religious leisure was moving rapidly in a secular and self-indulgent direction. An observer of presbyterian mores[8] noted in 1901 that amongst the many ways of spending 'pleasant religious evenings' there was a new arrival from America – the 'candy-pull': 'This agency, if that be the correct word, is a party of young men and women who meet for the purpose of pulling candy'. This United Free Church minister looked on rather bemused by the energy expanded on such activities, but whilst he felt increased congregational activity was a welcome reaction to the single-minded individualism of the past, he none the less expressed concern with the house of God becoming 'more concert room than church'. Congregations were becoming universal providers of second-rate entertainment 'so that a Christian will not need to go outside the Church for culture or amusement'. But the trend became dominant in the twentieth century. By 1913, the Young Men's Guild Literary Society at St Matthew's was experiencing a fall in attendances due to competition from literary societies organized by Heriot's, Watson's and Stewart's – three of Edinburgh's private schools. This was an interesting illustration of how organized middle-class leisure became, and to a significant degree has remained, dominated by the dual focuses of the school (in the form of extra-curricular sports, clubs and uniformed youth organizations for children and former-pupils' clubs for adults) and the church. But in order to fit into this duopoly, much of the serious religious and 'improving' content disappeared after 1890 from the curricula of church organizations, displaced by peripheral attractions originally introduced an enticements.

It was in this context that the middle classes withdrew from evangelization. The collapse of Queen's Park Free Church Evangelistic Association, noted earlier, was duplicated throughout the suburban congregations of Scotland in the 1890s and 1900s. Such associations in the Free and United Presbyterian Churches, which were the most active in evangelization and the most popular denominations in the suburbs, reported severe shortages of voluntary helpers. Really quite quickly, middle-class evangelicals became less willing to undertake their established duties: entering working-class streets, knocking on doors of tenement flats up gloomy staircases, and enquiring as to the 'religious state' of the occupants. There was waning interest in asking the traditional and fundamental evangelical questions, and there was embarrassment about the very recent heritage of religious 'enthusiasm' and revivalism. One Glasgow congregation of the Free Church in

1899, being no longer interested in the trappings of revivalist liturgy, tried to withdraw the Sankey hymnbook from use in its working-class mission station – only to instigate a revolt amongst mission worshippers which forced a change of mind. The most serious decline in religious voluntary work took place in the Sunday schools. The number of teachers in these schools reached its peak in the 1890s with some 50,000 operating in the three main presbyterian churches in the middle of that decade. But the numbers started falling in the Free Church from 1890, in the United Presbyterian Church from 1895, and in the Established Church from 1907, and by 1910 there had been a net loss of 4000 from these churches; during a twelve-month period in 1905–6, the United Free Church lost 300 teachers in Glasgow alone. Whilst congregational Sunday schools for the middle-class children had been growing since the 1860s, what had happened in the last decade of the century was the beginning of a very rapid decline of the older mission Sunday schools for working-class children of non-churchgoing parents. As congregations moved to suburban areas, mission Sunday schools in inner-city areas collapsed as teachers switched to the more pleasant task of supervising scholars from the neighbourhood. One factor in this change may have been the shift in the sex-balance of teachers; in 1850 more than two-thirds were male, but by 1890 the majority were female. The committed evangelical businessman, such as Lord Overtoun and Sir Michael Connal, who in their younger years worked actively in the home-mission field, was disappearing.

These changes in middle-class presbyterianism had several consequences for the nature of the relationship between the working classes and the churches. In the first place evangelization was increasingly left to the care of full-time missionaries and 'Bible women' who were being recruited in significant numbers in the last quarter of the nineteenth century from working-class converts of religious revivalism. This created a surfeit of presbyterian divinity graduates after the 1880s, and, with poor promotional prospects in the context of suburbanization and rationalization of congregations, careers were made out of evangelizing city slums. The records of congregations which maintained evangelistic associations during this period give a strong impression of 'social distance' and diverging interests emerging between middle-class churchgoers and the missionaries they employed; as at Queen's Park Free Church in Glasgow, these missionaries were by 1900 having to conduct most of the work themselves unaided by lay district visitors. Furthermore, as evangelistic associations collapsed as suburbanization proceeded, home-missionary enterprise came increasingly under the superintendence of general assembly committees and proletarian organizations. Though supported financially by Protestant firms, these independent organizations developed as an important feature of urban proletarian Protestantism between the 1880s and 1950s: organizations like the United Evangelistic Associations of Glasgow and Dundee which ran 'Tent Halls', the City Missions of the major cities, the United Working Men's Christian Mission, the Working Men's Evangelistic Association, the Protestant Missionary Society of Glasgow, the Salvation Army, temperance friendly societies such as the Rechabites, and the Independent Order of Good Templars, started in Scotland in 1869 and having some 84,000 members within seven years. This professionalization and proletarianization of evangelism represented a narrowing of the power base of evangelicalism as a whole, and, as we shall see later in the chapter, had a profound impact on the strategy of religious social reform.

The secularizing trend in leisure also had an important impact on the working classes. Religious organizations remained of great importance to all sections of the working classes at the turn of the century. In a 1904 survey carried out by the Charity Organization Society in Edinburgh, more of the working classes were found to have affiliations with religious, church and temperance organizations (28 per cent of skilled workers and 22 per cent of semi- and unskilled) than with working men's clubs, sports clubs, political parties and hobby clubs (17 per cent of the skilled, 11 per cent of the semi- and unskilled).[9] Yet there was a widespread recognition by churchmen that religious leisure was being increasingly rejected by the working classes after 1890. Attendances at Sunday schools and mission stations were starting to fall whilst 'secular' leisure was booming. Among the many forms of non-religious pastimes, football mania was probably the most important with crowds of around 15,000 attending the big matches by the late 1880s and as many as 120,000 by 1907. Participant football also became enormously popular, and religious organizations (notably the Bands of Hope and the Boys' Brigade) had by the early twentieth century organized their own teams, leagues and knock-out cups. The churches were being drawn inexorably into competition with commercial and secular leisure. In 1887-9, a fad for orchestras and brass bands swept through Established and dissenting congregations. More fundamentally, the collection plates were dispensed with in many mission stations to permit them to compete, and to be seen to be competing, with secular alternatives. One mission hall for boys in the Townhead district of Glasgow had a sign outside its door in the 1890s which proclaimed boldly:[10]

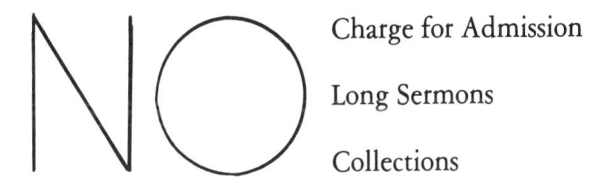

NO Charge for Admission

Long Sermons

Collections

Religious voluntary organizations were shifting the basis of their activities from 'improving' educational classes in religious instruction, or from revivalism, to sport, outings and militaristic youth movements. The YMCA is a case in point. It had started in Glasgow in the 1840s as an institution providing educational lectures, and then in 1876 overhauled its curriculum with a revivalist bent after the Scottish visit of Moody and Sankey. But in the 1880s it tilted with the wind by becoming a predominantly sporting outfit providing opportunities in athletics, swimming, rambling, cycling and curling. In the same way, Band of Hope meetings were transformed in the 1890s by children's demands for wizardry: 'novelty' classes showing the workings of tramways, electricity, phonographs and other technological miracles of the age; even the temperance message was put across using the ubiquitous magic lantern. And for many working-class lads, the main attraction of the Band of Hope by the 1910s was its football teams.

But the success of religious compromises with secular pursuits was limited by the appearance of systematic proletarian rejection of middle-class paternalism. Whilst it would be wrong to suggest that there was a sudden surge in working-class irreligion, deferential submission to bourgeois proselytization markedly diminished. In trying to reach the 120,000 'unchurched' of Glasgow in 1892, Christian socialists of the Church of Scotland arranged an elaborate event of amusements and concerts in the East End Exhibition Centre. But as the Rev. Donald Macleod, the convener of the project, reported to the general assembly, the result was a 'bitter disappointment' with few of the working classes attending:

> I am sorry to say that what occurred has made me fear that the gulf which separates class from class in our great centres of industry is wider, and the class feeling deeper, than we had dreamed. I fear that the very name of our Association as being for the Social Improvement of the People gave offence, and that inference on the part of those who are called 'the upper classes' is resented. I believe that to gain success you must act somehow through the working classes themselves. You must get them to move; or, still better, you must have it done by bodies like the Corporations of our great Cities, which represent the whole community.[11]

Macleod not only signals here the decay of the churches' organizing role, but acknowledges the decay of working-class acquiescence with middle-class patronage. This was the *quid pro quo* of the withdrawal of the middle classes. The 'suburban captivity of the churches', to borrow an American phrase, interacted with the rise of the labour movement and of socialism to segregate urban social classes both spatially and ideologically.

The challenge of labour and the loss of 'social prophecy'

Until the last decade of the nineteenth century the centrality of religion to industrial and urban society – and thus the basis for

Victorian church growth – had lain in the ubiquitous relevance of evangelicalism to modern class relations, social mobility and the solution of social problems amongst the 'residuum'. Religion held the key to social salvation by offering on the one hand an ethos of individualism which permitted 'improvement' to the receptive, and on the other an evolving agenda for social action for the rescue of the degenerate through a combination of evangelization, legitimate philanthropy and selective intervention by the state. Evangelical values were the bedrock on which personal worth was fixed, and they delineated the means – the only means – for advancement by individuals, social groups and the country as a whole. In early and mid-Victorian Britain social mobility, progress and prosperity had been seen almost without challenge in terms of personal 'improvement' through combined endeavour in the religious, moral and economic spheres.

But around 1890 this hegemonic evangelical grasp of public ideology started very suddenly to slip. The tangible effects of declining churchgoing, Sunday-school attendance and Sabbath sanctity were only part of the story. They were merely elements in the great 'social question' – a complex national issue subsuming themes like the physical and moral fitness of Britain as a Christian and imperialist power, class divisions represented in the rise of trades unions and labour political parties, and the role of the state in ameliorating poverty, low wages, poor housing and industrial disputes. The period from the late 1880s until 1920 witnessed a heightening awareness of inequality through the work of social investigators and royal commissions on the poor law and housing, and through the generation of intensified debate on the causes of social problems and on the ethics of permitting their continuation. The churches were stunned by the implications of the 'social question'. On one level it undermined their monopoly of 'respectability'; on another it removed religious concerns from the centre-stage of social action. 'The Social Question', wrote a United Presbyterian minister from Dumbarton in 1893, 'being the greatest national question of our time, is at bottom a religious question, affecting the whole status, spirit, and health of modern society.'[12] A major change was under way, not only in the functions of the churches and evangelical agencies, but in the perceived role of religion in society generally. Leisure for pleasure was displacing rational and improving pastimes, but in the process a wider transformation was taking place in popular ideology. Rationalized religious doubt was the common currency of the 'man in the street'. 'Let us be certain', said Donald Macleod in striking up the crisis theme in his moderator's address to the Established Church general assembly in 1895, 'that these larger discussions are reaching into the very heart of society around us; they are entering our warehouses and offices, and clerks at the desk are accustomed to exchange doubts respecting matters which a few years ago were regarded as stable as the everlasting hills.' He had noted, really in the space of six years, the very sudden appearance of 'a stormy and dark cloud over the horizon of our faith'.[13]

Macleod's credentials for the moderator's office were themselves confirmatory of the crisis. He was appointed convener of the Home Mission Committee in 1888 on a remit which implied emulating the evangelization work of the dissenters. By 1893 he reported to the assembly that mission work had merely resulted in religion being 'handed over to the monied classes' whilst the poorer classes were segregated by 'sending down bands of workers to Mission Halls and Mission Churches, whose very names are stamped with separateness'.[14] The evangelical design was manifestly failing, and this theme was taken up by many commentators. Established churchmen exploited it to attack the dissenters who were clamouring for disestablishment; a parish minister from Argyll harangued the 'millionaire congregations' of the United Free Church: 'A Church conducted on ordinary commercial principles is not a Church of God.'[15] The parish church was viewed by the Church of Scotland as a hope for religious democracy, to attract back the alienated working classes. Donald Macleod told the commissioners of the general assembly 'to distinguish between non-churchgoing and irreligion' and 'to consider how we can best bless the people'. This was to be an issue which agonized the presbyterian churches for over twenty years.

'The poor worker is having his revenge', wrote Keir Hardie, the Scottish Labour leader and MP in 1898, '. . . by not attending church.'[16] The economic function of churchgoing was diminishing. Evangelical palliatives were of diminishing importance to social improvement, and the churches' claim to confer respectability was losing credence. Social progress by individual action was being overtaken by collectivist action by the state: the 1886 Crofters' Act, the slow advance of council housing from the late 1880s, national insurance, old-age pensions, medical inspection of schoolchildren, and expanding municipal ownership of utilities and control over building. Such a pragmatic advance of state responsibility was not entirely new, nor something that evangelicals had been resistant to in the past. But what was new and daunting for the churches was that this agenda of action did not emanate from an evangelical nor any other religious source, but from the labour movement. The initiative in social and political action was passing out of the hands of activists inspired by religion and the bearers of social salvation were now trades-union leaders, socialist intellectuals and labour politicians.

The undermining of evangelical thinking was nowhere more apparent than in the ideological change within the labour movement. Radicals and Chartists of the first half of the nineteenth century were strongly imbued with evangelical precepts, initiating for instance the teetotal movement, and in a more general sense deriving from puritanism the values which bred solidarity and class consciousness in many industrial communities and occupations. The coming of greater prosperity after 1850 confirmed the relevance of evangelical self-help ideology to the organizations of Protestant skilled artisans – the 'aristocracy of labour' – which dominated the labour movement of mid-Victorian Britain. This ideology created broad trades-union agreement with the churches and the middle classes on the economic system and its social conventions – economic liberalism, free trade, sabbatarianism and the local veto. Trades unions supported church candidates at school board elections in the 1870s and 1880s and joined with the churches in opposing the Sunday opening of art galleries and the Sunday running of trams. Working-class friendly societies, invariably 'temperance friendly societies' like the Independent Order of Rechabites, promoted the very values of thrift, self-reliance and teetotalism which were central to the strategy for social reform put forward by evangelicals. However, church and labour had very little contact before 1890. Artisans might express their aspirations in terms redolent of the middle classes and the evangelical churches, and might indeed constitute the majority of church members. But between trades unions and the churches as organizations there was a significant antipathy caused by fundamental disagreement on the righteousness of combination and holding strikes, and over the association of labour with violent popular protest of the sort that characterized the period from 1790 to 1848. Church and labour vied for 'moral righteousness'. In the early 1880s, for example, the general assemblies of the Established and Free Churches criticized the railway servants' union for holding meetings on the Sabbath. The Glasgow trades council retorted that the kirks should be 'denouncing the great amount of unnecessary [Sunday] work now done by public companies in our midst, the shareholders of which are, we believe, in many cases, strong stoops in the Church'.[17]

But church–labour relations were radically transformed by the changing character of the labour movement in the 1880s and 1890s. The rise of unions for the semi-skilled and the unskilled worker enlarged the scope of industrial combination and, irrespective of the effectiveness of strike action, offered a widely available alternative, or at least addition, to evangelical 'improvement'. Labour representation emerged after 1890 on town councils, school boards, parochial boards and in the House of Commons, providing for the first time an effective challenge to the ideology and policies of competitive individualism. Despite the slow electoral progress of the labour movement before 1914, the interests of the working classes became quickly associated with the outlook it represented and the policies it promoted. In an important sense, its lack of success in the polls accentuated the ideological transformation because the 'social question' became seen by many, especially in the churches, as an ethical issue rather than a political one. Churchmen in Scotland were moved by revelations of social conditions provided by studies like *The Bitter Cry of Outcast London* of 1883, Charles Booth's volumes on the London poor published in the 1890s, and Rowntree's

1901 examination of poverty in York. The Established Church, the most affected by this social-reform concern, undertook its own studies; notably the Glasgow Presbytery Commission on the Housing of the Poor in Relation to their Social Condition, of 1888-91, and the general assembly Commission on the Religious Condition of the People of 1889-96. In carrying out such inquiries the churches were brought into contact with trades unionists, Labour activists and left-wing intellectuals, and were driven to reassess traditional religious and especially evangelical thinking. This produced from the Church of Scotland's most radical presbytery, Glasgow, the conclusion in 1888 that 'existing agencies and methods have not hitherto proved adequate to cope' with poverty and poor housing.[18] What emerged in Glasgow in 1888-94 was a small band of non-political Christian socialists who sought a new social theology incorporating ideas drawn from a nexus of social reformers including representatives of organized labour. The issue was not one of overturning the existing political parties but of creating a consensus in favour of increased social action by public authorities. Urged on by philosophers like T. H. Green in England and Edward Caird in Scotland, and by an emerging breed of 'social scientists' like Patrick Geddes, churchmen went beyond traditional evangelicalism - which viewed social problems as the products of immorality - to regard poverty, insanitary and overcrowded housing, and ill-health as in themselves immoralities which could not be countenanced in a Christian country. Therefore, it became necessary and ethically justifiable for churches to work with the labour movement and to pronounce upon issues of the day. As one minister said, 'we are at a point of social pressure where to keep silence is little less than immoral'.[19]

The new social theology produced a deluge of books of biblical reinterpretation between 1890 and 1918 - the majority written by Established Church ministers but with other contributions by dissenting presbyterian clergy; very little was produced by Episcopalian or Catholic clergy. The starting point was the strike of London dockworkers in 1889 which spread to other ports and attracted national attention of an unprecedentedly sympathetic nature. A United Presbyterian minister wrote immediately after it:

> Who were the spokesmen of these miserable dockmen in making a righteous demand? Not the ministers of Jesus Christ; not the magnates of the religious world; but a few socialists who, amid the starving multitudes, kept themselves and the sufferers in such moderation and self-control as to be the admiration of the world.[20]

In the new social theology, strikes and other social protests acquired a legitimacy not recognized by churches before. A leading Christian socialist in the Established Church commented in 1908: 'Social unrest itself is a good sign, a mark of vigorous life, not of decadence. It is a divine discontent with social wrong.'[21] But churchmen regarded it as 'the bitterest drop to us that social progress is mainly effected by men opposed to our churches and our religion', and sought to sustain their relevance to 'social prophecy' by mixing socialism with Christianity: 'The fact is that socialism needs to be Christianised, and that Christianity needs to be socialised.'[22]

The principle of the new social theology was that 'the objective of all social effort is the realisation of the Kingdom of God on earth'.[23] Reward in this world through social justice became emphasized, and led clergy to attack *laissez faire* and big business. Speculators were denounced as 'the hungry parasites of our industrial order',[24] and the proper stewardship of wealth was promoted as a means of balancing the respective rights of entrepreneurs and workers. Compromise was sought between the basic tenets of evangelicalism, in which religious and economic salvation was perceived as arising from the individual as a 'free moral agent', and the need to regulate capitalism in order to reduce exploitation: 'Individualism is only a half truth; solidarity is the other half.'[25] Various ideals were drawn into the theology: that of co-operativism represented by David Dale, Robert Owen, the Rochdale pioneers, and the Scottish Co-operative Wholesale Society whose educational work was supported by many Christian socialists in the Edwardian period; the garden-city movement of

The 'social question' and the crisis for religion 191

Ebenezer Howard; and perhaps most importantly municipal socialism which between 1890 and 1914 was a popular and virtually apolitical trend in Western city government, and turned Glasgow Corporation into what one minister described as 'the mecca of the municipal reformer'. The new social theology derived much from evangelicalism – its concern for cities, its 'call to action', and its enthusiasm. The Christian socialist vision was for churches and society 'to be alit with civic ideals, to be alive with civic ardours, to be aglow with civic pride and patriotism'.[26] But it differed from evangelicalism in several important respects. It rejected the primacy of religious conversion with its attendant moral virtues as the source of social salvation, though it failed ultimately to resolve the conflict between the socialist aim of freedom from economic want and the evangelical principle of freedom from state restriction which even the Christian socialists acknowledged was necessary for the cultivation of those values. It differed also in that it was overwhelmingly a movement of clergy with the support of church courts, and lacked any real base amongst the laity. Its call to social service – to running baby clinics, undertaking sociological investigations and to providing homes and holidays for slum children – was one which was answered more by professionals and by institutions rather than by the church membership. From the outset, Christian socialism displaced religious objectives and assisted rather than stemmed the secularization of social policy.

The new social theology gave rise to the formation between 1890 and 1914 of a church–labour group, based mostly in Glasgow but with outposts in Edinburgh and Dundee. This group was composed of less than a hundred individuals of whom around thirty were clergy drawn from the Established, Free, United Presbyterian, Episcopal and Catholic Churches, and the remainder were trades unionists, Labour activists, medical officers of health, academics, town councillors and MPs. Few of the clergy were socialist; the only one of note was John Glasse, minister of Old Greyfriars' Church in Edinburgh who was a devotee of Marx and Proudhon, an ILP sympathizer, and a friend of William Morris. For the remainder, a network of interlocking voluntary organizations provided an apparent ecclesiastical influence upon social-reform initiatives: organizations including, on the labour side, trades councils, the Scottish TUC and the Scottish Labour Party; on the church side the Scottish Christian Social Union, the Ruskin Society and the Social Unions of Glasgow, Edinburgh and Dundee which were all active in philanthropic renovation and building of working-class housing, social surveys, refuges, medical clinics and other enterprises between 1890 and 1914. And in the 'middle' between church and labour was the Scottish Council for Women's Trades, founded in Glasgow in 1894, which through its focus on the plight of women and children in 'sweated' industries, provided an area in which all were agreed that unionization and legislation to curb exploitation were vital. But the network of organizations created a united support on a whole range of issues from free school meals to national insurance. It led ministers to conclude that 'if such things as Old Age Pensions, State intervention in Labour disputes, Labour Exchanges, and the Trades Boards Acts are Socialism, then Socialism is not a thing to be greatly dreaded'.[27]

The church–labour group had several short-term consequences. A small number of clergy were recruited to the labour movement and were elected to local authorities; as a result, opposing ministers started to stand as Tory candidates, especially in rural areas. Another consequence was an attempt by the Established and Free Churches to negotiate in industrial disputes involving railwaymen in 1891 and miners in 1894, but 'wholly without effect'. Obversely, the church–labour group gave the labour movement an entrée into the world of social-policy formation with access to experts in the caring professions: teachers, poor-relief administrators, doctors, nutritionists, and others. This gave the labour movement both expertise in the field and the ability to draw up detailed and workable manifestos with which to attract electoral support and to fight for reforms in local and national government.

But in the process the churches passed the banner of social progress into the hands of others. The churches' own investigations spelled out a socialist message rather than a Christian one. The final report of the Established Church's Commission into the Religious Condition of the People stated that 'the

The 'social question' and the crisis for religion 193

Christian conscience has been aroused; and all persons, with some sense of justice as well as generosity, feel that the chasms between wealth-land and woe-land are a symptom of social unrighteousness'.[28] The churches' solutions to unemployment now became unevangelical. From 1892, congregations of the Established Church were handing out money to unemployed members in an effort 'to save all from want'. The dissenters clung on longer to traditional policies, avoiding handouts and social service in the 1890s as 'action that could not well be taken' by them. By 1904, the Established Church general assembly was persuaded by the Glasgow Christian socialists to abandon evangelization in favour of social work in homes and 'labour colonies' for the elderly, disabled, inebriate, delinquent and unemployed, and the United Free Church followed suit after the depression of 1908–9 in which both denominations carried out systematic payments to unemployed adherents. Whilst evangelization continued on a much-reduced basis, the fundamental attachment to evangelicalism was abandoned.

The attempt to compromise with the labour movement was a wise strategy in the circumstances. To have directly opposed labour and adopted a coherently reactionary political stance would have intensified working-class alienation from the churches – as happened in some countries. But the attempt to form a church–labour accommodation came to an abrupt halt after 1914, and by 1920 non-political Christian socialism was virtually dead in Scotland, the product of various changing circumstances. Most of the leading clergy in the church–labour group died during the 1910s, and those who were left found their visions of social justice out of step with the times. The agreed agenda of social action of church and labour had been virtually completed by government legislation, and the major outstanding issue of subsidized council housing had proved too controversial for ministers to support. But the major factor was the myth of Red Clydeside that arose from the First World War – the labour disputes and rent strikes which the churches, as clarions of the patriotic war effort, had to denounce. Despite inter-denominational support for worker democracy in the later stages of the war, Scottish Labour's fiery band of leaders such as James Maxton, Willie Gallacher and the maverick John Maclean gave the movement a transformed image. The Bolshevik Revolution threw a new light on working-class politics in Scotland, and few in the churches were willing to subscribe to a movement which seemed to flirt with revolution. Even mundane issues became controversial, and Christian socialists struggled to keep socialist social-reform matters alive in church courts. In the main they failed in Scotland as they did in England, and Christian socialists became a politicized and ineffectual minority in the presbyterian churches.

A contributory factor to the Protestant churches' alienation from the labour movement in the 1910s and 1920s was a dramatic switch in Catholic opinion away from the Liberals towards Labour. During the Victorian period the Catholic hierarchy and the Catholic press in Scotland had been very hostile to organized labour. In part this can be seen in terms of ideological defensiveness by the priesthood which discouraged support for trades unions, but it can also be regarded as a product of sectarianism. Not only were Catholics excluded from many skilled occupations by Protestant employers; Protestant workers excluded them from unions and some friendly societies. Despite increased unionization amongst Catholics in the 1890s and 1900s, caused by recruitment to skilled jobs in mining for instance and by unionization amongst the unskilled, the majority of Catholics did not align with Labour politics but continued to vote Liberal until 1918. The Catholic newspaper, the *Glasgow Observer*, stated in 1895 that 'the ILP is in effect the workman's wing of the Tory Party', whilst it described the Conservatives as 'hopelessly an anti-Catholic Party – the Party of ascendency and bigotry'.[29] But indications of a swing to Labour were evident by the early 1900s. Co-operative societies in the west of Scotland were split by sectarian dispute in the decade before the outbreak of war, with independent Catholic co-ops being formed in Motherwell, Wishaw, Renfrew and parts of Glasgow. Catholics in Coatbridge were starting to vote Labour by 1906, and in the next three years the Church's open hostility diminished markedly. A correspondence in the *Observer* in 1906–8 hotly debated Catholicism and socialism, and from it John Wheatley of the Catholic Socialist Society emerged as an acceptable leader of the laity. In 1908 the

The 'social question' and the crisis for religion 195

archbishop of Glasgow gave a speech which softened the hierarchy's attitude: 'What did capital risk? – Its money. What did labour risk? – Its life.'[30]

Increasing access to skilled jobs over the next ten years, and especially during the war, infused Labour attitudes amongst Catholics, and the independence of Ireland and collapse of the Liberal Party released them to vote Labour. By the early 1920s, the Scottish Labour vote was highly reliant on the support of Catholics and the membership and leadership of the left wing – notably communists – became strongly associated with lapsed Catholics. This merely confirmed, as far as many Protestants were concerned, that 'popery' and atheism went hand-in-hand. However, the inter-war Scottish Labour leadership had a highly variegated religious composition: out of forty-two identified by William Knox, 31 per cent were members of the Church of Scotland, 26 per cent to the United Free Church, a further 17 per cent belonged to minor Protestant churches, and 14 per cent were Catholic. This has led Knox to suggest that the Scottish labour movement owed more to presbyterianism than is commonly acknowledged, and particularly to the United Free Church and its antecedents which, in the 1920s he feels, had 'the most enlightened social programme drawn up by the churches in Scotland'.[31] Whilst several United Free churchmen, and notably a few ministers, were prominent in reformist Labour politics, the Church of Scotland had established a much more comprehensive social-work scheme – and at an earlier date – than the dissenters. None the less, a general point can be made that Labour activists might tend to come from a dissenting rather than establishment tradition. But as the twentieth century proceeded, the popular association of Labour voting with Catholics hardened, reinforcing the reason for the Protestant churches to shed Christian-socialist rhetoric.

But the rise of Catholics in the labour movement merely confirmed the end of the 'social question' within Protestantism. In the attempt to compensate for the decay of evangelicalism in church life and popular thinking, the Christian socialists in the Church of Scotland and the United Free Church had failed to create a religious ideology of social justice which appealed to its middle-class congregations. Equally, respectability was no longer a purely religious concept but one which could be derived from secular ethical codes promulgated separately by upper-middle-class intellectuals and by some labour organizations. More importantly it was no longer a concept linked to churchgoing. The Socialists strove for respectability in the early 1890s by claiming that God was in the labour movement and founded labour churches and similar organizations to create what Stephen Yeo has described as a 'religion of socialism'.[32] But practically all the labour churches in Scotland had disintegrated between 1896 and 1900 as the Labour struggle became a purely political one which, in itself, was becoming respectable. Christian socialists helped to make the fight for state social reform a moral campaign. But in the process of promoting collectivism and the secularization of social policy an alarming change had taken place in the relationship between religion and civil government.

Church and state, 1873–1929

The crisis in popular presbyterianism fomented a profound change in the degree and in the nature of religious influence in the civil state. The change was not so much in the churches' connections with central government, which were remarkably little affected, but rather in the manner by which clergy and leading laity had traditionally exerted control over the *local* state. The rise of religious dissent in the eighteenth and nineteenth centuries had undermined the legitimacy and effectiveness of the Established Church's management of rural affairs through the board of heritors and the kirk session. As a result civil functions of the Church were gradually withdrawn by parliament and vested in new and apparently 'secular' bodies of local government. But the mode of administration created was the design of the presbyterian churches, and especially of the dissenters in the Free and United Presbyterian Churches. What developed in the second half of the nineteenth century was a system of popular control of traditional ecclesiastical functions, a system which did not terminate religious influence but perpetuated it. Mimicking the internal democracy of presbyterian church government, the local

The 'social question' and the crisis for religion   197

state became the arena for evangelizing by electioneering and the means for 'voting in' the kingdom of God. But from 1890 the 'social question' started to undermine the design. The decline of participation in Protestant religion – in churchgoing, voluntary work and teetotalism – propelled evangelical leaders and missionaries towards ever greater reliance on electoral support, culminating after the First World War in an intoxicating frenzy of evangelical canvassing from which only the Catholic Church benefited. The result was a marked diminution in the secular role of religion in Scottish civil life.

The conventional line of argument is that secularization in Scotland as in other Western countries was marked by the state's take-over of traditional church functions: notably the withdrawal of poor-relief management from the Established Church in 1845, and the setting up of the state system of education in 1872. In reality, both of these events were major victories for religious and particularly evangelical interests. The Free, United Presbyterian and Catholic Churches were keen to remove poor relief from the hands of Established Church elders who, it was commonly alleged in the first half of the nineteenth century, discriminated against dissenters who applied for financial aid from the poor fund. Similarly, the 1872 Education Act withdrew the privileged status of parish schools and sanctioned the creation of a popularly controlled system of administration which the churches contrived to dominate. The creation of apparently 'secular' authorities was thus designed to preserve religious control of civil administration by making it elective and subject to interdenominational rivalry at the ballot box.

And until the 1890s the churches were successful in their objectives. Between 1845 and 1894, poor relief was administered by parochial boards which were composed partly of elected members and partly of elders or heritors nominated by the local Established Church. In 1894 the boards were replaced by all-elected parish councils which continued to be dominated by representatives of the churches and of the landowners. In Glasgow church nominees were still present in 1910, and even two of the three Labour members were dissenting ministers. In one rural parish[33] near the Borders between 1894 and 1910, the parish council was invariably composed of the minister, one large farmer and three small ones, and it acted like a kirk session by stopping payments to claimants who were known to buy drink and by demanding that its medical officer – the local doctor – 'clear himself of the scandal' of adultery in a manner redolent of an eighteenth-century fornication case. The role of the school-board teacher exemplified the continuity between traditional kirk control of the community and the overtly 'secular' state. He was appointed virtually automatically by parish councils in country districts to the positions of clerk, rate collector and Inspector of the Poor; and his appointment by more distant authorities to the posts of librarian and civil registrar of births, deaths and marriages in the less populous parishes, and his obligatory appointment as an elder of one of the presbyterian churches, tended in practice to make the intrusion of state control little more than the continuation of the status quo.

But in the 1910s and 1920s, the continued presence of ministers and elders on parish councils masked a fundamental secularization of operations and rationale. In urban and industrial districts there was a great infusion of Christian socialists who agreed with new Labour representatives that the giving of relief should not be dependent on the appearance of evangelical virtues amongst the 'deserving poor'. Socially concerned clergy recoiled at what one of them described in 1905 as the 'brutal and vicious' interrogation of applicants by a relief committee in Glasgow in which 'man after man walked up to the bar and had his life-record read out to him . . . like judgement-day'.[34] Paradoxically, the keeping of records was pioneered by religious charities and the Charity Organization Society, but the practice became during the First World War and the economic depressions of the 1920s and 1930s the basis for professionalization of social service and for the better regulation of statutory relief agencies. In this process, the role of churchmen, of evangelical attitudes and indeed of popular election diminished, and parish councils were abolished in 1929.

Much the same happened in the more significant area of education. The establishment of elected school boards in every burgh and rural parish in 1873, coupled with the imposition of compulsory education, was widely welcomed by the presbyterian churches, though the Catholic Church refused to surrender its schools and continued to provide its own education. Virtually the only issue at the triennial elections between then and the late 1880s was the nature of the religious instruction to be given in board schools, and practically all presbyterian schools – especially in urban areas – were quickly handed over without compensation. Nearly all successful candidates at elections in those decades stood on 'religious tickets' of one kind or another – whether as informal representatives of their own denominations, as supporters of particular policies on religious instruction, or as Orangeists. In the vast majority of the 900 schoolboards, contested elections were avoided by inter-denominational agreement on the allocation of seats. In rural districts, this produced little change in education with old parish schools and schoolmasters continuing under the supervision of boards composed of the parish minister, a dissenting minister (if there was one), a few elders and the senior heritors or their factors. There were isolated religious feuds in country districts. At Clyne in the Highlands, the Free Church-dominated board inherited the old Established Church schoolmaster and tried to remove him by accusing him of fornication, adultery and drunkenness. Prosecuted by the board, the teacher was acquitted, awarded damages for defamation, and continued in the post for twenty years under the protection of the Scottish Education Department. In South Uist the overwhelmingly Catholic population was forced under pain of eviction to vote for the presbyterian regime and its teacher until the 1886 Crofters' Act gave them security of tenure.[35]

But in most school boards, education settled down quickly after 1873 into a pattern little changed since the days of church schools. Even in the largest school boards of Glasgow, Edinburgh and Govan, the contested elections regularly produced a denominationally balanced membership which instituted a solidly presbyterian form of religious education in the classroom. Catholic candidates, both clergy and laity, were elected to oppose the spending of ratepayers' money on presbyterian religious instruction, but they never gained more than a fifth of the seats on the city boards. School boards were thus able to sustain great continuity in the content and objectives of education. Despite a decline in the religious content of school books, caused by the government's insistence on 'timetabling' religion apart from other subjects, 'RI' was fixedly presbyterian and traditional, based on 'use and wont' when the schools were under church control. The Established, Free and United Presbyterian Churches were allowed by many boards to send in their own inspectors to check on the nature of religious education, and they came away completely satisfied – so satisfied that the Church of Scotland dismissed its Inspector in 1879. The furtherance of literacy and evangelical virtues was safely in the hands of church nominees on school boards and teachers trained entirely at denominational training colleges.

But circumstances changed in the late 1880s and 1890s. Labour candidates started to stand and were progressively elected in urban areas, gaining about a fifth of the seats. They stood on the general 'ticket' of representing the working classes, but their policy of free education was a matter of great concern to evangelicals. In the evangelical design, popularized by Thomas Chalmers in the 1810s, parents should be charged fees for the education of their children because it encouraged self-reliance and especially thrift. During the 1870s and 1880s, only the very and 'deserving' poor were excused payments, and even when parliament ordered in 1889 that fees be abolished some boards like that of Glasgow maintained them because of pressure from middle-class parents fearing an influx of working-class children into the more expensive board schools. Not until 1893 did the Glasgow board abolish fees and thus reduce the social segregation between its schools. The evangelicals resisted until the last, Sir Michael Connal speaking 'decidedly about Dr Chalmers' scheme as the best', and when the board 'freed the schools' the evangelicals resigned from management positions on the various committees. Henceforth, the Glasgow board was ruled by a loosely affiliated group of Christian socialists, Labour and Ladies representatives, with the occasional support of the Catholics. Thus there was no sudden removal of clergy from school-board management, but instead a fundamental shift in educational ideology. Issues of 'social justice', of providing free books, meals, spectacles and shoes, now symbolized the welfare function of education rather than its evangelical design.

The perception of fading evangelical, and indeed presbyterian, control of Scottish education was heightened by the government's decision in 1918 to make the country's Catholic schools the first in a predominantly non-Catholic nation to be incorporated within a state system. Historians of Scottish Catholicism and of sectarianism emphasize the importance of this aspect of the 1918 Education Act. For the Catholic community, it ended the discriminatory denial of full financial support from central government and local rates. Between 1873 and 1919, the Catholic Church was unable to meet the educational needs of the whole Catholic population: it had too few schools, too few properly qualified teachers, meagre post-primary provision, and in Lanarkshire at least gross overcrowding by 1918–19 with more than one-third of its schools enrolling more pupils than they had places. From 1900, the Church was keen to enter the state system on a basis that would protect its influence upon Catholic education, and many of the city school boards agreed. Negotiations were completed at the end of the war, and although the full absorption took ten years or more, the system of separate Catholic schools within the state system became an invaluable bulwark to the faith. The state now had to ensure that there were sufficient places for Catholic children, and Church funds were released for other vital purposes such as church-building.

Presbyterian hostility to the state take-over of Catholic schools was remarkably muted in 1918 as there were other aspects of the Education Act which raised greater concern. But a Protestant outcry arose the following year after the elections for the new county education authorities. The system of proportional representation led in Glasgow to the return of large numbers of Catholic candidates and Labour representatives 'lifted in by the Roman Catholics who gave them their second vote'. At the next election in the city in 1922, fierce Protestant canvassing halved Catholic representation, but it rose again in 1925. The education issue was one focus for widespread popular sectarianism after the collapse of the post-war economic boom in 1921. We shall examine twentieth-century religious bigotry in the next chapter, but it is important to note here that the Scottish presbyterian establishment, civil as well as ecclesiastical, became in the 1920s more profoundly anti-Catholic and anti-Irish than at any point in modern times. The general assemblies of the Established and United Free Churches demanded immigration control to protect the 'Scots race' and nation, and the police – apparently acting with the approval of the government's chief law officer in Scotland – tried to ban Catholic religious processions in Glasgow and to a new shrine at Carfin in Lanarkshire. Regarded by presbyterian ministers ever since as a burning issue and 'a tactical blunder', the Education Act became in the context of declining influence in civil administration in the 1920s a spark for Protestant reassertion in high as well as low places.

A sense of insecurity troubled presbyterianism in the 1920s. Whilst Catholicism appeared to be in a healthy state, the decay of evangelicalism and the advance of secular values was forcing Protestantism on to the retreat. In one sense, this increased the urgency for reunion between the Established and United Free Churches, but in another sense it heightened presbyterian alarm. Union was based on the appearance, at least, of disestablishing the Church of Scotland. This took various forms: new Articles for a refashioned Church of Scotland which were approved by both denominations in 1918–19 and by parliament in 1921; and a parliamentary Act of 1925 which commuted the teinds to a fixed payment of decreasing value, passed the ownership of churches from heritors, burgh councils and others to Church trustees, passed the ownership of churchyards to town and county councils, and deprived heritors of the right to own or allocate pews. The 1929 union of the two churches was welcomed by most members; only some 25,000 United Free Church adherents seceded over the course of the next twenty years as congregations merged. But the momentum towards reunion, which was well in motion by 1911, increased the presbyterian sense of crisis and retrenchment. For many Established churchmen, untying the knot with the state weakened the presbyterian character of Scotland, and the various measures enacted by parliament were carefully formulated to maintain the appearance of a church still protected by the state. For United Free churchmen, reunion was but a product of evangelical decay evident in low church growth and declining voluntary organizations.

In contrast, the professionalization and proletarianization of evangelicalism after 1890 appeared on the surface to herald a new and influential era in religious social reform. From the late 1880s, full-time missionaries campaigned strenuously for a parliamentary act to institute the local veto plebiscite by which communities could ban the sale of alcohol. At the same time, they used all means to attack the licensed trade. A court case of 1909 concerning the competence of teetotalers to sit as members on licensing authorities revealed how United Free Church missionaries in Glasgow canvassed for objections to licence application on behalf of the Citizens' Vigilance Association – an organization run by the Lord Provost who was a United Free churchman and chairman of the licensing appeal court. The tremendous force with which the temperance issue was thrust into the public arena in Scotland between the 1880s and 1920s gave it a moral righteousness which few politicians (including Labour leaders) and few even in the Established Church could actively resist. Dummy plebiscites were conducted which showed that once a cautious parliament consented, even major cities like Glasgow would vote 'dry'. In Dundee in the 1890s and 1900s, a working-class temperance movement became extremely popular, combining religious campaigning, trades unionism amongst mill girls, and anti-corruption drives on the town council, to develop into both a Labour sect and a millenarian movement – its members carrying 'purity badges' and being expected to 'Vote as you Pray'. In 1903 it became the Scottish Prohibition Party which had branches in many Scottish towns, but it was in the textile city of Dundee that it gained its biggest following and greatest political successes.

But with the partial exception of Dundee, the prohibition campaign was not a mass participatory movement. It developed after 1880 into a political concern reflecting the failure of teetotalism. Adult teetotalism was diminishing rapidly, and especially in the churches; in the 1890s only 14 per cent of the 34,000 registered abstainers in the United Presbyterian Church, and only 29 per cent of 48,000 abstainers and 'moderate drinkers' in the Established Church, were adults. Perhaps more compelling was the appearance of working-class rejection of 'improving' pursuits and 'moral suasion'. In this context, 'moral force' by the state, based on the 'popular will', grew to be the acceptable alternative. In the absence of the local veto before 1920, teetotalers in positions of political influence on town councils and other bodies did as much as they could to promote the temperance cause. In Glasgow, the school board introduced temperance lessons in the 1880s and objected to every application for a drinks licence within the vicinity of its schools. The town council in conjunction with the licensing authority used a variety of means to attack drinking between 1890 and 1914: banning licensed premises from municipal property (a ruling staying in force until the 1970s and accounting for the absence of public houses from council-housing schemes); banning barmaids since they enticed men to drink; making 'unreasonable' sanitary demands on publicans, with the effect of turning the toilets into the most salubrious parts of many pubs; and virtually quarantining public houses and their clients by insisting that passers-by be unable to see in, by banning 'family departments', and generally by preventing drinking from becoming a 'civilized' and 'respectable' pastime. The local state became an energetic agent of the temperance movement at the turn of the century, giving the impression that the reform of drinking habits fell within the same collectivist ideal as that being put forward by the Christian socialists. As Bernard Aspinwall has said: 'In the generation before the first world war, Scottish identity was found not in the church, established or free, but in the town hall; in an ethical Christian community faith rather than "churchianity".'[36]

But the 'moral force' strategy of late Victorian and Edwardian evangelicals was of a different character to Christian-socialist collectivism, and whilst the agendas of the two might intermix, they were fundamentally discrete. The Christian-socialist agenda was based on the socialist agenda, though deriving inspiration from a vision of social harmony rather than class conflict; Christian socialism decayed, but the agenda remained at the forefront of political debate. The prohibition cause, on the other hand, was a product of evangelical puritanism, born of the failure of evangelizing but emboldened by suburban middle-class hostility to the truculent and irredeemable proletariat.

The nature of the prohibition cause became clear when, after the First World War, parliament granted the local veto to Scotland. Under the Temperance (Scotland) Act of 1913, it became possible from June 1920 to hold local plebiscites on whether public houses should be banned or restricted in number. Since the government during 1914–18 had taken major measures to control the licensed trade to help in the war effort (by designating 'dry' areas near munitions factories, for instance), the evangelicals in the churches were looking forward to massive popular support at the polls. Evangelicals called plebiscites in over 500 local wards in Scotland in the first year, and city missionaries, women's guilds, Bands of Hope and other church agencies were marshalled into a massive canvassing campaign. Most of the effort was directed to the large cities since polls were generally not called for rural areas which were in many cases *de facto* 'dry'. But the results were a grave disappointment. Voting for 'No licence' and 'restriction' of licensing was strongest in the old evangelical strongholds of dissent – the Highlands, Hebrides, Northern Isles, fishing villages on the north-eastern and Fife coasts, and industrial communities in west central Scotland. Amongst the large cities, Glasgow returned the greatest number of votes for restriction of licensing, followed some way behind by Edinburgh, Dundee and Aberdeen. But few wards reached the necessary majority for going 'dry'. Outside of the north, most were working-class districts like Whiteinch and Parkhead in Glasgow, and small mining and industrial communities like Kilsyth, Kirkintilloch, Stewarton, Cambuslang and Airdrie, but most of the big-city 'dry' votes were returned in middle- and lower-middle-class suburbs of Glasgow like Kelvinside, Pollokshields, Cathcart, Camphill and Langside. The working-class temperance vote was strongest amongst women, but men seem to have looked upon the 1913 Act as 'class legislation' which attacked their public houses but did not affect licensed hotels and restaurants frequented by the middle classes. In all, only around forty of the 584 Scottish wards polled went 'dry' in the early 1920s, and with re-polls organized by the licensed trade, and with Labour switching its allegiance from prohibition to a 'wet' policy, only seventeen wards remained without public houses by 1927. Evangelicals regarded this as a final rebuttal of their social programme. By 1926, the churches noted that the Bands of Hope were in decline, and the chairman of the Church of Scotland's temperance committee resigned in a mood of depression.

Between the 1870s and the 1920s, the presbyterian churches revelled in electioneering and in promoting the idea that 'the vote is a sacred trust'. Evangelicals and Christian socialists alike sought to found democratic 'cities of God' through participation in civic affairs permitted by the agreeable manner of state intervention. In 1918, the government proposed to use the forthcoming Education Act to bring Scotland into line with England and Wales by abolishing direct elections to education authorities. The presbyterian churches revolted and forced a government retreat. With elections for parish councils, education authorities and the local veto, the evangelicals were convinced that the millennium could be voted in. As the general assembly of the Church of Scotland stated in 1919 of the local veto: 'the abolition of the common public-house, with its attendant evils, would be a step in the way of social reform, which all who seek the Kingdom of God should use their utmost endeavours to secure'.[37]

But there was little to comfort the churches in the 1920s. The unseating of Winston Churchill from his Dundee constituency in 1922 by a candidate of the Scottish Prohibition Party was an example of the electoral frenzy that could be induced in the early part of the decade, but it was short-lived. Within a few years the presbyterian churches lost enthusiasm for electioneering as the results became more discouraging for their various causes. The year 1929 concluded a period of profound change in the civil and secular significance of presbyterian religion. The union of the United Free Church and the Church of Scotland marked the end of dissenting evangelicalism and of the established state church; henceforth, the Church was 'National', recognized by the state and offered 'state protection', but in reality it was an independent entity relying on its own resources. Of equal significance, the *ad hoc* education and poor-relief authorities were abolished, depriving the presbyterian churches of the last means of major influence over their historic fields of interest. And although the

The 'social question' and the crisis for religion 207

local veto remained on the statute book until 1976, and a few places – most famously Kilsyth – remained 'dry', the prohibition cause and that of 'moral force' puritanism generally died for most of Scotland in the 1920s. The secular relevance of popular evangelicalism was channelled in its decay into electioneering where the sectarian element became unacceptable to a civil state that was already in command of the institutions and ideology of public social policy.

Notes

1 J. A. Campbell (1884) *Elders in their Relation to Church Work*, Glasgow, 5.
2 D. G. Barron (1884) *Our Lapsed Masses*, Edinburgh, 4.
3 J. Begg (1866) *Happy Homes for Working Men, and How to Get Them*, London and Edinburgh, iii.
4 Anon. (1906) *The Religious Doubts of Common Men: A Correspondence between Two Laymen*, Edinburgh, 2–3.
5 S. Yeo (1976) *Religion and Voluntary Organisations in Crisis*, London, Croom Helm, where the issues raised in this section are discussed in relation to the English town of Reading between 1880 and 1914.
6 J. C. Gibson (ed.) (1895) *Diary of Sir Michael Connal, 1835 to 1893*, Glasgow, 149, 334, 340.
7 Quoted in W. Grant (1913) *Edward Bayley: His Work Among Young Men and System of Guild Bible Classes*, Edinburgh, 30.
8 I. Maclaren (Rev. John Watson) (1901) *Church Folks*, London, 33, 41–2.
9 R. Q. Gray (1976) *The Labour Aristocracy in Victorian Edinburgh*, Oxford, Clarendon Press, 105.
10 M. Kay (1939) *Romance of the Martyrs' Christian Band*, Glasgow, 30.
11 D. Macleod (1893) *Our Home Mission*, Edinburgh, 12–13.
12 A. S. Matheson (1893) *The Church and Social Problems*, Edinburgh and London, 4.
13 D. Macleod (1895) *Lines of Progress*, Edinburgh and London, 21–2.
14 D. Macleod, *Our Home Mission*, 16.
15 M. MacCallum (1915) *Religion as Social Justice*, Glasgow, 6.
16 K. Hardie (1893) 'The church and the labour problem', *The Thinker*, iii, 108.
17 Glasgow United Trades Council, *Annual Report* (1882–3), 11.
18 Church of Scotland Presbytery of Glasgow, MS Minutes, 28 March 1888, SRO, CH3/171/12.
19 A. S. Matheson, op. cit., 2.
20 A. S. Matheson (1890) *The Gospel and Modern Substitutes*, Edinburgh, 176–7.
21 D. Watson (1908) *Social Problems and the Church's Duty*, London and Edinburgh, 5.

22 A. S. Matheson, *The Gospel and Modern Substitutes*, op. cit., 176–7, 184.
23 D. Watson (1905) *Perfect Manhood*, London, vii.
24 W. S. Bruce (1905) *Some Aspects of Christian Morality*, London, 237.
25 D. Watson, *Social Problems*, 109.
26 A. S. Matheson (1910) *The City of Man*, London, 196–9.
27 W. Muir (1910) *Christianity and Labour*, London, 26.
28 *Reports of the Schemes of the Church of Scotland* (1896), 806–7.
29 Quoted in J. O'Malley (1976) 'The Drift towards Socialism by the Irish Catholic Community in Glasgow 1880–1910', unpublished BA dissertation, University of Strathclyde, 9.
30 Quoted in ibid., 25.
31 W. Knox (ed.) (1984) *Scottish Labour Leaders, 1918–39: A Biographical Dictionary*, Edinburgh, Mainstream, 30, 33.
32 S. Yeo (1977) 'A new life: the religion of socialism in Britain, 1883–1896', *History Workshop*, 4.
33 J. Littlejohn (1963) *Westrigg: The Sociology of a Cheviot Parish*, London, Routledge & Kegan Paul, 40–4.
34 D. Watson (1905) *Perfect Manhood*, 98–9.
35 M. Monies (1974) 'The Impact of the 1872 Education (Scotland) Act on Scottish Working Class Education up to 1899', unpublished Ph.D. thesis, University of Edinburgh, 275–80.
36 B. Aspinwall (1982) 'The Scottish religious identity in the Atlantic world 1880–1914', in S. Mews (ed.) *Religion and the National Identity*, Oxford, Basil Blackwell, 505.
37 *Reports on the Schemes of the Church of Scotland* (1919), 512.

7
Religion in the secular century

War and depression

During the debates on the 'social question' in the quarter of a century leading up to 1914, pessimistic churchmen shouted long and hard about the decline in religious habits and thinking, and about the blurring of the division between the sacred and the profane. For all that, it is perhaps surprising how little had actually changed in the short term. Church membership figures indicate a rapid downturn in growth after 1900 but not a spectacular breaching of religious adherence. Churchgoing may have fallen as many Protestant clergy maintained, but rather than swelling the numbers of the 'lapsed' the trend was towards a more lax definition of 'vital church connection'. Just as double Sunday worship declined, so too did church attendance every Sunday. This helps to explain anomalies in the evidence. Amongst a cross-section of elderly Scots interviewed in the 1970s, over half claimed that both of their parents were regular churchgoers in the late Victorian and Edwardian periods – a figure higher than in any region of Britain except Wales.[1] Yet contemporary evidence would suggest that less than half this proportion of the people attended church each Sunday. The intensity of members' connection with their churches was slackening whilst the number in connection actually continued to rise. The crisis at the turn of the century gravely affected the viability of many Protestant congregations and the role of religion in civil social policy, but the people did not desert the churches.

By the middle of the First World War, it seemed to many in the presbyterian churches that popular religion was facing a crisis of different type and magnitude. Warfare was profoundly counter-religious:

> The manner of life of a soldier in camp, surrounded by all the most subtle temptations, and hardly a voice raised against them, save from chaplains (who mix with officers when not on Church parade), and in the trenches where they are out to slaughter their enemy, by sniping, bombing, raiding, or advancing, creates an atmosphere of sordid existence that has not an atom of faith or belief in the ideal life preached by religion.[2]

A Scottish officer in the Great War noted that sexual immorality at troop bases was matched at home: 'The lack of restraint and reserve since the war among women who were previously modest and respectable is an especially conspicuous and regrettable fact.'[3] Yet the short-term impact of 'total war' upon the Scottish churches was not uniform nor necessarily adverse. The outbreak of hostilities in 1914-15 initiated a surge in membership during a period of stagnancy; overall between 1913 and 1918, the number of members rose by 1.3 per cent in the Church of Scotland and by 3.3 per cent in the United Free Church. But the reverse happened in 1938-43 with a fall of 22 per cent in Church of Scotland members. From the outset, the First World War turned into a jingoistic moral crusade in which the churches, with the connivance of the state, hijacked war culture and focused it on a puritanical campaign which associated morale with morals. The government imposed severe licensing restrictions – including state management of the drinks trade around munitions factories (like Gretna) and military bases (like Invergordon). The churches, town councils and local élites generally urged complete prohibition, and the momentum of their wartime rallies and conferences led directly on to the local veto plebiscites of 1920-1 which, whilst disappointing, still attracted 40 per cent of votes for the temperance cause. The Second World War was different, with conservative churchmen out of step with government policy and the temper of the times. The Church of Scotland consistently castigated the BBC for radio light entertainment programmes like 'ITMA' which brimmed with 'vulgarity' and 'drink suggestiveness', and attacked the government for permitting beer consumption to rise and assisting the brewers in their efforts to 'capture the nation's youth'. The post-war consequence was the collapse of the temperance movement; plebiscites in 1946–7 turned most of Scotland's remaining 'dry' areas 'wet' (including Wick, Lerwick, St Monans, Balfron and Fenwick), and 1947 legislation instituting state management of the drinks trade in the Scottish new towns then under construction was repealed in 1952. The surge of popular puritanism after 1918 was not matched after 1945.

Evidence on the impact of the wars on combatants is confusing. One inter-denominational study conducted in the later stages of the First World War and during demobilization found that 20 per cent of troops in Scottish regiments had a 'vital relationship' with a church compared to 11.5 per cent in English regiments. However, higher figures were returned from largely middle-class Territorial regiments from Scotland, and a Church of Scotland survey of one large troop base in France produced a figure of 40 per cent amongst Scottish soldiers (with all Catholics counted as 'vitally connected'). The lowest figures came from working-class battalions raised in industrial cities of both Scotland and England, and it was amongst these troops that the churches feared the greatest defection after the war. Yet churchmen sensed that the war itself did not generate anything new in the way of working-class alienation from religion, but tended instead to heighten existing dissatisfaction with the churches as upper-class institutions. The men in a Highland regiment, according to one chaplain, considered the churches to be bastions of 'formality and class separateness' whilst avoiding 'social questions, moral reefage and wreckage, brotherhood and brotherliness'.[4] The message in war remained the same as in peace, only it reached the churches louder.

One of the reasons for this was the apparently greater role and more puritanical tenor of religion in the British armed forces of 1914–18 than in those of twenty years later. Chaplains in 'the line', and YMCA canteens and 'church huts' at base camps were extensions of the army system and constituted the 'respectable' competition to the brothels and alcohol. By the 1940s, army morale rested on escapism and organized entertainment with the Church of Scotland canteens providing refreshments and, particularly, writing-paper for troops on the move in a mobile rather than static war. Moreover, the nature of the clergy had been radically changed between the wars with the minister's office now concerned as much with organizing social and sporting events as with saving souls. Lavinia Derwent describes how the ageing incumbent of a Borders' parish had been in the 1920s 'awful holy and awful upright, . . . awful strict, awful old, but not, I gathered, awful human', and how the new minister, her brother, brought a new style to church life; whilst the 'auld meenister' 'kept his place, aloof from his parishioners', the new one 'appeared in plus fours and an open-necked shirt' and not only organized but joined in sporting events and Scout camps.[5] Such a change became apparent in the Second World War as ENSA entertainment shows for troops displaced the stark dichotomy between 'respectable' and 'rough' in the First World War, and diluted the 'religious' content of military life. On the Home Front in 1939–45, the establishment of military installations in coastal communities of the north of Scotland brought southern urban ways into conflict with strongly religious communities. The army, navy and air force condoned drinking in 'dry' areas, and in the parish of Evie and Rendall in Orkney for instance the military and the locals clashed over the hanging out of washing on the Sabbath. Similarly, servicemen from rural areas were found by ministers in the late 1940s to have lost their previous regard for religion, and they were widely attributed with initiating a sharp fall in churchgoing after demobilization. None the less, the end of the war brought a major return to presbyterianism with the number of communicants rising by 175,000 in 1946 – almost a quarter higher than in the last year of the war. However, the Church of Scotland did not regain its 1938 level of active communicants until 1959, indicating that the war had seriously retarded the already slow growth of the first half of the century.

As in other branches of social history, it is difficult in the sphere of religion to separate the long-term effects of twentieth-century war from the consequences of change during peacetime. A major theme in historians' analysis of Scotland since 1918 – perhaps the dominant one – has been economic decay and its impact on popular culture. The country's economy has suffered badly since the end of the Great War due to the structural decline of her nineteenth-century staple industries (textiles, iron, coal, shipbuilding and engineering) and to the sluggish development of new industries which have tended to locate in the south of Britain away from traditional manufacturing and coal-mining areas. Indices of the quality of life, such as morality rates, ownership of domestic appliances and especially standards of housing, have, despite major improvement since 1900, lagged considerably behind those of most other parts of Britain. The state has had to compensate with disproportionately extensive programmes of council-house building, regional aid to industry, and subsidized work schemes such as the construction of the Cunard liner Queen Mary at Clydebank in the 1930s. The slow withering of once-common occupations produced highly diverse political and religious responses similar to those elicited from the handloom weavers between 1815 and 1850, and short-term depressions could foment both religious frenzy and increased disaffection with the churches.

Because of their strongly proletarian composition, Catholics have probably been more affected as a group by economic decline than Protestants. Certainly, of all the Scottish denominations the Catholic Church has responded most consistently and vigorously to the rise of counter-religious influences such as communism amongst its constituency. It seems that a disproportionate number of Communist Party recruits in Scotland were Catholic in the inter-war period, and fierce local contests built up between 'renegade' Catholics and priests during the General Strike and the Spanish civil war. In Fife during the coal strike of 1926 the scabs were identified as 'almost without exception composed of the religious fraternity', and when priests started anti-communist campaigning Party recruits 'vanished like snow off a dyke'.[6] The Catholic Church was probably the best equipped and certainly the most experienced denomination in tackling the adverse effects of economic depression, and does not seem to have suffered serious losses arising from recessionary periods. It is an implicit assumption in the writing of the modern history of British Catholicism that the faith has been invigorated by the combined and apparently connected effects of poverty and discrimination. Priests tended to be drawn from the working classes and to relate well to economic hardship amongst their parishioners, and chapels provided a welcome to all adherents irrespective of financial means. There was certainly social differentiation amongst Catholic worshippers, and increasingly during this century as job opportunities opened up in commerce, local government and the professions, but the sustained numerical importance of the working-class element prevented a major social division from emerging, certainly before the 1970s, between a practising Catholic bourgeoisie and a lapsed proletariat.

The effects of economic depression and industrial decay were more complex upon the Protestant community. On the one hand, social divisions tended to become more marked with middle-class congregations pulling further away from working-class ones. But on the other hand, the ideological schism within the working classes between the opposing ideals of evangelical Protestantism and organized labour was accentuated. Since the 1880s, a proletarian evangelicalism had been developing into the major counter-socialist influence in industrial districts, and in the depressed economic conditions of the 1920s and 1930s this split grew to be a major feature of working-class culture.

Proletarian evangelicalism was highly fragmented and loosely organized, and though extremely visible within working-class areas, it has been and remains relatively elusive to the historian. It was characteristically composed of the very popular temperance friendly societies, and of small missions operating out of hired halls, converted shops or churches bought cheaply from the large denominations during the rationalization of 'over-churched' inner-city areas. Before 1900, independent working-class missions were usually run by committed laymen and devoted most of their efforts to street preaching and anti-Catholic agitation. Whilst the sectarian element did not disappear this century, as we shall see shortly, there was a significant transformation of many missions by the 1920s into self-supporting and semi-permanent congregations under evangelists trained and ordained by larger denominations. Many of these evangelists emerged from localized evangelizing work carried out by the Free Church in the 1880s (in north-eastern fishing villages for instance), but after training at divinity colleges they came to exist on the fringes of mainstream Protestantism. The manner of their work created a separate though inchoate evangelical 'underground' which emphasized the abdication of home-mission endeavour by the principal denominations, and opened the way to unregulated Protestantism in the depressed conditions of the inter-war years.

Economic depression and industrial disputes were often the trigger for outbursts of religious expression amongst the working classes of isolated communities or occupations – outbursts sometimes accompanied by other expressions of civil distress. In Stirlingshire during the depression in the coal industry in the winter of 1921–2, pitched battles erupted between gamekeepers and miners hunting for food, but in the pit village of Plean a religious crusade by a local mission organization led to a revival amongst young people at late-night open-air prayer meetings. As so often in the history of popular religion in Scotland, the authorities frowned upon this disturbing enthusiasm, and on one occasion 'the village constable deemed it his duty to order the meeting to disperse'.[7] The simultaneous depression in the fishing industry caused by a disastrous herring season in the autumn of 1921 led to a millenarian revival guided by Jock Troup amongst the fishermen gathered in East Anglia and subsequently brought home to the coastal villages of the Scottish north-east. At Inverallochy work stopped as children knelt in prayer in the road, bonfires of cigarettes, playing cards, snakes-and-ladders boards and dancing shoes were started, and fishermen at the harbour told Bible stories and 'knelt down together on the shore and engaged in silent prayer, wringing their hands and swaying their bodies to and fro'.[8] News of an 'awakening' would bring evangelists from far and wide to assist and promote the religious work, and in the main they were not sent by the larger churches which became increasingly isolated from those most likely to be affected by emotional religion.

Such outbursts were generally short-lived, and the two cases cited coincided with intense evangelical activity connected with the local veto plebiscites. But proletarian evangelicalism was not limited to occasional revivals. It has had a sustained influence in many sections of Scottish working-class life. Fishing villages have remained, since a crucial revivalist period in the early 1880s, strongholds of temperance culture (such as annual parades) and highly independent and congregationalist churches. Christopher Rush described how his native St Monans has been regarded during this century as the Holy City of the East Neuk of Fife with a 'polyglot of sects': the Church of Scotland, Baptists, Evangelists, Catholics, Congregationalists and four brands of 'fawn-overcoated and bowler-hatted' Brethren who 'hell-fired at you in the streets and summoned you to judgement through your letter box'.[9] Economic prosperity as much as depression has characterized many fishing villages, but misfortune at sea, shifts in fishing stock, and changing forms of organization in the industry are the cause of recurrent uncertainties which seem to play a part in the religious equation of such communities. But proletarian evangelicalism has had a general importance to Scottish Lowland villages, both coastal and inland. Sometimes assisted by visiting Ulster presbyterians and American 'Bible belt' evangelists, *ad hoc* seasonal missions have continued to come to the smaller industrial and formerly industrial communities in the central counties, where they have exploited – perhaps unwittingly – the last vestiges of dissenting presbyterianism amongst mill workers, bleachers and their descendants. Church union after 1900 removed the distinctive preachers and church life which distinguished the old dissenters of industrial villages, and produced an upper-class eldership apathetic to their traditional duties. In this void, periodic evangelistic tours could satisfy a latent presbyterian need left by the 'lukewarmness' and episcopal tendencies of the modern Church of Scotland.

The evangelical 'underground' also had before the 1960s a tremendous appeal in the larger cities. Molly Weir recalls of inter-war Glasgow that as well as 'the big Church, where we went

Religion in the secular century 217

to Sunday School and Bible Class, and had our church parades of Girl Guides and the Boys' Brigade, we had the excitement in summertime of tent missions coming to Springburn to convert us'. The main attraction was Jock Troup who was such 'great value' that he could 'make the flames of hell so real, we felt them licking round our feet, and the prospect of heaven so alluring we often stood up to be saved several times during the week'. She gives a strong impression of the way in which Protestant working-class adults distributed their religious favours amongst a variety of religious organizations (like the Salvation Army, the Church of Scotland and evangelist meetings) for nothing but 'the sheer enjoyment', and how some of the children went along indiscriminately to Sunday schools of Protestant, Catholic and Methodist churches 'just because one gave tattie scones, the next sausage rolls and the other gave pies'.[10] In this way, independent missions fitted into a very variegated religious culture amongst the Protestant working class. It is extremely difficult to hazard a guess at the number of 'adherents' of these missions, in large part because they were a supplement and not an alternative to membership with a mainstream church. But one indication of their influence may well be the significantly high proportion of religious marriages (over 10 per cent) performed in the inter-war period by non-mainstream churches (see Table 5, page 76).

Tent missions, the Salvation Army and the like were sanctuaries to many of the working classes during the depressed 1920s and 1930s. They offered an open and effectual door to those suffering through unemployment and poverty, and made little financial demand upon followers who could in any event adopt an irregular connection with such organizations. The main presbyterian churches, because of their more rigid organization and system of permanent membership, could make fewer concessions to fluctuating fortunes. During the slump of the early 1930s, working-class congregations of the Church of Scotland experienced as much as 60 per cent unemployment among male members, and it was reported that church attendance and recruitment of men fell sharply because those on the dole would not appear in church without suitable clothes and money for collections. Seat rents continued to be set and exacted, and impoverished worshippers seem to have been required – as in the nineteenth century – to apply for suspension of payments or for use of free seats. Whilst church courts noted falls in revenue from seat-renting during depressions and prolonged strikes, there was no general effort made before the 1950s to abolish a system which so clearly symbolized the conjunction of worldly prosperity and churchgoing. The stigma of the gratuitous sitting remained, and the costs of renting the ordinary seats deterred the unemployed and very poor. The system was still in use in forty-nine out of fifty-five Church of Scotland congregations in Dundee in 1961 and the majority of seats were taken, but its abandonment was well under way in other regions during the 1950s and seems to have extended to all parts of Scotland by the end of the 1960s. Its demise was hastened by inflation which reduced the value of rents set during the Victorian period, but more acutely it was prosperity rather than poverty which by then was the churches' main problem.

The Church of Scotland response to poverty and unemployment seems if anything to have aggravated proletarian disaffection, and specifically by perpetuating notions of 'us' and 'them'. Socially concerned ministers opened day centres and canteens in urban and industrial districts, but despite the good intentions and the undoubted succour given, the image was still of philanthropic endeavour by a distant institution for outcast social casualties. The general assembly's Church and Nation Committee, which since the Great War has been the denomination's mouthpiece on political affairs, merely ascribed the cause of unemployment to spiritual and moral decay, and suggested in a half-hearted way that the Church might 'in a limited measure' assist in the search for remedies. The conviction of Victorian evangelicals and turn-of-the-century Christian socialists that social redemption lay in somewhat different forms in Christ's teaching dissipated after 1920, with the result that radicals like the Rev. George (later Lord) MacLeod, who in 1938 founded the semi-political Iona Community in Glasgow, were fairly isolated and often controversial figures within the Church.

During the course of this century, the leadership of the Church of Scotland has become increasingly out of step with the political views of the country as a whole, and to a certain extent also of the

Church's membership. Whilst the Labour Party has risen since the inter-war period to account for around 60 per cent of Scottish MPs, a survey of elders attending the general assembly in the mid-1960s found that three-quarters voted Conservative. This is hardly surprising since of every ten elders, four considered themselves upper or upper-middle class and a further three middle-middle class. Amongst Church of Scotland members in the mid-1980s, 45 per cent voted Conservative with only 17 per cent voting Labour, less than for the centrist Liberals.[11] As in the eighteenth and nineteenth centuries, the eldership has been during this century highly unrepresentative of the church membership, whose social composition has in fact changed little. In a major survey of Falkirk in the 1960s,[12] church affiliation was found to be strongest amongst the small number of the professional classes (who were entirely Protestant), whilst the proportion of lower-middle (or 'intermediate') classes in both Protestant and Catholic churches was between two and three times higher than in the town's population as a whole. But as in Hillis's study of Victorian Glasgow, the bulk of church members came from the skilled working classes who made up just over half of the total population and of Church of Scotland members, 60 per cent of Catholic adherents, and two-thirds of the members of minority Protestant denominations. The partly skilled and unskilled were under-represented, making up a third of the inhabitants but only a fifth of Catholic adherents and 8 per cent of Church of Scotland members. Thus, church membership fell further down the social scale, and became weighted towards the Catholic Church. On the other hand, the most active church members were in the lower social groups; 80 per cent of members amongst the partly skilled and unskilled claimed weekly church attendance compared with around 60 per cent for each of the higher social classifications. In other words, there was a very sharp distinction amongst the working classes between a highly committed though small group of churchgoers and the vast bulk of the 'unchurched'. Taken as a whole, the working classes attend church less frequently than others. In another 1960s survey, of the Prestonfield district of Edinburgh, two-thirds of the working classes were non-attenders ('dormant') compared with 38 per cent of middle classes and 29 per cent of the lower-middle ('borderline') class.[13]

Whilst the twentieth-century Lowland kirk has been dominated by the socially aspiring rather than the proletarian, the self-employed rather than the employed, and fishing-boat skippers rather than crew, the most committed churchgoers in the strongly religious Highlands and Hebrides have been overwhelmingly drawn from relatively poor crofting communities. In an area where state economic aid has been extensively used in trying to slow down the contraction of crofting, the disintegration of townships and out-migration of the young, southern commentators have pointed to 'the tyranny of religion' of the puritanical Free Church, Free Presbyterian Church and even of the Church of Scotland in this region. The dissenting clergy disapprove of sport, secular Gaelic song and dance, and even of religious voluntary organizations. Priests in the strongly Catholic southern Hebrides encourage such activities, contributing to a vibrant secular and Gaelic culture which co-exists happily within religious culture, leading one observer to suggest in the 1950s that a small Hebridean community 'would have a greater chance of survival if it were Catholic than if it followed one of the stricter sects of presbyterianism'.[14]

Amongst adherents to the Free and Free Presbyterian Churches, there is a fierce grip on the outward face of popular culture. Sabbatarianism is strict with Sunday activities centred on churchgoing and other tasks reduced to precisely catalogued acts of necessity (such as milking the cattle) and mercy. Cockerels are tethered to keep the Sabbath quiet, washing is taken in (or if wet rolled up to prevent drying), tourists are discouraged from arriving for bed and breakfast on Sundays, and those already in residence tend to be served food prepared the previous day. At Inverasdale in Wester Ross, motorists are reminded by a large sign of the Lord's stricture in the Fourth Commandment. So vigorously opposed to Sabbath desecration is the Free Presbyterian Church that in 1928 it ruled out the use of public transport by adherents for going to church. Its synod stated:

> allowing for the exteme exigencies of necessity and mercy, no one can lawfully make use of such services, whether for the

Religion in the secular century 221

purpose of attending church or for any less worthy purpose. Any use made of them on the part of an individual entails the giving by that individual of a certain proportionate moral and material contribution towards the support of evil, thereby making him a party to it and involving him in the guilt of it.[15]

It thus became better to miss church than face exclusion for promoting conveyances conducted for 'worldly or carnal expedience'.

The summer communion season survives still in the Hebrides as an intensified and elongated Sabbath stretching from Thursday till Monday with fringe prayer groups as well as church services twice daily. The devout take in successive communions, moving from village to village and staying in homes packed with relatives and friends from other parishes. Apart from the use of the Gaelic language, the tenor of worship is akin to that of eighteenth-century Lowland Seceders with a long sermon delivered with such power and perspiration that some ministers require a towel and change of clothes; the singing is of psalms (since human hymns are unworthy of praising the Lord) unaccompanied by any musical instrument as they too are unworthy.

The message of sermon and prayer is didactic, focusing on the sins and 'backsliding' of the flock. Denunciations of dancing, drinking and Sabbath breaches like watching television (including 'Songs of Praise') flow from the pulpit, and can spill over into civil government. Though the Free and Free Presbyterian Churches do not challenge overtly for political power, many elders and a few clergy are elected as councillors, and since the creation of a separate Western Isles Council in 1975 the opportunity for influencing the local state has risen. Throughout this century, the power of strict presbyterianism has prohibited public houses from practically all non-Catholic districts, and pressure has been brought to bear through elected representatives and petitioning to reduce Sabbath profanation. In the mid-1930s, MacBrayne's ferry services to Lewis on Sundays were stopped, and since then virtually only Catholic islands are visited on the seventh day. In the 1950s BEA had to stop Sunday flights; in the 1960s the new NATO base became the object of presbyterian scrutiny; and in the 1970s oil-related industries had to give undertakings about Sabbath work. Other forms of conflict can arise. Religious conscience forced a strictly presbyterian headmaster to resign from a state school in Easter Ross in the 1970s after considerable media attention had fallen on his refusal to allow a Christmas tree for the children.

An important aspect of such conflict lies in the Gaelic culture of dissent, which certainly in the past has segregated not only Highland from Lowland Scotland but also the native crofters from the incoming 'white settlers' who have customarily dominated professional occupations in the north-west. The Gaelic-speaking area of Scotland has long been contracting – very rapidly during the course of this century, indicated by the demise of Gaelic worship and of dissent in much of the Highlands between the 1880s and 1940s. Even in the Gaelic areas of the west Highlands in recent decades, there has been a drift towards bilingualism in the Free Church; indeed, English services may even be attracting more worshippers than Gaelic services in Wester Ross. Whilst the 'Wee Frees' have been instrumental in suppressing much of the secular and, from their point of view, 'frivolous' activities of Gaelic culture, they have also traditionally been important to the survival of the language. Now that the retreat of Gaelic is entering the heartland of conservative presbyterianism in the extreme north-west, non-Gaelic influence may be increasing in the Free churches – not only in the handful of long-standing urban congregations of migrant Highlanders in Edinburgh and Glasgow, but in other areas both Highland and Lowland. In at least one instance, an immigrant American minister has set up an entirely new Free Church congregation drawing upon non-Highland adherents. More broadly, the dissenting churches and especially the Free Presbyterian Church have in recent years cultivated strong links with English-speaking clergy and laity in the proselytizing and book-trade network of British, Irish and American evangelicalism. However, the base of these smaller denominations remains in the Western Isles, the last bastion of both Gaelic and high churchgoing.

It is prudent, though, to be cautious about the apparent 'religiosity' of the Highlands and Hebrides, for an inherent element in the presbyterian society there is 'backsliding'. Church strictures against drink do not prevent the existence of many illegal 'bothans' or shebeens in unused but often well-appointed croft houses or byres; those on the Isle of Lewis can be thronged until morning, contributing to a high rate of alcoholism. Churchgoers are notorious for their irreverence, especially in the less-populated districts where often poorly educated and elderly lay missionaries may be received with less than full solemnity in the characteristic cream, green or brown corrugated-iron churches shared by congregations of the Free and Free Presbyterian Churches. In a more general way, on Sundays as on other days of the week, outward piety is tempered by pragmatism and silent revolt (especially amongst men and the young) which led one post-war observer to remark that the crofters were 'no more interested in the destiny of their souls than they were in the destiny of their poultry'.[16] The religion of the Highlands, but more particularly of the Hebridean crofting areas, is in many ways pre-industrial in form. Whilst church attendance is strongly promoted in the 'modern' fashion, the modest pace of social and economic change perpetuates rites and practices of popular religion as a communal experience which embraces both the ardent and the apathetic.

Prosperity

Despite the trauma of industrial decay in the Lowlands and the lack of self-sustained growth in the Highlands and Hebrides, there has been for all Scots a marked improvement in standards of living and quality of life since 1900. Although one historian has summarized Scotland's recent history as a progression from 'a substantial world industrial power in 1914 to its present insecurity and insignificance',[17] it is arguably in rising real incomes and consumption that the origins of modern religious change are located. As far as the working classes are concerned, and for many of the lower-middle classes as well, the most profound transformation took place in housing. Because of the depth and extent of the housing crisis inherited from the nineteenth century, Scotland has had to rely more than any other country in the non-communist world on public-sector house-building and subsidized renting to reduce overcrowding (especially in one- and two-roomed tenement flats in which more than half the population lived before 1914). Between 1919 and 1965, 87 per cent of all houses built were rented out by state agencies (more than twice the rate for England and Wales), and the way in which slum clearance and rehousing was managed in massive programmes presented the churches with an enormous logistical challenge. The ecclesiastical response has been variable, and together with the grave problems of depersonalization, isolation, high unemployment, vandalism and poor sense of community that afflicted many of the new sprawling 'schemes', this has created a different and difficult role for organized religion.

In the main, the 'leakage' of church members seems to have been relatively low in the early housing schemes of 1920–35. The people affected were mainly the 'respectable' working classes who were rehoused close to existing housing and churches. Still, the church response was slow; the Church of Scotland built only twenty extension churches in 1920–32, and the Catholic Church twelve in west central Scotland. The more sweeping slum clearance and erection of large estates in the later 1930s was more serious. The Church of Scotland was reluctant to raise money for new congregations, though thirty churches and twenty church halls were started. In 1940–1, the Church lost some 20,000 communicants as a result of out-migration from city centres due to rehousing and wartime dislocation. From 1945, greater efforts were made to stem the tide. The Catholic Church was the most energetic in the west of Scotland, founding thirty-five new parishes in 1945–50, a further forty-one in 1951–60 and twenty-six in 1961–70 to cater for its adherents who were proportionately the most affected by rehousing in the post-war period. The Episcopal Church was also active, especially in the new towns, but the efforts of the Church of Scotland remained sluggish despite the use of temporary 'hall-churches' after the war. The surfeit of Victorian churches in wrong locations remained a millstone round the presbyterian church, exacerbated by its traditional inability to respond quickly to demographic changes.

Whilst council housing did not necessarily mean an age of luxury for the Scottish working classes, it interacted with other

Religion in the secular century 225

developments to throw up new forms of leisure and culture which helped to undermine the role of religion. For one thing, the dramatic increase in the space available in the Scottish home permitted the development of domestic leisure pursuits which have arguably become more important in Scotland than elsewhere in Britain. Clergymen identified the radio and, by the late 1950s, the television as major causes of declining religious interest and churchgoing, and the relative cheapness of councilhouse tenancies together with the later development of working-class car-ownership (from the late 1960s) initiated a strong trend towards quick adoption of every new home entertainment device: colour televisions, music centres, video games. Alternative communal activities also competed with the churches and church organizations; bingo developed very rapidly in the late 1950s as an alternative activity for working-class women, and in the same vein filling in and checking football-pool coupons became an important element in the domestic liturgy of men which ministers found in the 1950s to be usurping religious concerns and morals. In one sense, the growth of bingo was an aberration, for the trend was away from communal leisure pursuits (including spectator sport) towards domestic leisure in which the family spent time together either in the home or elsewhere. In the shift from public house, cinema and dance hall, the churches and religious voluntary organizations have also suffered, for they could no longer provide the comfortable surroundings nor the form of activities which the post-war generation came to expect. In an important sense, the evangelical structure of voluntary organizations, in which leisure was segregated into separate age, sex and occupational groups, was not suited to the trends of the twentieth century, and the churches found that their activities just could not attract families on a regular basis.

In reflection of this, the most popular and well-supported church occasions of the post-war period have been glittering grand events: most notably for Protestants the Billy Graham crusade in 1955 and for Catholics the visit of Pope John Paul II in 1982. The first was preceded by some eight years' evangelistic campaigning by 'Christian Commandos' and by the 'Tell Scotland' movement led by a few energetic Church of Scotland ministers and to which BBC radio in Scotland lent a degree of air-time and co-operation that would doubtless be prohibited today. The efforts of these campaigns probably appeared more successful than they really were because of what followed. For six weeks around Easter 1955 nightly mass rallies of some 10,000 people packed the Kelvin Hall in Glasgow, and for two of those weeks others attended churches and halls around the country to participate in the services via relay television. The concluding Good Friday service at Hampden Park attracted just short of 100,000 people, and throughout the crusade both the BBC and especially the Scottish press were carefully and successfully manipulated by the inter-denominational organizing committees. But it would be a misnomer to call the crusade a 'revival'. Only 20,000 (or under 3 per cent) of the 830,000 who attended the principal rallies in Glasgow came forward to 'make decisions for Christ': of these 70 per cent were women, 73 per cent were under thirty years of age (11 per cent under twelve), and 62 per cent were already regular church attenders. The occasions were visual spectacles, carefully orchestrated and designed, but not emotional outpourings. The audiences seem to have been composed overwhelmingly of the middle-aged and the elderly, mostly middle class, sitting stiffly erect and defensively muffled in sturdy overcoats with many of the women in their finest fur hats, coats and tippets. The 'enquirers' were the young, often the very young, and the lasting effects were slight. The bulk of the Protestant clergy were faintly hostile to the crusade and to the 'Tell Scotland' movement with which it was connected. Nearly 70 per cent of Church of Scotland ministers reported that all forms of evangel-ization in 1954–6 had 'little or no effect' on their congregations, and from 1956 the communicants' roll started its inexorable decline.

The papal visit twenty-seven years later generated a greater show of enthusiasm, predominantly amongst the young – especially schoolchildren – at rallies in Edinburgh's Murrayfield stadium and Glasgow's Bellahouston Park. The visit to presby-terian Scotland was of enormous symbolic importance, but like the Billy Graham crusade it seems to have had little effect on

Religion in the secular century 227

long-term trends in Catholic adherence. It was significant that the vigorous and irrepressible children's chanting, which nearly overwhelmed John Paul's addresses, was not delivered in any available religious vocabulary but in the tunes and rhythms of the pop world and the football terracing. In terms of church connection, the papal visit does not seem to have stemmed the outflow which set in during the late 1970s in west central Scotland. Whilst the Catholic population of the country grew from 446,400 in 1901 to 823,500 in 1977, it then fell by just under 10,000 in the next six years with the losses occurring entirely in the archdiocese of Glasgow and the dioceses of Motherwell and Paisley. Although twentieth-century statistics are probably not responsive to year-by-year fluctuations in church adherence, it seems clear that religious 'spectaculars' made no impression on established downward trends.

The inability to maintain religious or church-based leisure in the weekly life of the people has been a major cause of the declining role of the church as a focus in urban community life. This change has been more slow and more uneven in rural districts, but all forms of voluntary organization arrived quite late in country areas – mostly between 1880 and 1950 – and interacted with the transition to urban-style social divisions. An important perspective here is the erosion of the introspective parish community in which civil and religious authority rested with local élites. The loss of local autonomy in the 1920s and 1930s, through the demise of parish councils, parish school boards and boards of heritors, ended the secular functions and symbolism of the minister, the schoolmaster and the parish church. But in a wider sense the decline of the self-sufficient parish economy and improved transport to nearby towns for leisure, administrative and other purposes destroyed parochial deference and gave birth in the middle decades of the century to a rural egalitarianism. A Peeblesshire minister noted in 1963 that with 'the development of democracy and the claim for personal liberty of thought there has been a lessening of authority in the realm of the spirit'.[18] Declining church connection went hand in hand with the rise of an industrial relationship between farm workers on the one hand and farmers and landowners on the other. The final ending of the practice of heritors reserving pews for tenants seems to have instigated a major breach in church connection amongst the rural middle ranks in the inter-war period; and with continuous advances in farming techniques, a falling workforce, and the wartime need for improved food supply, farmers were by the 1940s and 1950s pressing their employees to use the Sabbath not for churchgoing but for the utilization of expensive capital machinery in ploughing, harvesting and tending to livestock. The church union of 1929 also had an effect with many lower social groups in the United Free Church being unable to countenance amalgamation with the traditional 'opposition' in the 'Auld Kirk'. Whilst a few rural parishes maintained very vigorous community religion – as in the village of Craigie in Angus where it was claimed in the late 1960s that every child was a member of the United Free Church Band of Hope – in general the arrival of improved bus services to nearby towns distracted the attention of the young from the local church, and with its decline the heart of many rural parishes was torn out. The fate of the rural kirk in large measure reflects the fate of Lowland rural society as a whole. Where town–country commuters have moved in since the late 1960s, the churches become imprisoned by suburbia; where they don't, paths to churches become overgrown, rights-of-way lapse, and many attend church only for marriage, baptism, and funerals, and perhaps also for annual communion after which a herdsman in the south of Scotland was heard to exclaim around 1960: 'Ah well, that's it by for another year.'[19]

At the beginning of the century, the slowing down of church growth to a level which barely kept pace with population growth was due to the failure in recruiting from children of those who were not church members. A key element in the fall in church membership which started in the 1950s was an alarming failure to recruit even the offspring of adherents. This change in the religious attitudes of the young has not been straightforward. For instance, there was between the 1930s and the 1950s a revolution in the manner of presbyterian baptism and marriage which seemed to indicate increasing 'religiosity'. Since the eighteenth century, it had been customary for both ceremonies to take place in the home, or in the case of marriage, by the inter-war period, in hired halls or dining suites in which the reception was also to take place. This applied across the social spectrum, but was radically transformed in mid-century by the demand for the romance of the church wedding and the baptism of children before a congregation. Ministers welcomed this as a sign of greater interest in the solemnity of religious rites, and in the same way were delighted with the young's demand in the 1950s for Christmas watchnight services – an occasion like all others in the Christian year which it had been anathema for presbyterians in the past to celebrate. But the bemused delight of ministers barely concealed their unease with the secularizing romance and ill-formed church connections which this 'religious' enthusiasm gave rise to. One Dundee minister observed in the 1950s that the new-fangled watchnight services were being covertly used by young lovers to exchange engagement rings, and church baptism was patently not ensuring the church connection of either the child or the parents. Between the mid-1950s and 1980, the number of Church of Scotland Sunday-school pupils almost halved, and a spectacular fall in church baptisms followed: between 1967 and 1982, they fell by half in the Church of Scotland and by almost 40 per cent in the Catholic Church. This rate of decline is higher than the fall in the birth rate, and would seem to indicate a considerable loss of church connection amongst young married couples.

The origins of this alienation lay at a younger age. A Falkirk survey of over 200 schoolchildren in the 1960s found that 27 per cent stopped attending church before the age of ten, and that by the age of thirteen two-thirds had given up church connection. The crisis of the young reached its peak in the Church of Scotland between 1967 and 1974. The Church's preoccupations with promoting the temperance movement and opposing gambling virtually disappeared to make way for agonizing over the revolution in youth culture. In abandoning the temperance cause, the Church also tried to move with the times by seeking compromises with the hippy-inspired culture of love and opposition to war. There was much in the young's hostility to the Biafran and Vietnam wars, and in their humane and liberal outlook, with which the younger clergy could sympathize. The general assembly was clearly affected by the mood of the times, and for example was remarkably uncritical of the legalization of abortion, the decriminalization of homosexuality, and the liberalization of divorce. In a more profound way, the Church was affected at all levels by the 'moral metamorphosis'. The committee on moral welfare advised the assembly in 1970:

> Need the Church always deplore this new 'permissiveness' as an unalloyed disaster? If the sanctions of commandment and convention are gone, people are set free to respond to goodness for its own sake, under no compulsion, constrained and sustained by the love of Christ and not by the fear of a lost respectability.[20]

And the Church tried to envelop this conventionless morality of western youth within its pale. Energetic youth leaders started church dances and discos in 1966-9, but kirk sessions quickly became concerned with the frequency with which the police visited their premises late on Saturday nights to sort out minor gang fights and complaints from neighbours. The problem became, as one Angus church put it in 1970, to put youth activities on an 'acceptable footing'. It became clear by the early seventies that the Church could not pursue and court youth culture whilst retaining its traditional public standing. The Moral Welfare Committee changed its approach radically between 1970 and 1972. In the first year it found 'the spirit of the age with its new found freedom' providing a healthy challenge to Christians 'to re-think the implications of Christian morality', though in an arch piece of sexism it considered that 'it is the promiscuous girl who is the real problem'. But by 1972, the committee was quite exasperated with 'the turbulent continent of morality' and virtually ceased trying to construct responses to the unfolding 'promiscuous age'.[21]

The decay of church connection amongst Scotland's youth seems to be closely connected with the burgeoning prosperity which, despite the economic difficulties of the later 1970s and early 1980s, has continued to dominate the economic experience of the vast majority of the population. It was during the seventies that the Catholic Church first had to come to terms with a sizeable upwardly mobile and young middle class within its constituency which, in the suburbs of Glasgow and in new towns like East Kilbride, has pushed the Church towards a more bourgeois outlook. Catholics have really only broken through in significant numbers into middle-class occupations since the Second World War, and mainly since the late 1960s, creating a growing section of prospering lapsed Catholics with which the Scottish Church might be particularly unpractised at dealing. But the problem is arguably more acute in the Church of Scotland which has felt uneasy in its relationship with the generation that reached its teens in the mid-1960s. Their disaffection with organized religion was of a scale and nature which confounded both the liberal compromisers and the conservative hard-liners in the Church, and has been compounded since as those who breathed in the heady atmosphere of rebellion, soft drugs and sexual 'freedom' in the decade from 1965–75 have established careers in the professions, married (and increasingly divorced), and reared unbaptized children who never see the insides of a church or a Sunday-school hall.

Explaining the reasons why prosperity appears to be undermining church connection is more difficult than merely drawing the correlation. One strain of analysis, common in the churches and in religious psychology, is to regard religious faith as being displaced by 'substitute religions' – materialism, consumerism or, as in some countries, Marxism. As far as Scotland and Britain are concerned, there has been no state-prosecuted frontal assault on religious habits or thinking as in communist countries. But this is not to deny the possibility that a significant ideological change may be taking place in regard to popular attitudes both to the churches and to the lexicon of precise 'beliefs', doctrines and practices they uphold. Trends in lifestyle – towards materialism, if you like – are important here, and notably amongst the younger generations of the upper working classes and the middle classes. A key factor is home ownership which is growing rapidly in Scotland from a very low base, and which is effecting a marked distinction between the generations. For children brought up in either middle-class or council housing, the future has for more than a decade lain in 'starter' homes sited in isolated estates with minimal provision for community facilities like shops, schools or churches. This is not a planning 'fault' like the lack of amenities of the council-housing schemes of the inter-war period and the 1950s. It is a part of the culture and lifestyle being sought by two-income families, for whom a car gives access to amenities. Pervasive and representative in the Lowlands is Sunday shopping at hypermarkets, DIY warehouses and general markets. The advance of Sunday trading since the 1960s has occurred in a part of Britain that was previously thought to be so Sabbatarian in its inclinations that prohibitive laws of the kind still in force in England and Wales were considered unnecessary. The paradox is acute. In Scotland the most institutionally secular Sundays in Britain co-exist with those of the most vigorous churchgoing. The 'adherents' of the two are not mutually exclusive; Sabbath shopping, work and DIY in the home and on the car stand not as denunciations of religious faith. But they do represent collectively a profound undermining of traditional Scottish presbyterianism.

Prosperity works against the churches in another way. With the advance of the state in social amelioration since the 1890s, the churches and religious charities have found a role in filling the social-work gaps in statutory provisions whilst at the same time pressing for legislation to eliminate those gaps. A case in point is the adoption of children which was fairly free of state regulation until 1948 when children's officers were appointed to enforce an earlier enactment of 1930. Agencies such as the Church of Scotland and the St Margaret of Scotland Catholic Adoption Society continued to work with the state until the 1970s when the local authorities assumed the bulk of adoptions – and when in any event opinion moved in favour of supporting one-parent families, leading to a marked drop in the number of children available for adoption. The diminution of poverty, promoted mainly by the state's actions, has turned many religious charities into pressure groups which tend not to involve large numbers of laity. Religious pressures and ethics become subsumed in a secular welfare morality, and the churches' visible role becomes increasingly hazy.

Religion in the secular century

Such trends do not intimate the decay of religious faith, but they do demonstrate the declining social significance of religion. In a society which in historical terms is prospering, diminishing numbers of people are driven by religion to social action, and few believe that the churches have any bearing upon social change. More broadly, the prosperity of the sixties, seventies and eighties is destroying the community-based value systems, the localized network of friends and relatives, and the very communities themselves which formerly sustained church congregations, religious organizations and Christian ritual. It was issues of socialism, the treatment of poverty and social inequality that lay at the root of defection from organized religion in the first half of the century; the second half is demonstrating that worldly success comes unaided by religion.

Sectarianism and ecumenicalism

On 31 May 1982 Pope John Paul II entered the precincts of the Church of Scotland divinity college and general assembly building in Edinburgh, and beneath the statue of the Scottish reformer, John Knox, shook hands with the assembly moderator. This was a major symbolic occasion in Scottish church relations, the culmination of some eight decades of ecumenical advance. Yet two years earlier there had occurred a major riot at Hampden Park in Glasgow at the end of the Scottish Cup Final when Protestant–Catholic hatred fired Rangers and Celtic supporters to running skirmishes on the pitch with mounted police attempting to restore order by repeated cavalry charges. These two phenomena – sectarianism and ecumenicalism – have both been pronounced features of twentieth-century Scottish life through prosperity and depression. Until the middle of the century they were not opposing trends but in many ways mutually reinforcing ones. Increasing church co-operation was almost entirely within presbyterianism, bringing about the unions of 1900 and 1929, and responding to the perceived crises first of the 'social question' between 1890 and 1914 and then of Catholic advance in the 1920s. In the context that prevailed up to the Second World War, ecumenicalism was accepted by many presbyterians because it united and strengthened Protestantism in the face of diminishing kirk influence in civil affairs. But after 1945 the ecumenical agenda had to be expanded if Christian unity was to be furthered, leading after the 1950s to the opening up of 'conversations' not only with other reformed churches such as the Methodists and the Congregationalists, but also with the Scottish Episcopal Church and, though more cautiously, with the Roman Catholic Church. From this point, it was apparent that ecumenicalism and sectarianism were tugging in opposite directions with the first emerging as an affair of church governors (and especially the clergy) and the second developing a secular and 'unchurched' character.

The foundations of anti-Protestant feelings amongst Scottish Catholics may be fairly easily explained. Both the Catholic Church and its constituency were persecuted by the early-modern Protestant state, and despite the slow erosion of discriminatory laws between 1793 and 1926 Scottish society (and the British constitution) has continued to be viewed by Catholics as hostile. With the immigration of large numbers of Irish Catholics in the nineteenth century, the Catholic Church considered that its interests were best served by encouraging a 'fortress' mentality amongst its adherents. The result was a certain paranoia in the defensive attitude of Catholic institutions in Scotland. At the turn of the century Celtic Football Club believed that there was overt discrimination against it in the area of public transport; Glasgow's underground railway provided a convenient station for the Rangers' stadium but passed nowhere near Celtic's, and higher prices were allegedly charged by railway companies for Celtic supporters' trains. When in the early 1960s the Catholic Church of St James in Renfrew was the target for sectarian attacks (from uprooting the flagpole to arson in the church hall), the priest questioned whether the police were doing sufficient to catch the culprits. In this context, attempts to abolish the religiously divided state education system set up in 1918 are looked upon by the Catholic Church as attacks on its schools and the bulwark to the faith they provide. The Catholic schools are regarded as the only major concession wrung from a Protestant state, and their continued survival is taken as a measure of religious emancipation. For Catholic adherents, discrimination has in the past taken many forms – most importantly in employment where entry to skilled occupations has been slowed down by the hostility of Protestant employers (apparent during the slump of the 1930s when 'No Catholics need apply' signs appeared at some factories) and of Protestant artisans and their trades unions. Catholic entry to higher education and thus to many professions was until the 1960s and 1970s restrained by poverty and lack of opportunity, and although for many of the young in the west of Scotland going to college at seventeen or eighteen now provides the first encounter with those of the 'opposing' faith, the universities of Glasgow and Strathclyde still administer bursaries which are restricted to Protestants. As older industries have declined and been replaced since the 1930s by employment in companies whose bases are located outwith Scotland, so job discrimination has diminished, though it is still said by some Catholics to continue.

Protestant anti-Catholicism is complex – in part because it has assumed diverse forms, and in part because of the impact of secularization. Its origins lie in the anti-papist theology and political philosophy of the early-modern period, the strains of which were resilient both in the presbyterian churches and in the civil state in Scotland until well into the twentieth century. In presbyterian political theology, Catholicism is an undemocratic tyranny which represses civil rights and individual conscience. From Rome, the 'anti-Christ' (the Pope) usurps the Protestant constitutions of other countries by employing unbiblical rites and practices (such as the mass) to destroy rationality. Thus, religious worship has political implications. In 1778, the Glasgow synod of the Church of Scotland warned against giving freedom to the Catholic Church because people 'are seduced into that detestable superstition whose peculiar worship is idolatry . . . which, the more it advances, the more powerfully it operates in pulling up the foundations of the Protestant state'.[22] The notion that popery diminishes liberty is central to the ideology of anti-Catholicism, giving rise to the Protestant march which in Scotland since the 1870s has been taken as the acid test of 'freedom': if the police and civil authorities prevent Orange marchers from going where they please – in practice through Catholic districts – then the Protestant state is crumbling. In most communities in the west of Scotland, Orange marches have generally been permitted to traverse or at least skirt Catholic quarters, and on many occasions in the 1920s and 1930s this led to severe rioting. Whilst the level of violence attending such occasions has fallen since then, the marching season from March to August (with a high peak in July) still foments disturbances: in 1986 at Dumbarton, for instance, and at Cowie near Stirling where the first Protestant march ever was permitted by the local authority but broken up by the police after the local Catholic priest and Church of Scotland minister lay down together in its path.

This last incident illustrates the declining church contribution to anti-Catholicism. Until the nineteenth century, anti-popery was orchestrated by the presbyterian churches with the overt assistance of the political establishment. But from the 1790s, there began a protracted ecclesiastical disengagement from sectarianism. Ministers developed an ambivalent attitude towards it, characterized on the one hand by distaste for the crudity and 'roughness' of popular bigotry, and for the social disharmony it created in an increasingly sophisticated society, but tempered on the other hand by an awareness that anti-Catholic feeling was a major 'religious' sentiment amongst the Protestant working classes – especially of the west of Scotland – which could be, or perhaps had to be exploited by the churches in their home-mission work. By 1829, significant numbers of presbyterian clergy, notably Thomas Chalmers and dissenters, supported the Catholic Emancipation Act; yet such was the strength of hostility of the skilled working class to Catholic Irish immigration into the Glasgow region in the next three decades that some ministers, particularly from the Calvinist wing of the Free Church, developed links with artisan Protestant defence organizations. The range of Protestant attitudes was apparent during the celebrations in 1860 for the tercentenary of the Scottish Reformation when most church courts declined to participate. The principal event was a four-day conference in Edinburgh which awkwardly combined academic historical lectures by divinity professors with rousing anti-Catholic speeches by vociferous anti-papists. The organizers invited every Protestant clergyman in Scotland, but were disappointed when only 150 turned up, outnumbered by ministers from Ireland and overseas. But in August 1860, just when the presbyterian churches were playing down what one newspaper called 'the hackneyed subject of Popery', disturbances erupted on successive Sundays in the Catholic Briggate district of central Glasgow in response to anti-Catholic preaching by a Free Church minister from an elevated external pulpit attached to a mission church built for the religious revival of the time. The scheme 'to harangue the multitude on Sundays' was described by a Catholic newspaper as 'an audacious impertinence', but the local Protestant press regarded the unrest and the eventual police instruction to desist preaching as 'a plot . . . of the Romish authorities matured in cold blood, for the purpose of putting down the right to proclaim the Gospel'. Sixteen hundred Orangemen, ready to fight, congregated at the end of the month to disperse 'groups of navvies, mechanics, and masculine-looking women, of unmistakeable Hibernian aspect, [who] might be seen laying their heads together in a low earnest manner, that meant mischief'.[23]

The sectarian appeal to the Protestant working class, and attempts to convert Catholics, were significant ingredients in Victorian evangelization. But they lacked the enthusiastic sanction of the presbyterian churches as a whole, and with the decay of church missions after 1890 the leadership of the Protestant crusade visibly passed to mostly independent and proletarian missions.

Despite the development of harmonious links between presbyterian and Catholic clergy at the turn of the century (through joint work for school boards and Christian socialist campaigns, for instance), the 1920s and 1930s were characterized by a frenzy of anti-Catholicism to which the Church of Scotland and the United Free Church felt compelled to contribute. The evangelical electoral campaign for the local veto in the early 1920s also encompassed a strong and popular Protestant reaction, heightened by the post-war depression, to the advent of 'Rome on the rates' in the form of the Catholic state schools. A high-powered report of the Church of Scotland general assembly of 1923 urged the government to stem Irish immigration (although it was fairly low by then), stating of Irish Catholics:

> They cannot be assimilated and absorbed into the Scottish race. They remain a people by themselves, segregated by reason of their race, their customs, their traditions, and above all, by their loyalty to their Church, and gradually and inevitably dividing Scotland, racially, socially, and ecclesiastically.[24]

The Irish were undermining Scots' thriftiness, independence and reverence for the Sabbath; and having already destroyed 'the unity and homogeneity of the Scottish people', what was next in prospect was 'the loss of the Scottish race to civilisation'. But despite the vigour of the language in this report, the Church sought to appear responsive to the feelings of its constituency without fanning the flames of bigotry. A committee of the assembly merely went through the motions for the remainder of the inter-war period, making an annual appeal to the Secretary of State for the ending of immigration.

Through their public stance on the Catholic 'threat', the presbyterian churches remained in the 1920s a focus for popular Protestant opinion at elections for the education authorities and, in west central Scotland at least, at local veto plebiscites. But the repeated failure of the plebiscites in Catholic districts, and the abolition of the directly elected education authorities in 1929, contributed greatly to the secularization of sectarianism. Small political movements of Protestant extremists started in the early 1920s, but they only emerged as significant electoral forces after 1930 when the presbyterian churches had been effectively prevented by the abolition of *ad hoc* authorities from continuing to be the rallying point for the popular Protestant vote. The Scottish Protestant League and Protestant Action gained sizeable numbers of votes and several councillors in municipal elections in Glasgow and Edinburgh respectively; the League attracted as much as a third of the votes in Glasgow in the early thirties, and Protestant Action achieved a dominance in the Leith area of Edinburgh. These two parties, which had links with Protestant gangs and a style and rhetoric borrowed from the fascists, seem to have had little overt or covert support from the churches. Moreover, the vocabulary they employed was markedly devoid of the political theology that had underpinned earlier articulations of anti-Catholicism. Though their popularity hinged on Protestant unemployment during the slump, and was all but destroyed by economic recovery in the later 1930s, they marked an important stage in the separation of the churches from Protestant extremism.

The decline of anti-Catholicism in the mainstream presbyterian churches is associated with the ecumenical momentum which started with presbyterian reunification early in the century. Within three years of the final and major reunion in 1929, 'conversations' commenced between the Church of Scotland and the Scottish Episcopal Church, and a report on the common ground between the two denominations was issued in 1934. The anti-Catholic tide of opinion ensured it a hostile reception in the presbyterian church, but discussions were resumed in 1949, culminating in the so-called 'Bishops' Report' of 1957 in which the presbyterian promoters of Christian unity urged the general assembly to institute bishops in the Church of Scotland as a prelude to union. A strong Protestant outcry erupted, setting back formal negotiations for a decade, at which point an enlarged 'Multilateral Church Conversation' commenced involving not only the Church of Scotland and the Episcopal Church but also the Congregational Union, the Methodist Synod in Scotland, the United Free Church and the Churches of Christ (now the United Reformed Church within Scotland), with the Roman Catholic Church and the Baptist Union as 'participant observers'. The stated aim of the Conversation is 'the visible unity of the People of God' and the erasing of Scotland's inheritance of 'a multiplicity of Churches working in latent or open rivalry'.[25] Discussions hitherto have concentrated almost entirely on doctrinal issues, and whilst reasonable progress has been achieved on baptism and even the Eucharist, the sticking point for the presbyterians has been the recommendation, reiterated in 1985, for the Church of Scotland to adopt bishops. But though the general assembly seems on the surface resolute in rejecting this step, the weight of opinion is behind the continuation of the Conversation and an accommodation with episcopacy.

It is not entirely clear why the ecumenicalists in the Church of Scotland have been able to enjoy quite such freedom to negotiate with the fundamental elements of presbyterian church government, nor why it should be that the pressure for unification and willingness to make the greatest concessions for that end should emanate from what is by far the largest denomination in the Conversation – the membership of the Church of Scotland outnumbering that of the Episcopal Church by more than twenty to one. The reasons may derive from the earlier presbyterian reunions which necessitated the weakening of doctrinal and liturgical control to the point that extensive variation in practice and attitude could co-exist in a very broad church. One consequence has been, since the 1960s, a modest though significant growth in *ad hoc* church union at congregational level. In some large housing schemes, new towns and over-churched city districts (which now include middle-class suburban areas, especially in the east of Scotland), congregations of various denominations have come to arrangements to share the same churches and to amalgamate voluntary organizations; the most notable example is probably the 'ecumenical parish' at Livingston new town. In other places, especially older communities in inner-city or outlying industrial districts, such ecumenical *rapprochement* is unthinkable – or at least very unlikely if church membership is to be sustained. At a general level, it seems that ecumenical pressure tends to come more from the east of Scotland than the west, and more from the clergy than from the laity. Divinity students of various denominations in Scotland train in common university classes, and are taught by lecturers now representing a wide cross-section of faiths. The geographical origins of new Church of Scotland clergy have shifted markedly; between 1910 and 1950 the proportion drawn from the unecumenical Highlands fell from almost half to a fifth, and the proportion from rural areas generally from nearly three-quarters to a half. Younger ministers from urban backgrounds bring to congregational life a strong desire for Christian union, and though many older presbyterians baulk at the erasure of schismatic tradition, a money-conscious church bureaucracy will welcome the disposal of church buildings.

Arguably, there is a more fundamental factor behind the influence of church-union negotiators: the progressive though uneven weakening of the presbyterian character of the Church of Scotland. The trend towards 'high churchism' – towards liturgical practices, church architecture and an ambience redolent of episcopacy or, as some would see it, 'Romanism' – has been by no means confined to the twentieth century, but can be discerned for instance in eighteenth-century Moderatism and in nineteenth-century worship reform. Some of the reforms of worship (such as the introduction of hymns and organs), carried out in the context of Victorian evangelical revival, stood at the head of a series of twentieth-century changes which have dissolved much of what used to be considered central to the traditional style of Scottish presbyterianism. The fast days which until the late nineteenth century constituted the presbyterian calendar have been slowly substituted by the episcopal Christian Year: initially Christmas and Easter in the first half of the century, and more recently the other episodes in Christ's progress. The celebration of communion has become more frequent (weekly in some cases), and in the last twenty years a number of congregations – again particularly in the east of Scotland – have moved considerably towards 'high church' practices, instituting for instance responses during prayer, and kneeling. In decoration, presbyterian churches in Lowland areas have during this century replaced the traditional plain glass windows with 'idolatrous' stained glass. Most symbolically, perhaps, has been the reinstatement of the quasi-episcopal dignity of pre-Reformation cathedrals. Until the mid-nineteenth century, these were much and deliberately neglected, having been shorn of their saints' titles and status when in the sixteenth century pre-eminence passed to the other municipal kirks (such as the Tron Church in Glasgow). But between the 1850s and 1930s, the Crown and county élites restored and refurbished them, adding unpresbyterian architectural embellishments such as ornate screens and choir stalls, and creating or reinstating side chapels. With this came a reversion from presbyterian names to Catholic ones: the plain 'High Kirks' of Edinburgh and Glasgow becoming St Giles' and St Mungo's Cathedrals. This episcopal trend, though meaningless in terms of church government, has gone further in an unofficial but, to the visitor, quite pronounced way with St Giles' Cathedral assuming a notional position as Scotland's premier kirk. Its interior layout has been changed in the 1980s to a modern 'central sanctuary' style with the communion table draped in white, adorned with candles and spotlighted, illuminating the white-frocked minister and orange-frocked choir in a manner much closer to episcopal or Catholic practice than to the pulpit-centred tradition of presbyterianism.

This trend is not ubiquitous in the Church of Scotland and by no means without controversy. Strong Orange areas in the west are very resistant to such innovation and, indeed, to ecumenical advance of the 'high church' strategy which has since the 1950s taken precedence in the Church of Scotland. A request by the Catholic archbishop of Glasgow to conduct the first mass for four centuries in St Mungo's Cathedral as part of anniversary celebrations for the city's oldest church was turned down by the minister and kirk session. The public manner of this request and rebuttal reflects the confrontational arena for ecumenicalism in the west of Scotland; it is probable that in the east it would have been discreetly handled in private. Ministers in the west are more likely than their brethren in the east to be members of the Orange Order, or in many cases to merely associate with the Order in an attempt to stay in touch with the Church's working-class constituency. For the same reason, some Church of Scotland ministers in the Glasgow area associate with the Protestant-aligned Rangers' Football Club. However, the numbers who do this are small, for they court the stigma of sectarianism and risk the loss of ecumenical respectability.

In this way, the Church has decreasing contact with proletarian sectarian feeling, and the Orange Order and Rangers' Football Club have come in the post-war period to represent the secularized nature of modern anti-Catholicism. Inspiration has emanated less and less from the tradition of the Scottish covenanters, for whose seventeenth-century battles there has been dwindling anniversary attendances, and more and more from the Protestant loyalists of Northern Ireland. The images and slogans which attract the Orange Order's 80,000 members are the Red Hand of Ulster and 'No Surrender', and splinter groups have a small but energetic following who find the main Order too passive in its anti-Catholic stance. The same images and slogans and their Catholic equivalents relating to Irish republicanism are to be found on the terraces of Rangers and Celtic football grounds and represent the best-known feature of religious bigotry in modern Scotland. Since the turn of the century the rivalry between these clubs has been an important focus for tension within the working-class culture not only of Glasgow but of the industrial Lowlands as a whole. Whilst sectarian associations of other clubs have softened (as with the Protestant Hearts and Catholic Hibernian in Edinburgh) or disappeared (as with the formerly Catholic Dundee United), the two Glasgow clubs attract more supporters from other cities than do local teams. Celtic have employed Protestant players and managers, but Rangers have a strong tradition of not recruiting Catholics. Irrespective of club policy the two sides have remained focuses of sectarian identity symbolized in the different flags (the Irish Tricolour and the Union Jack) which fly above their stands, and manifested in the violence which has punctuated the history of the 'Old Firm' fixtures.

For some historians,[26] Rangers–Celtic rivalry is the last vestige of a sectarianism that has declined markedly since the Second World War. Evidence for its diminishing relevance includes the general decay of religious affiliation, the secularization of society at large, the reduced extent of religious discrimination in employment, and the 'de-ghettoization' of Catholics and Protestants through slum clearance and council-house building. In politics, the former association of the Scottish Conservative and Unionist Party with the Orange Order has been considerably modified, and there are now Catholics amongst Scottish Tory MPs and government ministers. The Glasgow sectarian street gangs of the 'Norman Conks' (Catholics) and the 'Billy Boys' (Protestants) – the latter reputedly 800-strong in its heyday in the early 1930s – have virtually disappeared, and by comparison with religious conflicts in other parts of the world (including

Ulster) institutions like the Orange Order seem more like social clubs than manifestations of serious civil schism.

But such a sanguine view based on studies of organized sectarianism may underestimate the vibrancy of the popular culture of bigotry. In part, prosperity and better education have, in the words of one commentator, taught bigotry 'good manners', and though violence has decayed the disease 'survives to distort the thoughts and actions of men and women who would now be ashamed to admit it'.[27] Sectarianism is still a factor in the day-to-day lives of working-class Scots. It can be seen in popular graffiti which are almost entirely sectarian – 'FTP', 'FTQ' and 'FKB' (short-hand expletives addressed at the Pope, the Queen and King Billy), and in lapel badges which proclaim unhistorically 'I've been a Rangers supporter since 1690' (the year of the Protestant King William's victory at the Battle of the Boyne). Whilst religious ghettoization has been much reduced in Glasgow, in surrounding towns it is still significant – even perhaps heightened by council-house letting policy which in Greenock, for instance, produces schemes like 'the Shamrock' which are popularly identified as Catholic. Flute and pipe bands of both religions train every year to lead marches in Scotland, Northern Ireland or the Irish Republic, accounting for a significant part of youth voluntary activity in west-of-Scotland towns. The Scottish establishment – press, local authorities and government – has long tried to play down the sectarian division. In 1986, the leader of Midlothian District Council was forced to resign after describing Catholics as 'the enemy' at an Orange rally, and a sheriff-court judge in Kilmarnock was disciplined for demanding that the defendant in an assault case sing the sectarian Protestant tune 'The Sash' and, when the latter refused, for singing two versions of it himself from the bench. Mass marches of upwards of 15,000 Orangemen tend to be ignored by press and television whilst much smaller marches of trades unionists receive considerable attention. The silent hope is that by ignoring Protestant–Catholic antagonism, and by denying it political relevance, an unhealthy and illiberal atavism might disappear. But sectarianism runs deep in Scottish popular culture, especially though not exclusively in the industrial west. At one level, zealous propagandists fuel the flames, as in the following passage from a Protestant Loyalist broadsheet of 1983 which describes how a sixteen-year-old Catholic youth on a Youth Opportunity Programme course at a west-of-Scotland factory

> went to dry himself at a heater unaware that his boilersuit was soaked in paraffin. He immediately turned into a human torch and died in agony in hospital five days later. Everybody say Aah. [His father] said it was a pity this had happened as [his son] was just warming to the job. The company involved was fined £800 for the incident which is outrageous as [the boy] was only an RC and no friend to the Protestant Community. [He] disproved the old theory that Shite does not burn and it is thought that his parents are keeping his ashes for Ash Wednesday. We can safely assume that [he] is still feeling the heat where he is now but cannot confirm that his favourite record was 'Great Balls of Fire'.[28]

An another level, there is often popular reaction to the seemingly mundane – particularly by Protestants to the colour green, even when worn on articles of clothing. Associations are drawn when they may not be intended, as is evident from a letter in 1985 in the biggest-selling Sunday newspaper in Scotland, published under the headline 'Disgraceful Sight':

> I could hardly believe my eyes when a lorry drove down our street. The cab was painted white. The sides and top were bright green. The rear of the vehicle had been left the original orange. This [housing] scheme is already smothered in IRA grafitti [sic], but to have this blatant display on the streets is a disgrace. I'm a pensioner, born and brought up in this city, and feel sad and sickened at what's happening.[29]

Protestant insecurity gives rise to perceptions of Catholic invasion at many turns. Bigotry survives in part because of the religiously-segregated state schools, but also because of the strong links which are maintained between Scots Protestants and

Ulster Loyalists, and between Scots Catholics and Irish republicans – connections which have been enlivened since the outbreak of the Troubles in 1969. Crucially, economic decline has been most severe, protracted and agonizing in the very industries with the strongest traditions of religious segregation and sectarian militancy: shipbuilding, coal-mining, iron and steel, and the docks. Where those industries have dominated, especially in Glasgow's satellite towns such as Greenock, Larkhall and Motherwell, and in the industrial and mining areas of north Ayrshire, Orangeism and religious rivalries remain pronounced. Nor has the actual demise of pits and iron works weakened sectarianism, certainly in the short term. Rather, it has tended to make smaller communities with high levels of unemployment susceptible to heightened religious tensions – especially in places where the Orange Club assumes a new popularity as occupational social activities (like the Miners' Welfare) wind down. The future of bigotry depends in part on the extent and nature of economic recovery in such areas, but institutionalized sectarianism in education, winter football and the summer marching season seems sufficient to ensure that its decay will at best be slow.

It is in this unlikely context that ecumenical discussions have enjoyed such apparent fruitfulness in Scotland. Whilst unification with the Catholic Church is not even on the visible agenda of the Church of Scotland (as it is of the Church of England), traditional presbyterians perceive accommodation with episcopacy as the vital breach with the nation's religious heritage. Bearing that in mind, it is remarkable how far union negotiations have proceeded across the divide between episcopal and non-episcopal churches, and must be taken as a measure of the loss of popular Protestant reverence for, and interest in, the presbyterian church. In the long term – the very long term – the trend towards 'high churchism' may assist church unity, but the short-term cost seems to be the angering of 'low-church' presbyterians and increasing alienation amongst the working and lower-middle classes. In this way, secularization, sectarianism and ecumenicalism have emerged since the 1950s in a mutually reinforcing triangle with the first two in antagonistic but beneficial relationship with the third. It was perhaps coincidence, but perhaps not,

Religion in the secular century 247

that the absolute decline in the number of Church of Scotland members began in the same year as the furore over the 'Bishops' Report'. More instructive is the fact that despite fierce and violent religious hatred surrounding the 'Old Firm' football clubs and the marching season in the 1980s, only one hundred demonstrators, led by the Rev. Ian Paisley from Northern Ireland, turned up to protest at the admission of the Pope – the Protestants' 'anti-Christ' – to the palace of world presbyterianism in Edinburgh.

Notes

1. H. McLeod (1986) 'New perspectives on Victorian working-class religion: the oral evidence', *Oral History Journal*, 14, 33.
2. Quoted in D. S. Cairns (ed.) (1919) *The Army and Religion*, London, 89.
3. Quoted in ibid., 145.
4. Quoted in ibid., 223.
5. L. Derwent (1985) *Lady of the Manse*, London, Arrow, 65–6.
6. Quoted in I. MacDougall (ed.) (1981) *Militant Miners*, Edinburgh, Polygon, 301.
7. *Stirling Observer*, 12 January 1922.
8. *Fraserburgh Herald*, quoted in P. Thompson et al. (1983) *Living the Fishing*, London, Routledge & Kegan Paul, 205.
9. C. Rush (1983) *Peace Comes Dropping Slow*, Edinburgh, Ramsay Head Press, 7, 131.
10. M. Weir (1972) *Best Foot Forward*, London, Hutchinson, 69–71.
11. D. R. Robertson (1966) 'The Relationship between Church and Social Class in Scotland', unpublished Ph.D. thesis, University of Edinburgh, 364–6; *The Scotsman*, 15 May 1986.
12. P. L. Sissons (1973) *The Social Significance of Church Membership in the Burgh of Falkirk*, Edinburgh, Church of Scotland.
13. D. R. Robertson, op. cit., 48.
14. F. Fraser Darling (ed.) (1955) *West Highland Survey*, London, Oxford University Press, 315–16.
15. Quoted in A. McPherson (ed.) (c. 1973) *History of the Free Presbyterian Church of Scotland*, Inverness, Free Presbyterian Church, 359–60.
16. L. Beckwith (1968) *The Sea for Breakfast*, London, Arrow, 104.
17. C. Harvie (1981) *No Gods and Precious Few Heroes: Scotland 1914–1980*, London, Edward Arnold, vii.
18. Rev. B. Preston in J. M. Urquhart (ed.) (1964) *The Third Statistical Account of Scotland: The Counties of Peebles and Selkirk*, Glasgow, Collins, 171.
19. ibid., 75.
20. *Reports to the General Assembly of the Church of Scotland* (1970), 399.

21 ibid. (1970), 407, 410; (1972), 448.
22 Quoted in Senex (pseud.) (1884) *Glasgow Past and Present*, Vol. II, Glasgow, 265.
23 *Glasgow Free Press*, 25 August 1860; *Scottish Guardian*, 28 August 1860; *North British Daily Mail*, 27 August 1860.
24 *Reports on the Schemes of the Church of Scotland* (1923), 750–61. Some authorities wrongly cite the title of this report as 'The Menace of the Irish Race to our Scottish Nationality' (which was a pamphlet by the leader of the Scottish Protestant League); it was actually headed, more prosaically, 'Report of the Committee to Consider the Overtures on Irish Immigration and the Education (Scotland) Act 1918'.
25 *Christian Unity – Now is the Time: The Multilateral Church Conversation in Scotland Report* (1985), Edinburgh, Quorum, 7.
26 Such as Steve Bruce and Tom Gallagher; see bibliography.
27 G. Scott (1967) *The R.C.s: a Report on Roman Catholics in Britain Today*, London, Hutchinson, 25.
28 Quoted in S. Bruce (1985) *No Pope of Rome: Anti-Catholicism in Modern Scotland*, Edinburgh, Mainstream, 151.
29 *The Sunday Post*, 22 December 1985.

8
Conclusion

The emphasis of this book has been on religious change. The purpose has not been to chronicle unremitting religious decay since the industrial revolution, for that did not happen, nor to dismiss religious belief and observance as a peasant 'hangover' of a pious pre-industrial society. Conversely, there has been little lingering on the immutable significance of Calvinism and Scottish church tradition in the life of the people, for much of that, though not all, is romantic illusion or convenient misinterpretation. The quest has been for marker posts and leading edges of change: indicators of the timing and characteristics of the major shifts in direction for the social significance of religion.

One major theme of the early chapters was the agricultural origins of modern religious change: of religious pluralism which created dissenting churches, and of the popular religious values of self-help and 'respectability' which came to be associated with urban bourgeois ideology. A second major theme was the way in which religion became highly relevant to industrializing society, and how by many measures (though only partially quantifiable) the social relevance of religion did not fall with urbanization but grew. The evangelical conjunction of religious and economic individualism was the Victorian orthodoxy for Catholics as for Protestants – however it might be interpreted differently in denominational, regional or class contexts. The social and personal ideals of aggressive Christianity found their greatest representation in the dissenting presbyterian churches which in different regions, types of community and periods attracted support from a surprisingly wide range of social groups. Enterprising religion adapted to an enterprising society, and whilst an older pre-industrial form of religion was overtaken, religious ideology maintained a firm grasp of the public consciousness through control of organized leisure and social policy.

This control broke down in the late Victorian and Edwardian periods. The unchallenged hegemony of evangelicalism was confronted by secular progress in the form of the labour movement and state welfarism. The mainstream Protestant churches were fairly sharply separated from the working classes whose cultural experience fell under the dominance of an internal contest between essentially opposing ideals of labour and proletarian evangelicalism – a contest which the latter seems to have lost by the 1950s, compounded by the secularization of leisure and sectarianism. From the turn of the century, the major barometers of religious activity and affiliation swung one by one from growth to decline: Protestant churchgoing probably in 1880–1900; evangelization, Sunday-school and Bible-class membership, and presbyterian marriage between 1895 and 1920; most church youth and social organizations from the 1920s; Protestant church membership in the 1950s; and Catholic Church affiliation and baptisms in the late 1960s or 1970s. Whilst long-term decline has sometimes been interrupted by short-term growth (as in the late 1940s and early 1950s), there is little comfort for the churches in the failure of any of the indices to 'bottom out' by the mid-1980s.

There are many fragments to this religious jigsaw, including several which have not been commented upon in the preceding chapters. One is the difference between the sexes in religious ideals and participation. Troubled observers of church decline in the 1960s were concerned that around two-thirds of worshipping Protestants and Catholics were female with the imbalance rising to well over 70 per cent in a significant number of Church of Scotland congregations. But the greater religious enthusiasm of women is nothing new. Kenneth Logue has shown that in the late eighteenth and early nineteenth centuries women made up 46 per cent of those charged with mobbing and rioting at patronage

Conclusion 251

disputes – by far the highest female participation in any form of popular disturbance of the time, and very probably not a true reflection of the prominent part women took in patronage riots.[1] One result was the widespread though not general granting of voting rights to women in the Secession Church, especially Burgher congregations. Similarly, a vociferous though unsuccessful campaign was mounted just after the Disruption to extend the same rights to women in the Free Church. In the Church of Scotland in 1874, women made up 57 per cent of the communicants, and some acknowledgement of their importance in the kirk was made by the establishment of the Women's Guild in 1887.

Still, there are some grounds for believing that the disparity between women's religious observance (especially working-class women) and that of men has widened in the context of twentieth-century secularization. Many ministers noticed that middle-class servicemen returned to churchgoing after 1918 and again after 1945, but that there was a significant tendency for working-class servicemen not to. Throughout the history of local veto plebiscites, evangelical canvassers found the greatest support from women in working-class wards, and strenuous efforts were directed at turning out the female temperance vote. More generally, working-class women remained closely in contact with religious ideas and institutions. Codes of female respectability derived strongly from religious or semi-religious concepts transmitted by mothers, aunts, and girls' magazines and books, and were reinterpreted and enforced with each generation within the comparatively narrow confines of women's daily contact with peer-group pressure and female leisure activities. It is noticeable, for instance, that whilst religious and voluntary organizations for adults were generally in decline after 1900, the ones that survived best were female such as the Women's Guild and the Women's Rural Institute. By the 1960s, church organizations were so important to women's social life that as much as half of the membership did not belong to the church. The trend seems to have continued in depression and prosperity. Male church membership fell sharply during the slump of the 1930s in working-class presbyterian congregations, but membership and attendance amongst women and girls was reported as being little affected. Perhaps most striking was the quite remarkable fact that in Falkirk in the mid-1960s, only 37 per cent of boys who attended church expressed a belief in God compared to 47 per cent amongst non-attenders; in contrast, the situation was reversed amongst girls with figures of 75 per cent for churchgoers and 40 per cent for non-churchgoers.[2]

Presbyterianism seems to have long been close to sexual egalitarianism, but it was only in the 1930s that the very liberal remnant of the United Free Church admitted women to the eldership and the ministry, followed in the late 1960s by the Church of Scotland; in the mid-1980s, women account for around ten per cent of the clergy in the Kirk. This reflects in part the wider changes in the role of women in modern western society, but in part also the greater endurance of their church connection.

Another important feature of secularization has been the two-stage decline of presbyterianism. The first was the downturn in church activity (churchgoing, evangelization and recruitment through Sunday schools) which set in after 1890. Though the rate of growth in church affiliation fell after 1900, the second stage – the decline of church membership – did not start until 1957. If anything, church connection grew in importance between 1900 and 1950, though only slightly, indicating a popular desire to remain in institutional association whilst participating substantially less. An explanation for this may rest in the connection between presbyterianism and Scottish national consciousness. Until the 1950s the Church of Scotland and the dissenting presbyterian churches were symbols of the nation's Protestant heritage, expressed through identification with church-aligned candidates at elections to *ad hoc* authorities, in low presbyterian voting for Catholic candidates of whatever party at municipal or parliamentary elections, in the confused nationalist sentiments aroused in campaigns both for the maintenance of the Established Church and for dissenting voluntaryism, and in the equally confused patriotism for the preservation of Scottish parish schools as well as for their abolition as symbols of an educational heritage allowed to atrophy under English government neglect. But since the 1950s, the drift away from presbyterian standards and practices in the Church of Scotland, the clergy's hostility to expressing even an intellectual anti-Catholicism, and the rise of political nationalism in the form of the Scottish National Party in the 1960s and 1970s have assisted in the displacement of the churches as focuses for national identity. For the non-churchgoing majority of Scottish presbyterians, church membership was maintained for so long as the Kirk stood for the nation's religious heritage. However strongly the nation's heritage is seen in other, non-religious ways, it is now little regarded in religious terms.

Whilst the Protestant churches are well in decay and the Catholic Church appears to be embarking on the same process, there has been an interesting growth since the 1960s of new religions and religious movements. The numbers of Asians and especially blacks in Scotland have remained very low, though the Woodlands Asian community in Glasgow is now overspilling into other parts of the city and eliciting the first major signs of Scottish racism. The figures for the active Moslem population in Scotland, based on religious marriages in 1984, may be somewhere in the region of 14,000; this is likely to increase as a result of migration from English cities. Hitherto, the main support for overseas religions has come from the educated middle classes. Since 1970, Buddhism, Zen, Krishna Consciousness, Transcendental Meditation and many other groups attracted first the disaffected young and then members of the prospering intelligentsia, notably English immigrants to Edinburgh. However, this cannot be taken as evidence of 'de-secularization' as the numbers of people involved are very small, and because in many cases, such as that of meditation, the attraction is not of a religion requiring adherence to firm doctrines but of activities which aid personal orientation and development. At the same time, there has been a limited development of modern religious movements within and across the Scottish churches. The charismatic movement is a case in point, creating small circles of enthusiastic followers in the Baptist, Episcopal, Catholic, presbyterian and other churches. There are difficulties in assessing the significance of such trends for they most frequently do not result in the formation of organizations which count 'members'. But in any event, such developments are reactions against a perceived 'hostile' world, and they accentuate the division between the highly committed religious minority and the unchurched majority.

The emergence of new religious movements can be seen as part of the evidence of social changes which in the later twentieth century are proving to be far more antipathetic to religious adherence than anything thrown up by the agricultural or industrial revolutions. The social mould in which the relevance of religious values and the churches was cast in the previous two centuries has been progressively cracked and destroyed. Social improvement has been divorced from issues of religion, and has in itself assisted in the disintegration of communal activity and community identity. Prosperity has withdrawn people from assembled gatherings in halls, cinemas and churches, whilst modern social values are transmitted via radio, television, pop records, and domestic activities. Arguably, there has been little change in the basic values. Self-reliance and respectability are still powerful themes in popular ethics, but they are no longer conferred by parading in church pews on a Sunday.

We should not look upon Scotland's religious progress as idiosyncratic. The timing and characteristics of change find strong parallels in the rest of Britain: the eighteenth-century rise of nonconformity; the interaction between religious and class identity in the industrial revolution; the ubiquitous evangelical ideology of the Victorian period; the crisis of evangelicalism and religious leisure at the turn of the century, accompanied by progress towards ecumenical union initially amongst a frantic Protestant dissent and latterly between the 'high' section of the Church of England and the Catholic Church.[3] Whilst levels of churchgoing and membership remain higher in Scotland, the direction and pace of change is very similar to that in England and Wales. Moreover, church connection is kept strong in Scotland because of puritanical presbyterianism in the Highlands and some other remote communities, and because of sectarian identity in Catholic regions of the Lowlands. In the last area, Catholic religious observance is starting to fall as it is amongst Catholics in nearly every European country, and as sectarianism becomes increasingly secularized the high levels of Protestant church

Conclusion 255

observance of the sort found in Northern Ireland are also falling. More representative are the east, south, and north-east of Scotland where levels of churchgoing range between 9 and 14 per cent of the population – figures close to England's average of 11 per cent. In short, Scotland has shared with the rest of the first industrial nation a very similar pattern of growth and decline of organized religion.

Secularization pushed forward but did not initiate the erosion of Scotland's distinctive religious character. The advent of urbanization and modern social structure in the eighteenth and nineteenth centuries gave pre-eminence to evangelicalism as a religious system for defining and increasing church adherence and popular attachment to religious values. In the process, doctrinal peculiarities like Calvinism became of diminishing importance. In the present century, not only has presbyterian doctrine and practice withered considerably as prosperity pushed out puritanism, but the distinctive denominational structure of Scotland has for some time been open to tender. A united Christian Church may be a noble dream, but historically it is a characteristic of the pre-industrial theocratic state. The modern attainment of ecumenical objectives may well become the mark of a secularized society.

This is not to say that Scotland is becoming a 'godless' country. There is a vast array of religious or quasi-religious beliefs present in the population: superstition, belief in the supernatural, and indeed belief in a God, which is held by probably four out of five adults. Rationalism and the growth of science have clearly had adverse effects on people's willingness to accept church or biblical doctrines, yet they have done nothing to undermine basic, gut feelings about the existence of God. The consequence is that religious belief has been considerably shorn of Christian theology, and even when residual understanding remains of church teachings learnt as a child, adult concepts of the unanswerable questions about life, death and the life hereafter tend to stray from ecclesiastical wisdom. Even the Church of Scotland has found in the mid-1980s that over 13 per cent of its own members hold agnostic or atheistic views.[4] The possibility of conflict over modern liberal theology infecting the Church of Scotland as it has the Church of England could elevate fundamental Christian issues concerning the miracles and 'the empty tomb' into further causes for alienation for both active and lapsed presbyterians. Moreover, the removal of social pressures to attend church has made congregations smaller but more committed and more likely to be concerned with such matters. This may well enhance the position of the smaller and more conservative Protestant churches, and even make them less likely to decline.[5] However, the churchgoers are no longer the substantial minority of the nineteenth century, the custodians of social respectability and society's operative values. The stewardship of Scottish society is vested in generations which are becoming increasingly secular in their culture and thinking, and whilst the churches will not disappear, organized religion appears at present to be on the path towards the margins of social significance.

Notes

1 K. J. Logue (1979) *Popular Disturbances in Scotland 1780–1815*, Edinburgh, John Donald, 199–200.
2 P. L. Sissons (1973) *The Social Significance of Church Membership in the Burgh of Falkirk*, Edinburgh, Church of Scotland, 325.
3 For the English setting, see for example, A. D. Gilbert (1976) *Religion and Society in Industrial England: Church, Chapel and Social Change, 1740–1914*, London and New York, Longman; S. Yeo (1976) *Religion and Voluntary Organisations in Crisis*, London, Croom Helm, a study of Reading in 1890–1914; and J. Cox (1982) *The English Churches in a Secular Society: Lambeth, 1870–1930*, Oxford University Press. A wider perspective is given in H. McLeod (1981) *Religion and the People of Western Europe 1789–1970*, Oxford University Press.
4 *The Scotsman*, 15 May 1986.
5 S. Bruce (1984) *Firm in the Faith*, Aldershot, Gower, 37–40.

Bibliography

Whilst the literature on the Scottish churches and on their intellectual impact is vast, research in the social history of modern Scottish religion is comparatively scarce. The following is a selective guide to some of the most useful items of ecclesiastical and social history, and sociology. Some major topics such as the Enlightenment and education have been omitted.

So much research waits to be undertaken that four types of source are worth publicizing. Firstly, *The Statistical Account of Scotland* (21 volumes, 1791–99), *The New Statistical Account of Scotland* (15 volumes, 1845) and *The Third Statistical Account of Scotland* (many volumes published between the 1950s and 1980s), which all have much information on the geographical distribution of the churches. Secondly, the published annual reports of the general assemblies of the Church of Scotland, the Free Church and the United Free Church, and the synod of the United Presbyterian Church, which contain a wealth of material on Scotland's social and religious life. Thirdly, the MS records of presbyteries and kirk sessions (less usefully synods) of all the presbyterian churches contained in SRO and regional archive file numbers CH2 and CH3. And lastly newspapers, which in the nineteenth and early twentieth centuries devoted considerable space to church stories, including generally verbatim reports on meetings of church courts.

Chapter 2

Amongst works of ecclesiastical history, a general introduction to the presbyterian perspective is J. H. S. Burleigh (1960) *A Church History of Scotland*, London, Oxford University Press. More detailed accounts, though hostile to the presbyterian dissenters, are given in three books by A. L. Drummond and J. Bulloch, *The Scottish Church 1688–1843: The Age of the Moderates* (1973), *The Church in Victorian Scotland 1843–1874* (1975) and *The Church in Late Victorian Scotland 1874–1900* (1978), all Edinburgh, Saint Andrew Press.

258   The Social History of Religion in Scotland

An illuminating perspective on kirk disputes is given by a leading expert on Church law in A. Herron (1985) *Kirk by Divine Right: Church and State: peaceful co-existence*, Edinburgh, Saint Andrew. Moving a little further towards social history is A. C. Cheyne's (1983) *The Transforming of the Kirk: Victorian Scotland's Religious Revolution*, Edinburgh, Saint Andrew Press, whilst K. M. Boyd (1980) *Scottish Church Attitudes to Sex, Marriage and the Family 1850–1914*, Edinburgh, John Donald, is extremely detailed on church debates on these issues. There is no thorough modern treatment of presbyterian dissent, forcing reliance at present on the books by J. McKerrow, G. Struthers, T. Brown, M. Hutchinson and J. Barr cited in the notes, together with D. Scott (1866) *Annals and Statistics of the Original Secession Church*, Edinburgh; A. McPherson (ed.) (c. 1973) *History of the Free Presbyterian Church of Scotland*, Inverness[?], Free Presbyterian Church; and D. Woodside (c. 1918) *The Soul of a Scottish Church*, Edinburgh, on the United Presbyterian Church. On Independency see D. B. Murray (1977) 'The Social and Religious Origins of Scottish Non-Presbyterian Dissent 1730–1800', unpublished Ph.D. thesis, University of St Andrews; and H. Escott (1960) *A History of Scottish Congregationalism*, Glasgow, Congregational Union. For presbyterianism in politics, see G. I. T. Machin (1977) *Politics and the Churches in Great Britain 1832 to 1868*, Oxford, Clarendon Press, on the Ten Years' Conflict leading to the Disruption; and the recent detailed study by I. G. C. Hutchinson (1986) *A Political History of Scotland 1832–1924*, Edinburgh, John Donald, which reveals the intricacies of the churches' party alignments.

Scottish Catholicism is becoming well served, especially by the early books of J. E. Handley, *The Irish in Scotland 1798–1845* (1945) and *The Irish in Modern Scotland* (1947), both Cork University Press; C. Johnson's (1983) *Developments in the Roman Catholic Church in Scotland 1789–1829*, Edinburgh, John Donald; and D. McRoberts (ed.) (1979) *Modern Scottish Catholicism 1878–1978*, Glasgow, Burns. Useful on Methodism is W. R. Ward (1978) 'Scottish Methodism in the age of Jabez Bunting', RSCHS, xx; and covering a wider timespan than the title suggests is M. Lochhead (1966) *Episcopal Scotland in the Nineteenth Century*, London, SPCK. For a revealing though sensationalist account of the Exclusive Brethren in the north-east, focusing on the 'unmasking' of their apparently libidinous American leader of the early 1970s, see N. Adams (1972) *Goodbye, Beloved Brethren*, Aberdeen, Impulse.

Chapter 3

By far the best compendium of national religious statistics is R. Currie, A. Gilbert and L. Horsley (1977) *Churches and Churchgoers: Patterns of Church Growth in the British Isles since 1700*, Oxford, Clarendon Press. Post-1970 figures can be found in church yearbooks like *The Church of Scotland Yearbook* and *The Catholic Directory for Scotland*. Amongst other sources not cited in the chapter, crucial to the difficult calculations on Catholic data are J. Darragh (1953)

Bibliography

'The Catholic population of Scotland since 1680', *Innes Review* iv, and the same author's 'The Catholic population of Scotland, 1878–1977' in D. McRoberts (ed.) (1979) *Modern Scottish Catholicism 1878–1978*, Glasgow, Burns. Also of enormous value are two volumes by J. Highet, *The Churches in Scotland Today* (1950), Glasgow, Jackson, and *The Scottish Churches: A Review of their State 400 Years after the Reformation* (1960), London, Skeffington, which discuss statistics and general characteristics of not only the large but also the small churches. For analysis of the main source on churchgoing see D. J. Withrington (1974) 'The 1851 census of religious worship and education: with a note on church accommodation in mid-nineteenth century Scotland', *RSCHS*, xviii. K. J. Panton (1973) 'The Church in the community: a study of patterns of religious adherence in a Scottish burgh', in M. Hill (ed.) *A Sociological Yearbook of Religion in Britain*, 6, London, SCM, is an interesting statistical investigation of religious segregation in Alloa in the 1960s, though it is weakened by over-simplification of the social structure.

Chapter 4

On what I have described as the pre-industrial form of religion, A. A. Cormack (1930) *Teinds and Agriculture*, London, Oxford University Press, explains one part of Established Church finances. For the other major part, see J. M. McPherson (*c.* 1941) *The Kirk's Care of the Poor: With Special Reference to the North-east of Scotland*, Aberdeen, John Avery; J. Lindsay (1975) *The Scottish Poor Law: Its Operation in the North-east from 1745 to 1845*, Ilfracombe, Stockwell; and T. Hamilton (1942) *Poor Relief in South Ayrshire 1700–1845*, Edinburgh, Oliver and Boyd. No wholly satisfactory account of kirk-session justice exists beyond the seventeenth century, but useful are T. C. Smout (1972) *A History of the Scottish People 1560–1830*, Glasgow, Fontana/Collins; B. Lenman and G. Parker (1980) 'Crime and control in Scotland 1500–1800', *History Today*, 30 (January); S. J. Davies (1980) 'The courts and the Scottish legal system 1600–1747: the case of Stirlingshire' in V. A. C. Gatrell *et al.* (eds), *Crime and the Law*, London, Europa; W. Makey (1979) *The Church of the Covenant 1637–1651*, Edinburgh, John Donald; and J. Di Folco (1977) 'Discipline and welfare in the mid-seventeenth century Scots parish', *RSCHS*, xix. In many ways more useful are A. Edgar (1885) *Old Church Life in Scotland*, Paisley and London, and especially the excellent J. H. Gillespie (1939) *Dundonald: A Contribution to Parochial History*, vol. 2, Glasgow, Wylie, which must be the best existing model for the study of pre-industrial Scottish religion.

Little has been written on levels of religious observance before 1800. D. J. Withrington (1970) 'Non-churchgoing, *c.* 1750–*c.* 1850: a preliminary study', *RSCHS*, xvii, examines the rising level of ministers' criticism, partly directed at episcopalian landowners. The 'Cambuslang Wark' of 1742 is a well-quarried source on religious enthusiasm, including T. C. Smout (1982) 'Born again at

Cambuslang: new evidence on popular religion and literacy in eighteenth-century Scotland', *Past and Present*, 97, and A. Fawcett (1977) *The Cambuslang Revival*, London. For the clearest statement of the difficulties in measuring 'religiosity' in the early-modern period, reference must be made to the English position, cogently put in M. Spufford (1985) 'Can we count the "godly" and the "conformable" in the seventeenth century?', *Journal of Ecclesiastical History*, 36.

Nineteenth-century rural religion is poorly covered. Notable exceptions are I. Carter (1979) *Farmlife in Northeast Scotland 1840–1914: The Poor Man's Country*, Edinburgh, John Donald, and the same author's (1974–5) ' "To roose the countra fae the caul' morality o' a deid moderatism": William Alexander and *Johnny Gibb of Gushetneuk*', *Northern Scotland*, 2. The Horseman's Word is discussed in H. Henderson (1980) 'The ballad, the folk, and the oral tradition' in E. J. Cowan (ed.) *The People's Past*, Edinburgh, Polygon. On patronage disputes, K. J. Logue (see note 9, p. 128) provides data on social composition of those charged with offences, and R. Sher and A. Murdoch (1983) 'Patronage and party in the Church of Scotland, 1750–1800' in N. MacDougall (ed.) *Church, Politics and Society: Scotland 1408–1929*, Edinburgh, John Donald, is an interesting reassessment of 'party' attitudes to the system. On the particular urban context of patronage and secession, see R. B. Sher (n.d.) 'Moderates, managers and popular politics in mid-eighteenth-century Edinburgh: the Drysdale "Bustle" of the 1760s', in J. Dwyer *et al.* (eds) *New Perspectives on the Politics and Culture of Early Modern Scotland*, Edinburgh, John Donald; and A. T. N. Muirhead (1983) 'Religion, politics and society in Stirling during the ministry of Ebenezer Erskine 1731–1754', unpublished M.Litt. thesis, University of Stirling.

The Highlands and Hebrides have been more fully covered, certainly until 1850 when historians' interest in popular religion tends to wane. The starting point is J. MacInnes (1951) *The Evangelical Movement in the Highlands of Scotland 1688 to 1800*, Aberdeen University Press, and taking the story on are J. Hunter (1974) 'The emergence of the crofting community: the religious contribution 1798–1843', *Scottish Studies*, 18; the same author's (1976) *The Making of the Crofting Community*, Edinburgh, John Donald; J. Mackay (1914) *The Church in the Highlands*, London; and S. Bruce (1983) 'Social change and collective behaviour: the revival in eighteenth-century Ross-shire', *British Journal of Sociology*, 34. It is impossible to separate the growth of Highland evangelicalism from the issue of the Clearances, for which find an opposing apologist position to that of Hunter in P. Gaskell (1968) *Morvern Transformed: A Highland Parish in the Nineteenth Century*, Cambridge University Press, and E. Richards (1982, 1985) *A History of the Highland Clearances*, 2 vols, London, Croom Helm. For the devastating though probably unique effect of the puritanical version of Free Churchism on an economically precarious community, see C. Maclean (1983) *Island on the Edge of the World: The Story of St. Kilda*, Edinburgh, Canongate; and T. Steel (1975) *The Life and Death of St. Kilda*, London and Glasgow, Fontana/Collins. The role of

Gaelic in Highland religion is examined in some depth in V. E. Durkacz (1983) *The Decline of the Celtic Languages*, and C. W. J. Withers (1984) *Gaelic in Scotland 1698-1981*, both Edinburgh, John Donald.

Chapter 5

There is a highly diverse literature on urban religion. Debate tends to start with social composition of churchgoers, for which consult the seminal works of A. A. MacLaren cited in note 13, p. 167, plus his (1967) 'Presbyterianism and the working class in a mid-nineteenth-century city', *SHR*, 46, and (1983) 'Class formation and class fraction: the Aberdeen bourgeoisie 1830-1850' in G. Gordon and B. Dicks (eds) *Scottish Urban History*, Aberdeen University Press. An important difference of interpretation is given in P. Hillis (1981) 'Presbyterianism and social class in mid-nineteenth century Glasgow: a study of nine churches', *Journal of Ecclesiastical History*, 32, 47-64. Also relevant is B. M. Thatcher (1976) 'The Episcopal Church in Helensburgh in the mid-nineteenth century' in J. Butt and J. T. Ward (eds) *Scottish Themes*, Edinburgh, Scottish Academic Press. On the wider British context, see H. McLeod (1984) *Religion and the Working Class in Nineteenth-Century Britain*, London, Macmillan.

On the churches and urban social policy, see S. Mechie (1960) *The Church and Scottish Social Development 1780-1870*, London, Oxford University Press; C. G. Brown (1982) 'Religion and the Development of an Urban Society: Glasgow 1780-1914', unpublished Ph.D. thesis, University of Glasgow; idem (1981) 'The Sunday-school movement in Scotland, 1780-1914', *RSCHS*, xxi; O. Checkland (1980) *Philanthropy in Victorian Scotland*, Edinburgh, John Donald; R. A. Cage and E. O. A. Checkland (1976) 'Thomas Chalmers and urban poverty: the St. John's experiment in Glasgow 1819-1837', *Philosophical Journal*, 13, and S. J. Brown (1978) 'The Disruption and urban poverty: Thomas Chalmers and the West Port operation in Edinburgh 1844-47', *RSCHS*, xx. R. S. Blakey (1978) *The Man in the Manse*, Edinburgh, The Handsel Press, provides an extensively researched though ultimately romantic view of the lives of nineteenth-century presbyterian ministers.

Insights into working-class religion are contained in N. Murray (1978) *The Scottish Hand Loom Weavers 1790-1850*, Edinburgh, John Donald; A. B. Campbell (1979) *The Lanarkshire Miners 1775-1874*, Edinburgh, John Donald, which describes the early stages of Protestant-Catholic segregation; so does R. D. Lobban (1971) 'The Irish community in Greenock in the nineteenth century', *Irish Geography* 6, though he probably exaggerates the extent of desegregation after 1900. But for a study of how the first ethnic minority was absorbed in Scottish cities, see C. W. J. Withers (1985) 'Kirk, club and culture change: Gaelic chapels, Highland societies and the urban Gaelic subculture in eighteenth-century Scotland', *Social History*, 10. On radicalism and religion, see H. U. Faulkner (1916) *Chartism and the Churches*, New York, and

262 The Social History of Religion in Scotland

A. Wilson (1970) *The Chartist Movement in Scotland*, New York, Kelley, whilst religion and Protestant artisan 'respectability' is illuminatingly discussed in R. Q. Gray (1976) *The Labour Aristocracy in Victorian Edinburgh*, Oxford, Clarendon Press, and the Catholic Church's promotion of the same values is reviewed in W. M. Walker (1972) 'Irish immigrants in Scotland: their priests, politics and parochial life', *Historical Journal*, xv. Amongst first-hand accounts about working-class life, start with the unmatched *Christian Watt Papers*, ed. D. Fraser (1983), Edinburgh, Paul Harris; and try A. Somerville (a Seceder) (1848) *The Autobiography of a Working Man*, London, and *Autobiography of Robert Flockhart, the Street Preacher*, (orig. 1858, 1977 reprint, Grand Rapids, Baker).

Chapter 6

Literature on the changing position of the churches at the turn of the century is growing. Particularly relevant are D. J. Withrington (1977) 'The churches in Scotland *c.* 1870–*c.* 1900: towards a new social conscience?', *RSCHS*, xix; W. M. Walker (1979) *Juteopolis: Dundee and its Textile Workers 1885–1923*, Edinburgh, Scottish Academic Press; B. Aspinwall (1984) *Portable Utopia: Glasgow and the United States 1820–1920*, Aberdeen University Press; R. Q. Gray (1977) 'Religion, culture and social class in late nineteenth and early twentieth century Edinburgh' in G. Crossick (ed.) *The Lower Middle Class in Britain*, London, Croom Helm, which is useful on suburbanization; and C. G. Brown (1982) 'Religion and the Development of an Urban Society: Glasgow 1780–1914', unpublished Ph.D. thesis, University of Glasgow. More particularly on the labour movement, see W. Knox (ed.) (1984) *Scottish Labour Leaders, 1918–39: A Biographical Dictionary*, Edinburgh, Mainstream; I. S. Wood (1980) 'John Wheatley, the Irish and the labour movement in Scotland', *Innes Review*, 31; S. Gilley (1980) 'Catholics and socialists in Glasgow 1906–1912' in K. Lunn (ed.) *Hosts, Immigrants and Minorities*, Folkestone, Dawson; the excellent D. F. Summers (1958) 'The Labour Church and Allied Movements in the Late Nineteenth and Early Twentieth Centuries', unpublished Ph.D. thesis, University of Edinburgh; and I. McLean (1983) *The Legend of Red Clydeside*, Edinburgh, John Donald. On teetotalism and prohibition, see Aspinwall, op. cit., and D. C. Paton (1977) 'Drink and the Temperance Movement in Nineteenth-century Scotland', unpublished Ph.D. thesis, University of Edinburgh; I. Wood (1973) 'Drink, temperance and the labour movement', *Journal of the Scottish Labour History Society*, 5; and E. King (1979) *Scotland Sober and Free: The Temperance Movement 1829–1979*, Glasgow Museums.

Chapter 7

Much research on the twentieth century waits to be undertaken, even by ecclesiastical historians. The area by far the best covered is Catholicism, including

D. McRoberts (ed.) (1979) *Modern Scottish Catholicism 1878–1978*, Glasgow, Burns; J. F. McCaffrey (1983) 'Roman Catholics in Scotland in the nineteenth and twentieth centuries', *RSCHS*, xxi; and T. A. Fitzpatrick (1986) *Catholic Secondary Education in South-west Scotland before 1972*, Aberdeen University Press, which has useful data and discussion on the growth of the Catholic Church. An agenda for research on the decline of presbyterianism was acutely predicted in A. H. Dunnet (*c.* 1933) *The Church in Changing Scotland*, London, Clarke. On the churches and war, see D. S. Cairns (ed.) (1919) *The Army and Religion*, London, and L. L. I.. Cameron (1972) *A Badge to Be Proud Of: A History of the Church of Scotland Huts and Canteens*, Church of Scotland.

Religion and social class in the Lowlands is discussed in P. L. Sissons (1973) *The Social Significance of Church Membership in the Burgh of Falkirk*, Edinburgh, Church of Scotland, and D. R. Robertson (1966) 'The Relationship between Church and Social Class in Scotland', unpublished Ph.D. thesis, University of Edinburgh; and in idem, 'The relationship of church and class in Scotland', in D. Martin (ed.) (1968) *A Sociological Yearbook of Religion in Britain*, 1, London, S.C.M.; and J. Littlejohn (1963) *Westrigg: The Sociology of a Cheviot Parish*, London, Routledge & Kegan Paul. Bridging from the north-east to the Hebrides and Shetland is the fascinating P. Thompson *et al.* (1983) *Living the Fishing*, London, Routledge & Kegan Paul, whilst on the Protestant Hebrides generally see T. M. Owen (1956) 'The "Communion Season" and Presbyterianism in a Hebridean community', *Gwerin*, 1; J. Ennew (1980) *The Western Isles Today*, Cambridge University Press; and a very useful section on religion in Harris in K. MacKinnon (1977) *Language, Education and Social Processes in a Gaelic Community*, London, Routledge & Kegan Paul; on the Catholic Hebrides, F. G. Vallee's (1954) study of Barra in 'Social Structure and Organisation in a Hebridean Community', unpublished Ph.D. thesis, University of London (LSE), is a good start.

Amongst the wealth of autobiographies, the first to look at on the Highlands is A. Phillips (1984) *My Uncle George: The Respectful Recollections of a Backslider in a Highland Manse*, Glasgow, Richard Drew, followed up by F. J. Macdonald (1982) *Crowdie and Cream*, and idem (1983) *Crotal and White*, both London, Macdonald. The many books by Lavinia Derwent (on the Borders) and Molly Weir (Glasgow) provide an introduction to the Lowlands.

Sectarianism is something of a growth industry. Most important are R. K. Donovan (1979) 'Voices of distrust: the expression of anti-Catholic feeling in Scotland, 1778–1781', *Innes Review*, xxx; I. A. Muirhead (1973) 'Catholic emancipation: Scottish reactions in 1829' and (1973) 'Catholic emancipation in Scotland: the debate and the aftermath', both *Innes Review*, xxiv. J. Smith (1984) 'Labour tradition in Glasgow and Liverpool', *History Workshop*, 17, Spring, underestimates the degree of sectarianism in Scottish working-class culture around 1900. Sanguine on its decline since the 1930s are S. Bruce (1985) *No Pope of Rome: Anti-Catholicism in Modern Scotland*, Edinburgh, Mainstream, and T. Gallagher (1985) in 'Protestant extremism in urban Scotland

1930–1939: its growth and contraction', *SHR*, lxix, and idem (1985) in 'Soccer: the real opium of the people', *Innes Review*, xxxvi. The last is a review of the excellent B. Murray (1984) *The Old Firm: Sectarianism, Sport and Society in Scotland*, Edinburgh, John Donald. For a Catholic view of the embattled religious minority, see G. Scott-Moncrieff (1960) *The Mirror and the Cross: Scotland and the Catholic Faith*, London, Burns & Oates.

The social history of Scottish ecumenicalism is untouched. The ecclesiastical starting points are J. R. Fleming (1929) *The Story of Church Union in Scotland*, London, Clarke; R. Sjolinder (*c.* 1962) *Presbyterian Reunion in Scotland 1907–1921*, Edinburgh, T. & T. Clark; and A. I. Dunlop (1980) 'The paths to reunion in 1929', *RSCHS*, xx; the politics of late nineteenth-century ecumenicalism are discussed in I. Machin (1983) 'Voluntaryism and reunion, 1874–1929' in N. MacDougall (ed.) *Church, Politics and Society: Scotland 1408–1929*, Edinburgh, John Donald. A useful source on the period between 1904 and 1950 is A. Muir (1958) *John White*, London, Hodder & Stoughton, a biography of a leading ecumenical minister. On liturgical trends, see A. C. Cheyne (1967) 'Worship in the kirk: Knox, Westminster, and the 1940 Book' in D. Shaw (ed.) *Reformation and Revolution*, Edinburgh, Saint Andrew; and D. B. Forrester and D. M. Murray (eds) (1984) *Studies in the History of Worship in Scotland*, Edinburgh, T. & T. Clark. An important factor may be the changing pattern of ministerial recruitment which is illuminated in M. Maxwell-Arnot (1974) 'Social change and the Church of Scotland', in M. Hill (ed.) *A Sociological Yearbook of Religion in Britain*, 7, London, SCM.

Chapter 8

Women and religion is a topic ready for exploration. A discussion of the double-edged effects of Calvinism on the status of post-Reformation women in Scotland is to be found in J. D. Young (1985) *Women and Popular Struggles: A History of British Working Class Women 1560–1984*, Edinburgh, Mainstream; whilst C. Larner (1981) *Enemies of God: The Witch-hunt in Scotland*, London, Chatto & Windus, clarifies the purpose and nature of this state-sanctioned activity. The historical survey in J. Kennedy, C. A. Smith and J. M. Fraser (1959) *The Place of Women in the Church*, Edinburgh, Saint Andrew, assumes too hastily that the presbyterian order was, by the standards of other churches, anti-women.

A convenient introduction to some of the perspectives on church and nationalism in Scotland is to be found in four papers by H. R. Sefton, B. Aspinwall, D. W. Bebbington and K. Robbins in S. Mews (ed.) (1982) *Religion and National Identity*, Oxford, Basil Blackwell.

Index

Aberdeen 39, 47, 80, 83, 98-9, 131, 150-1, 205
Aberdeenshire 39, 45, 103, 114-15
Aberfoyle 95
adultery 94-6, 199
agricultural improvement 27, 39, 89, 101, 105-6, 109, 112, 114, 120
agricultural occupations 45, 110-11
Airdrie 51-2, 205
Alloa 106
Alva 112
Angus 43, 49, 51
Anne, Queen 24
annuity tax 99
Antiburghers 35-6, 94, 105, 107-9, 139; *see also* Secession Church
Applecross 96
Ardnamurchan 126
Ardrossan 112
Argyllshire 65, 77, 82
aristocracy 49, 103
Arminianism 13, 53, 139-40, 157-60
Arran 119
Aspinwall, Bernard 204
Assynt 124
auction of pews 102
Ayrshire 45, 96

Baird & Co., William 164

Balfron 112
Band of Hope 115, 143, 160, 183, 206
Banffshire 77
baptism 92, 96, 228-9, 250
Baptists 1, 41, 43-4, 113, 121, 123, 137, 155, 239; rates of growth of 71-2
Barra 39, 45
Bathgate 29
Bearsden 80
Begg, Rev. James 172
Bereans 43
Berwickshire 7, 103
Bible Society Census 1984 19-20, 77-81
biblical criticism 173-4, 255-6
bingo 5, 225
Blairgowrie 112
Booth, Charles 188
Borders 39, 212; *see also by* county
Boys' Brigade 17, 143, 183, 217
Breadalbane 119
Brethren 1, 4, 54, 59, 216
British Broadcasting Corporation 211, 226
Buchanan, Rev. Robert 132, 143
Buchlyvie 112
Burgess, Keith 137
Burgess Oath 35-6

Burghers 35, 43, 107–8, 139; see also Secession Church
Burray, island of 123

Caird, Edward 189
Caithness 65, 77
Calvinism 8–9, 13, 16, 36, 38, 42, 44, 53, 136–41, 249, 255; see also Arminianism; predestination, doctrine of
Cambuslang 97, 205
Cambusnethan 112
Campbell, R. H. 137
Campbeltown 1–2, 4–6, 37, 142
Canna 45
Cardross 112
Carlyle, Thomas 34, 141
Catholic Church 1, 7, 19, 27–8, 39, 44–8, 58, 213–14, 226–7, 231; and education 200–2, 234–5; in the Highlands 116, 220; in housing schemes 224–5; rates of growth of 62, 72–7, 250; social composition of 161–2, 219
Catholics 1, 112, 124, 211–14; assimilation of 162–5; and the labour movement 194–5; see also Irish immigration
Catholic Socialist Society 194
Celtic Football Club 233–4, 243
Chalmers, Rev. Thomas 17, 40, 142–3, 200
charity 232
Charity Organization Society 182
Charles I, King 24
Chartism 106, 187
Chartist Churches 157
children 130–1, 226, 229–30, 252
Christian socialism 127, 173, 177, 184, 188–96, 200, 204
Christian Year, advance of 18, 229, 241
church accommodation: rural 91, 98, 100–3; urban 81, 99–100
church attendance: problems of analysing statistics of 57–60, 77; rates of 19–20, 45, 61–3, 77–85, 100, 169, 209, 226–7, 250, 252, 254–5
church buildings: construction of 81, 100, 125–6, 131, 133–4, 141–6, 156, 177–8, 224; disposal of excess 48, 179, 240–1; multiple congregations meeting in 99; poor state of 98; refusal of sites for 126; relocation of 114
church membership: problems of analysing statistics of 57–61; statistics of 64–77, 85–6, 209–12, 250
Church of England 49–51, 65, 114, 246, 256
Church of Ireland 15, 50
Church of the Nazarene 53–4
Church of Scotland 1–2, 4, 9, 15, 18, 23, 27–33, 35, 114, 216, 230; Commission on the Religious Condition of the People 189, 192–3; disestablishment of 33, 109, 206; Glasgow Presbytery Commission on Housing 189; in housing schemes 224–5; and the labour movement 188–95; patronage in 29–33, 35–6, 103–4, 114, 124–5, 250–1; in pre-industrial parishes 90–100; rates of growth of 61–70, 85, 210–12, 217; recruitment of clergy 240, 252; social composition of 151–2, 154–5, 217, 219–20; see also Evangelical Party; Moderatism
Churches of Christ 54, 239
cinema 225
Clackmannan 37
Claim of Right (1842) 32
Clearances, Highland 45, 119–20
Clyne 199
Coatbridge 50–2, 164, 194
Collins, William 133

Index

Commissioners for Forfeited Estates 118
communion 97, 118, 228, 241
Communist Party 195, 213
Comrie 108
Congregationalists 1, 41, 43–4, 121, 123, 137, 158, 239; rates of growth of 71–2
Connal, Sir Michael 176–7, 181, 200
Conservative Party 194, 243
covenanters 2, 24–6, 34–5, 242; *see also* Reformed Presbyterian Church
Crieff 94
Crofters Act (1886) 127–8, 187, 199
crofting society 3–4, 39, 44, 54, 120–8
Cumbernauld 76

Dale, David 37, 43, 148, 190
Darwinism *see* biblical criticism
Deanston 112
Denny 108
Derwent, Lavinia 212
Dingwall 81
Disruption, the 2, 9, 32–4, 38–40, 62, 70, 125–7, 133, 142, 151
Dornoch 98
Doune (Perthshire), 96, 112
Downie, Rev. Alex 120
drunkenness 96, 108; *see also* temperance
Dumbarton 39
Dumbartonshire 76–7, 80
Dumfriesshire 82, 95
Dunblane 95, 98
Dundee 14, 43–4, 50, 72, 80, 82, 99, 142, 148–9, 160, 203, 205–6
Dundee United Football Club 243
Dunfermline 98
Dunkeld 98
Dysart 112

Easdale 122
East Kilbride 76, 231
East Lothian 3, 80, 82
Eastwood (Renfrewshire) 80
economic decline 213–23
economic individualism 109, 136–8, 249; *see also* self help
ecumenicalism 17–18, 233–4, 239–42
Edinburgh 31, 35, 39, 50, 61, 76, 80, 83, 99, 179, 205, 219, 226
education: county education authorities (1919–29) 11, 201, 206, 238; Education (Scotland) Act (1872) 197; Education (Scotland) Act (1918) 201–2, 206; parish schools 43, 98–9, 201; private schools 180; ragged schools 17; school boards (1873–1919) 11, 99, 176–7, 187, 197–201, 227; urban schools 180, 245
Eigg 45
elders 28–9, 92, 117, 169; social composition of 150–2, 219
Elect, doctrine of the *see* predestination, doctrine of
Elgin 98
emigration 45, 121, 124
Enlightenment, the 16, 30
Episcopal Church 1–2, 4, 48–51, 58, 234, 239–40; episcopacy and monarchy 23–4, 27; rates of growth of 72–3, 76
episcopalians 2, 7, 18, 24, 116
Established Church *see* Church of Scotland
evangelicalism 4, 16–18, 255; crisis in 41, 169–96, 209, 218, 250, 254; and the middle classes 135–52; proletarian 203–6, 214–17; *see also* evangelization; home missions; revivalism
Evangelical Party (in Church of Scotland) 32, 63, 120, 133
Evangelical Union 44, 54, 158
evangelization 19, 141, 143–8, 166–7, 170, 174–7, 180–4,

evangelization—*continued*
225–6; *see also* home missions; revivalism
Eyre, Archbishop Charles 163

Falkirk 108, 219, 252
fast days 107, 137
Fenwick 96, 106
Fife 14, 34, 39, 43, 74, 80, 104, 213
Finney, Charles 159
First World War, the 64, 85, 87, 205, 210–12, 251
fishing communities 4, 39, 44, 52, 54, 71, 205, 215–16
football 182–3, 233–4, 242–4
foreign missions 32
fornication 94–6, 108
Fort William 45
Franciscans 116
Fraserburgh 158
Free Church of Scotland (1843–1900) 2, 4, 10, 32–3, 38–40, 42, 44, 96, 125–8, 147, 171, 173, 175; rates of growth of 62–5, 70; social composition of 114, 125–6, 150–2, 154–5
Free Church of Scotland (post-1900) 1, 38, 44, 128, 220–3; rates of growth of 71–2
Free Presbyterian Church (1893–) 44, 128, 220–3; rates of growth of 71–2

Gaelic 1–2, 14, 44, 117, 120, 127, 221–2
Gairloch (Wester Ross) 95, 118–19
Galloway 80; Levellers 26
Galston 96
Galt, John 103
Geddes, Patrick 189
Gillespie, Rev. Thomas 104
Glasgow 1, 14, 17, 35, 37, 39, 43–4, 49–52, 61, 72, 76, 81, 83–4, 99, 131–3, 135, 173, 179, 205, 226

Glasgow City Improvement Act (1866) 132
Glasgow Foundry Boys' Religious Society 143
Glasgow Religious Tract Society 145
Glasites 43, 59, 142, 148–9
Glasse, Rev. John 191
glebes 91–3, 107
Good Templars 1, 5, 182
Gorbals 53, 74
Graham, Rev. Billy 225–6
Green, T. H. 189
Greenock 17, 49, 163–4, 246

Haddington 98
Haldane, James and Robert 43, 121
Hamilton 37, 51
Hammond, Edward Payson 159
Hardie, Keir 175, 186
Harris, Isle of 125
Heart of Midlothian Football Club 243
Hebrides 3, 25, 28, 39, 43, 45, 48, 65, 71–2, 77, 80, 115–28, 220–3
Helensburgh 49
Helmsdale 126
heresy trials 137–8
heritors 91–3, 98, 101–4, 114, 117, 123, 227
Hibernian Football Club 243
Highet, Dr John 84
Highlands 1–3, 25, 28, 39, 43, 48, 65, 71–2, 77, 115–28, 220–3, 254; *see also by* county
Hill, Rev. Rowland 121
Hillis, Dr Peter 151–2, 154, 219
Hogg, James 9, 120
holidays 107
Holyrood (Dumfriesshire) 95
home missions 19, 32, 115, 121, 143–8, 164, 171, 180–1, 183, 186, 214–17; *see also* evangelization; revivalism
Horseman's Word, Society of the 113

Index

housing 131, 172, 223–5, 231–2, 243–4
Howard, Ebenezer 191
Hunter, Dr James 127

immigration 23, 74; *see also* Irish immigration; Jewish immigration
Independency *see* Baptists; Bereans; Congregationalists; Glasites; Old Scots Independents
industrialization 3, 14–15, 22, 31, 71
industrial villages 72, 112
industry, concentration in 175
Inveresk 112
Inverness 125
Inverness-shire 82
Iona Community 218
Irish immigration 4, 19, 23, 45–8, 50–1, 61, 74, 161–4, 234, 238; *see also* Catholics
Irish republicanism 47, 163, 195, 243
Irvine 150

Jacobitism 2, 29, 35, 48, 104–5, 116, 118
Jedburgh 31, 77, 109, 142, 148
Jehovah's Witnesses 1, 53
Jewish immigration 53, 74
Johnson, Christine 162
Johnson, Samuel 8, 49

Kilmarnock 244
Kilsyth 97, 205, 207
Kincardineshire 43, 49, 77
Kintail 45
Kintyre, Mull of 1, 125
kirk sessions 11, 28, 93–7, 152–3
Kirkudbrightshire 26, 82
Kirkwall 70, 98, 122–3
Knoydart 45
Knox, John 23, 98
Knox, Dr William 195

Labour Churches 169
labour movement 127, 164, 177, 187–96, 200, 205, 219
Lanarkshire 19, 45, 201
Lancashire 14, 20, 84
landowners 49, 51, 91–2, 116; *see also* heritors
Lauder 159
Laurencekirk 96
League of the Cross 160, 163
leisure 179–80, 182–4, 212, 224–5, 227, 230
Lennoxtown 80
Lerwick 122
Leslie (Fife) 107
Lewis, Isle of 94, 119, 125, 221, 223
Liberal Party 33, 41, 127, 194
Licht, New and Auld 36, 43, 109
literacy rates 98, 150–1
Livingston 76, 240
local veto plebiscites 203, 205–7, 210–11, 238
Lochalsh 77, 80
Lochcarron 96, 118–20, 124, 140
Lochgelly 112
Lochwinnoch 153
lofts, church 102–3
Logue, Dr Kenneth 103, 250
Long, Harry 164
Lothian *see* East; Mid-; West

MacInnes, Dr John 118
Mackenzie, Sir Compton 47
Mackenzie, Sir Hector 95
Mackenzie, Rev. Lachlan, 119–20, 124, 140
MacLaren, Dr Allan 53, 137, 150–3
Macleod, Rev. David 184, 186
Macleod, Rev. George (Lord, of Fuinary) 218
manufacturers 43, 49, 175–6
marriage, religious 76, 86–7, 92, 163, 217, 228–9, 250
Marshall, Dr Gordon 13, 137
materialism 231

Mathew, Father Theobald 163
medical missions 146
'Men', the 118, 121, 127
Methodism 1, 13, 51–3, 57, 112–13, 123, 137, 217, 239
middle classes 135–52, 177–82, 223–33
Midlothian 3, 80, 244
migration 45, 178
Miller, Hugh 126
Milngavie 80
Miners 45, 54, 71, 176, 215, 246
Moderatism 16–17, 30, 32–3, 108, 118, 120, 139
Moidart 45
Monklands 76
Montrose 83, 99, 108
Moody, Dwight 17, 114, 138–9, 147, 160, 183
Morar 45
Moray 39, 77
Morison, Rev. James 140
Mormons 53, 72–3, 173
Moslems 253
Motherwell 76
Moulin 119
Mull, Isle of 125

Nairn 39, 77
Napoleonic wars 32
nationalism 14, 252–3
Newfoundland 45
New Lanark 43
new religious movements 253–4
Niddrie 165
North, Brownlow 141
Northern Ireland 216, 242–3

Old Scots Independents 43
Orange Order 50, 235–7, 242–4, 246
Original Secession Church 43; rates of growth of 71–2
Orkney 39, 43–4, 54, 65, 68–71, 80, 122–3, 212

Overtoun, Lord 175–6, 181
Owen, Robert 190

paganism 116–18
Paine, Thomas 43, 121
Paisley 43, 52
Paisley, Rev. Ian 247
patronage *see* Church of Scotland
Peebleshire 227
penny savings banks 143, 148, 171
Pentecost, Rev. George 169
Perth 35, 43, 98–9, 148–9
Perthshire 34, 39, 49, 51, 104, 107–8
pew-renting 81, 92, 100, 102–3, 114, 133, 141–2, 153, 155–6, 162, 217–18, 228
poor relief 92, 144, 197–8, 206
Pope John Paul II 225–7, 233, 247
popular disturbances 25–6, 29–30, 103–5, 118, 124, 126, 131, 190, 193, 250–1
Porteous, Rev. William 131
precentors 98, 103
predestination, doctrine of 53, 137–41, 157–8; *see also* Arminianism
pre-industrial religion 23–8, 57, 90–100
presbyterianism: reunions within 33, 36, 41, 172, 179, 216, 233–4, 239; social cohesion produced by 12, 24, 100; system of church government 28–9; victory of in 1690 2, 24–5; *see also under* each Church
Prestonpans 104
Protestant Action 238–9

Quakers 53

railways 133
Ramsay, John 105
Rangers Football Club 233, 242–4
ranting 96

Index

Rechabites 182, 187
Reformation: (1560) 23, 44, 116, 131; Second Reformation (1638–50) 25
Reformed Presbyterian Church 2, 42, 139; *see also* covenanters
Relief Church 2, 4, 31, 34, 36–7, 121–2, 134; rates of growth of 63, 142; social composition of 149–50
Religious Census (1851) 20, 33, 38, 59, 61–2, 72–3, 75, 77–83, 86
religious instruction 199–200
Renton 112
respectability 97, 156, 171, 177, 196, 251
revivalism: in 1742 97, 114; in 1830–50 158; in 1859–62 147, 159; in 1873–4 17, 138–9, 147; in Highlands 119–20, 122, 125; in late-nineteenth century 169, 181; in twentieth century 215, 225–7
Rhum 45
Riddell, Sir James 126
Roman Catholic Church *see* Catholic Church
Ross and Cromarty 39, 65, 77, 220, 222
Rowntree, Seebohm 188–9
Royal Commission on Religious Instruction (1837–9) 59, 61–2, 82–3, 154–6

sabbatarianism 8, 93–4, 99, 132–3, 175, 188, 232; in the Highlands, Hebrides and Northern Isles 118, 212, 220–3; and proletarian identity 105–7
Sage, Rev. Aeneas 118–19
St Andrews 98
St Margaret of Scotland Catholic Adoption Society, the 232
St Monans 211, 216
Saltcoats 112
Salvation Army 1, 54, 182, 217

Sandemans of Perth 43, 148
Sankey, Ira 17, 114, 138–9, 160, 181, 183
Sanquhar 102
Scone 112
Scotch Baptists 43, 139
Scott, Bishop Andrew 162
Scottish Co-operative Wholesale Society 190
Scottish Council for Women's Trades 192
Scottish Episcopal Church *see* Episcopal Church
Scottish Society for the Propagation of Christian Knowledge 117–18
Scottish Prohibition Party 8, 203
Scottish Protestant League 238–9
searchers, Sabbath 99
Secession Church 2, 4, 26, 30–1, 34–6, 42–3, 104–5, 107–8, 121–2, 140; rates of growth of 62–3, 142; social composition of 109–12, 148, 150, 154–6; *see also* Burghers; Antiburghers
Second World War, the 210–12, 251
sectarianism 12, 19, 47, 163–5, 195, 201–2, 214, 233–9, 242–7
seers 116
segregation, religious 163–4, 243–4
self help, religious ideas of 103, 136, 143–4, 162–3, 165, 171, 249, 254
Selkirkshire 77, 82
Shetland 39, 43, 80, 122–3
Simeon, Charles 43, 121
Skye 119–20, 125
Slateford (Edinburgh) 112
slum clearance 132
slump, the 217–18
Smith, Rev. Dr John 5
social class and religious pluralization 4, 12, 18, 25–6, 29–30, 36, 38, 42, 46, 50
social mobility 148–52, 165, 214
social policy 143–6, 172–3, 187–94
Social Unions 192

Socialist Sunday schools 169
Society for the Propagation of the Gospel at Home 121
Spoutmouth Bible Institute 176–7
Stevenson, R. L. 10, 23
Stirling 36, 98–9, 135, 142
Stirlingshire 34, 39, 74, 107–8, 215
Strathaven 109–11
Stromness 122
Stuart Pretenders 48, 105
suburbanization 177–81, 228
Sunart 126
Sunday schools 32–3, 43, 85–6, 115, 131–2, 145, 181, 217, 229, 250
Sutherland 65, 77, 126
Sutherland, Duke of 126
Symons, J. C. 8

tacksmen 117
Tayside 80
teetotalism *see* temperance
teinds 91–2, 118, 202
television 5, 225–6, 254
temperance 5, 8, 10, 33, 132, 148, 166, 203–7, 222–3
Ten Years' Conflict, the 32, 125
textile occupations 43, 45, 52, 95, 101, 113, 130, 148–50, 157
Thurso 121
Tibbermuir 112
Tiree 121
town councils 131–4, 172, 191, 204, 210
tracts 145, 171
tradesmen 4, 109, 148–50
trades unions 164, 187–95
Treaty of Union 7, 9, 14–15
Troup, Jock 215, 217

Uist 39, 45, 199
Unitarians 53, 173
United Free Church (1900–29) 41, 44, 176, 179, 195, 228; rates of growth of 64, 210

United Free Church (1929–) 228, 239, 252; rates of growth of 71–2
United Presbyterian Church 4, 34, 37–8, 40–1, 96, 173; rates of growth of 62–5, 70; social composition 113, 150, 153–4
universities 155, 235
urban improvement 131–2
urbanization 18, 22, 42, 71, 81–3, 130–5; *see also* suburbanization

Veto Act 1834 32
voluntaryism 36, 41; *see also* Church of Scotland, disestablishment of

Wales 7, 10, 13, 52
water-kelpies 116
Watt, Christian 158, 166
Weber, Max 13
Webster, Alexander 45
Weir, Molly 216–17
welfare state *see* social policy
Wesley, John 51–3
West Calder 109–12
West Lothian 3, 29, 34, 77, 80, 82
Westminster Confession of Faith 28, 33
Wheatley, John 194
Whitefield, George 51
Wick 121
Wigtonshire 82
William III, King 23, 244
Willison, Rev. Archibald 108
Wilson, David 53
women: and kirk justice 94–6; and local veto 205; and religious participation 226, 250–2
Women's Guild 179, 251
working classes: alienation from organized religion 5, 19, 50, 130, 135, 152–3, 165–7, 184–8, 219–20; participation in organized religion 154–67, 177, 211–20

worship reform 18, 138, 141, 183, 241-2

Yeo, Dr Stephen 174, 196

Younger, John 105-6
Young Men's Christian Association 143, 183, 212